The B-25 in the Backyard

The B-25 in the Backyard

My Father's Historic Airplane Sanctuary

WALLY SOPLATA

McFarland & Company, Inc., Publishers
Jefferson, North Carolina

All photos are from the Wally Soplata collection unless otherwise noted.

LIBRARY OF CONGRESS CATALOGUING-IN-PUBLICATION DATA

Names: Soplata, Wally, 1953– author.
Title: The B-25 in the backyard : my father's historic airplane sanctuary / Wally Soplata.
Other titles: B25 in the backyard
Description: Jefferson, North Carolina : McFarland & Company, Inc., Publishers, 2020 | Includes bibliographical references and index.
Identifiers: LCCN 2020026701 | ISBN 9781476680668 (paperback : acid free paper) ∞
ISBN 9781476640297 (ebook)
Subjects: LCSH: Airplanes—Collectors and collecting—Ohio—Newbury Area. | Airplanes, Military—Collectors and collecting—Ohio—Newbury Area. | Airplanes—Conservation and restoration—United States. | Airplanes—Salvaging—United States. | Soplata, Walter A., 1923-2010—Estate. | Soplata, Wally, 1953—Family.
Classification: LCC TL506.U6 N49 2020 | DDC 623.74/6074771336—dc23
LC record available at https://lccn.loc.gov/2020026701

BRITISH LIBRARY CATALOGUING DATA ARE AVAILABLE

ISBN (print) 978-1-4766-8066-8
ISBN (ebook) 978-1-4766-4029-7

© 2020 Wally Soplata. All rights reserved

No part of this book may be reproduced or transmitted in any form or by any means, electronic or mechanical, including photocopying or recording, or by any information storage and retrieval system, without permission in writing from the publisher.

Front cover image: B-25 *Wild Cargo* relaxing in the snow (courtesy of Jason McKeon)
Back cover: the author in the snow by the Cutlass jet at age 10 (author's collection)

Printed in the United States of America

McFarland & Company, Inc., Publishers
Box 611, Jefferson, North Carolina 28640
www.mcfarlandpub.com

To the memory of all the brave men and women
who have gone before us that dared to live
the dream of soaring the wild blue skies.
That we may celebrate you,
honor you, and stand with you until
the last of us have all flown west.

Table of Contents

Preface 1

1. No Place Like Home 5
2. Airplane Siblings 13
3. Sky King 18
4. Scraping By 25
5. The Banana Bus 32
6. Walter the Conqueror 44
7. Heavy Metal 47
8. The Mother-In-Law 51
9. Wild Cargo 59
10. The Flying Zoo 66
11. The Little Six That Could 71
12. Wings of the Night 81
13. Treasure Hunting 84
14. On the Outside Looking Up 92
15. Chicago Clone 98
16. Plane Crazy 112
17. Delusions of Flight 124
18. Plane Folks 126
19. Along for the Ride 134
20. High Hopes 142
21. Carrying a Load Not Measured in Pounds 150
22. A Hollywood Part 159
23. As Is, Where Is—The Fate of the Hunted 166
24. "Your Place" 178
25. In the Grip of Obsession 182

Table of Contents

26. Mother Load 190
27. Chasing the Dream 199

Epilogue: Live and Let Fly 204
Appendix I: Walter Soplata's Airplanes: Where Are They Now? 209
*Appendix II: Aviatrix Marge Hurlburt's Hidden Treasure:
   Air Race Corsair* Lucky Gallon 213
*Appendix III: The Global Reach of Walter Soplata's Airplanes:
   Lockheed Neptune #40436* 217
Sources 221
Bibliography 223
Aircraft Make and Model Index 225
General Index 227

Preface

I was eight when I went on my first airplane-hauling trip with my highly unusual father in 1961. That was the beginning of an epic eleven-year run during which we hauled a wide variety of historic aircraft, most of which came perilously close to being destroyed and cut up for scrap metal. All of these airplane-saving efforts were done haphazardly on a shoestring budget with lousy and inadequate equipment—if we were lucky enough to even have that. Sometime in my teen years it hit me hard that I was both a participant and a witness to something extraordinary and in some cases nearly unbelievable. An early sense of obligation told me I had to write this story down. Fortunately, that feeling continued to nag me until I began writing down many notes and stories in the early 1970s while so much of this was fresh on my mind.

In this father-and-son story about my airplane-obsessed dad, my long journey in his shadow sometimes weaves a twisted path down a road of irony and contradiction. Typical aviation stories of those and earlier times tell of old speed and distance records broken and once unthinkable new records set. Other aviation stories vary from disaster avoided to exotic locations traveled to. This story is unlike those or any others. Instead, I will tell it by using a wide variety of airplanes that would never fly while in the eternally clenched hands of my father's tight grip. Under his watch, his airplanes sat in the same spot in Ohio for so many years; the only travel many of them did was for their landing gear to sink deeper into the soft soil below. Now presenting my own story of irony and contradiction, I will use these same airplanes to take you on an unimaginable journey like none other.

I don't remember who the aviation leader was who said this at one of the many large gatherings I've attended, but he reminded the audience to never forget that all aviation stories are actually stories about people. I can thank my father for making it easy to remember that. I use the word "unconventional" a lot in this story. I perhaps risk using it too much, but he often thought so far outside the box, he could almost be unconventional about being unconventional. And while that kind of out-there-somewhere thinking enabled him to accomplish so much, in other ways it was a trait that could imprison him. That said, while there is plenty of material here for aviation enthusiasts to discover and enjoy, I imagine a few case studies in sociology class could also emerge from this. While I also am a self-confessed aviation addict, the constant intrigue as Walter's son trying to know, trying to understand, trying to explain, and trying to love this most unusual father of mine has been truly most compelling.

Due to this focus on my father in the telling of our many airplane adventures together, it is beyond the scope of this story to go into extensive detail on the wide variety of airplanes we will encounter. Great aviation historians can, and often do, devote large manuscripts entirely to one aircraft such as the P-47 Thunderbolt. As a result, I have listed many references for readers to more deeply research and explore these historic aircraft. Likewise, these references tell the rich history of the brave pioneers who flew these planes that sometimes helped them make history at events such as the Cleveland National Air Races.

I have the tremendous good fortune to have many truly wonderful people to thank for enabling me to tell this story, beginning with my wife of forty years. Lisa today is the same kind, caring, sweet and generous lady I met early in my year of pilot training at Columbus Air Force Base in Mississippi. She and our two grown children, our son Austin and our daughter Avery, have endlessly poured out their support and encouragement for me in telling this story, which at times is a difficult personal journey.

Throughout the military, airline, and general aviation communities, I have countless people to thank who have taught me, inspired me, and kept me safe in a sometimes-dangerous profession. Among the many special people in this group, those who helped me in a wide variety of ways with this manuscript deserve special thanks. Most are from or have an aviation connection to what I call my Memphis airplane family. Here I wish to thank Bill Austin; Eddie Brewer; Jimmy Burkeen; the Davis brothers, Andy and Duke Davis; Jeff Dula; Ken Eckles; Don Eye; Kevin Gardner; Todd Gibbons; Rick Henry; Wally Knight; Ron Lundquist; Alexis Meaders; Chris Norman; Gilbert Pierce; Mike "Tuna" Pontoni; the Rice brothers, Jim and Rick Rice; Ron Stout; Scott Thompson; Steve Vihlen; the late John Boudreaux; the late Jack Kalemba; and the late Dwight Smith, who have each played some personal role in helping me and/or inspiring me with this project.

In November 2007, *Air & Space/Smithsonian* magazine published a section of this book about hauling B-25 *Wild Cargo* in "The Soplata Airplane Sanctuary" article I wrote then. I owe a special thanks to author Carl Hoffman and editors Pat Trennor and Caroline Sheen for their enormous help getting that story published.

I also need to thank author Simon Beck, who is an incredible aviation historian and writer with two great McFarland books published. He has likewise been an ever-helpful coach and mentor while continuing his many contributions to preserving aviation history from his home in New Zealand.

The photographs I used in this book came largely from a selection of photos and negatives my mother gave me in the 1990s. Using an old box camera, my father took almost all the photos of the airplanes as they were being hauled home. He thus appears in very few photos. Every photo he took until the mid-1970s was shot in black and white. A smaller but significant number came from photos I shot myself. Other photos, and in some cases negatives, have been provided to me by some very generous people including Larry L. Johnson, Robert E. Garrard at AirHistory.net, Jason McKeon, Alexis Meaders, Ron Muecke at skyking.com, and Rick Rice from the Shaw Creek Air Ranch. Some of the original Soplata photos have been through a bit of wear and tear in a photo album shown to countless visitors over more than thirty years. Whether it was digitizing negatives or performing restoration on some battered prints, Cliff Satterfield and his assistants Holly and Adele at Memphis Professional Imaging (MPI) did incredibly great work. Since almost none of these photos have been published or available online until now, I am deeply indebted to all of these wonderful people who have made the photo content of this book possible. Thank you all!

Preface

Finally, I need to thank my late parents Walter and Peggy Soplata for not only sharing the vision to save historic aircraft, but also keeping our family spirit strong through some very challenging times. An immeasurable blessing, they left me four of the most amazing and wonderful sisters on the planet. Each of them has led a life that in their own way has made the world a better place. Some of my sisters were involved with the planes now and then and certainly have many of their own stories to tell. I will leave it to them to tell those stories however they wish, and I forever encourage them to do so.

Among the experiences that best defined my relationship with my father, he was a total workaholic who figured the best way to raise his son to become a real man was to keep me working. The endless work was hardly limited to airplanes. Just the time the two of us spent fixing his overworked airplane-hauling Suburban and trailer was enormous. We changed so many major and minor parts on the Suburban that Mom joked its shadow was the only thing we didn't change.

Sorry, Mom, we did some of that, too. Altogether, there were few things both physical and emotional that my father's giant and ever-present shadow left unchanged. Though deceased nearly ten years now, his long shadow still looms large, just as it should. The shadows cast by the many airplanes he saved will be around for future generations to enjoy without end, exactly as he envisioned and wished for.

Blue Skies,

Wally Soplata
Collierville, Tennessee

1

No Place Like Home

The engines on the B-25 bomber hummed a powerful tune as we headed for our target. Just a few more minutes until we're over Tokyo and ready to let Japan have it for bombing Pearl Harbor. Then, suddenly:

"Zeros, twelve o'clock high," Rick shouted as he spotted Japanese fighter planes approaching us.

"Man the gun turrets!" I ordered.

"Bang, bang, bang," went the gun Rick was manning up front in the bomber's nose.

Convinced we would need some help, I called Bill. "We've got Zeros coming at us, Bill, how about some help?" I yelled.

"No sweat, I'm coming to the rescue," said Bill as he advanced the throttle on his big Navy Corsair fighter plane.

"Me, too," shouted Ed as he pursued the Zeros in another Corsair. More "bang, bang, bang" sounds as Ed's machine guns blasted away. Engine and propeller sounds filled the air. After about ten minutes, the battle was over. After the mission, we climbed out of the World War II planes my father kept in the yard by our house. At age 12, Rick and I were the oldest boys. Everyone was finished playing combat for the day, so we got on our bikes and left a small trail of dust as we rode off looking for something else to do.

Even as a young boy, I realized my father, Walter A. Soplata, was different. As a result, the way we lived was different. But though we had airplanes parked near our house, it wasn't anything I paid much attention to in my early years. The planes didn't fly or do anything. Days, months, and sometimes years would go by with the planes doing nothing but sitting in the same spot.

My earliest memory of seeing Dad work on a plane involved putting together a big airplane that was silver and had two giant propellers. I was about four. Just to see what he was doing, I had to stand up to see over the windowsill looking down from our second-story sunroom. I didn't want to miss a thing, so I stood there the whole weekend with my face glued to the window. I must have asked Mom a million times to let me go outside for a closer look. Each time she responded with a firm "no," telling with a sense of danger that Dad was using the boom tractor to put the plane together. Anytime he used the giant boom tractor, Mom kept us in the house under her watchful eye. Just for insurance, she had a latch high up on the rickety wood screen door that was far out of reach of all five children.

The plane Dad was reassembling was an F-82 Twin Mustang. A plane that would later deceive the eyes of countless visitors to our home, it looked like it was made by joining two P-51 Mustangs. In fact, it was a totally different airplane, yet it fooled almost everyone, because it was already a rare airplane by the time Dad got it. Fortunately for my anxious curiosity, Dad worked fast, and by the end of the weekend had the F-82 all put together. With him back at his carpenter job during the week, Mom took my sisters and me out to tour the new member of our airplane family. "Can we slide down it, Mom? Can we, can we?" my sisters and I asked as we jumped up and down. Mom previously let us use the steep sloping wing of Dad's Corsair as a sliding board when he wasn't home. Maybe she'd let us slide down the big silver plane, too.

"Well, I guess it will be all right, but don't tell your father," Mom answered our pleas. Using a wooden ladder, my sisters and I climbed up on the plane and stood on the wing next to one of the plane's two cockpits. Like a flight attendant assisting evacuating airline passengers, Mom stood at the back edge of the wing flap and caught us one by one as we slid down the wing and flap. Disappointed, we found the F-82 wasn't very good for sliding. Without a doubt, the Corsair wing remained the best slide in town.

My sisters and I would occasionally go through the family photo album. Of course, there were pictures of Mom and Dad getting married, as well as more family pictures of us. When we got to the few pictures of Dad as a young boy, he was always posing with his model airplanes. When Dad talked about his days as a kid, what he was most proud of were all the model airplanes he made from balsa wood. Many of them actually flew. Judging from the pictures, many of the models were quite big, with some having wingspans of three to four feet. Dad was born only 20 years after the Wright Brothers' first flight, so airplanes were a new and rapidly evolving phenomenon back when he was a kid. Thus, as a young boy, he set his sights on having his own airfield and an airplane he could fly.

As an adult, Dad pursued his dream of building an airfield at the same time he started a family. Initially, he began setting up his airfield on five acres of undeveloped farmland in Newbury, Ohio. He got the land as a wedding present from his mother and later bought thirteen more acres from her. On a hillside overlooking Hickory Lake, he planned to build a house. A quarter mile away next to some woods, he planned to build a small airplane hangar and workshop. Though he really couldn't afford to build either, by using surplus material from World War II, he was able to start on the hangar.

When the war ended, our military did virtually turn its "swords into plowshares," in the words of the prophet Isaiah, at a record pace. Steel, copper, aluminum, and other metals had been very scarce during World War II. There was an intense effort to melt down much of the huge military arsenal and recover the metals for consumer goods that had been in terribly short supply due to the war. Dad found a full-time job at a scrap yard on the east side of Cleveland. There, he and other men took apart thousands of warplane aircraft engines to separate the steel, brass, aluminum, and magnesium. After being separated, the metals were melted down and recycled.

Many of the large engines were new and most were still in their big shipping crates. There was so much crate lumber that several men worked all day burning crates. Dad went to his boss and offered to tow the crates away on his own time. The boss gladly let Dad have all the crates he wanted. So with a small homemade trailer, Dad started towing home a load of wood every day. Before long, he had a huge number of crates. Since it was free, he decided to use the wood to build an airplane hangar and workshop. While the crate lumber wasn't suitable for beams and other structures, it worked well when used for roofing, flooring, and walls. In just a few months, Dad quickly put up his hangar and shop, which had a total size of about 5,000 to 6,000 square feet.

After completing the building, he had a tremendous amount of wood left. Soon, he was selling the extra wood and found a lot of eager buyers. People liked it because it was treated and Dad sold it cheap. Sales of the crate lumber grew so much he employed his stepbrother Chuck and brother-in-law "John-D." After Dad hauled the big engine crates home, Chuck and John-D would take the crates apart and stack the wood by size for resale.

When Mom and Dad got married, they started off by living with Dad's mother and stepfather. A baby girl was born in the first year of their marriage, and Dad's stepfather Charlie had little tolerance for a crying baby. Realizing they couldn't wait on the house Dad planned to build, they came up with an alternative plan to move out. Dad figured the quickest way to have a home was to put a second story on top of the shop portion of his hangar. A little different, but it was home. Crate lumber was used where practical. A contractor was hired to put in all the drywall. Some of the floor was done in oak, while the rest was done in tile or linoleum. The outside of the house was finished with standard wood siding and white paint. When complete, it looked like a normal house except for an exceptionally large hangar and shop downstairs.

With our family living upstairs, Dad began working full time downstairs in his shop. Instead of disassembling aircraft engines in town, he now trucked the big engines home to do the work. After taking the engines apart, he got paid by the pound for separating the magnesium castings while also removing other metals such as steel studs and brass bushings from each piece of magnesium, which the company continued to melt and recycle. The work was hard and the pay was low.

Still, Dad made enough to support our growing family. In my early years, my sisters and I could hear his hammer tapping downstairs for hours on end, breaking steel studs and driving out brass bushings, among other uses. Eventually there were five children in our family with four girls and me as the only boy. I had three older sisters and one younger than me by two years. Altogether we were close in age, with only six years separating my oldest sister from our youngest.

As our family grew, Dad's hobby of collecting airplanes grew along with it. Through his contacts in the scrap metal business, he occasionally came across an unusual engine or a rare aircraft that was on its way to the recycling furnace. Each time he was stunned that the item wasn't going to a museum, but instead was about to become part of someone's new aluminum screen door. He snapped the items up and bought many of them at scrap-metal prices. Besides buying the F-82 Twin Mustang from NASA's predecessor, NACA, Dad had earlier purchased the XP-82 from them, which was the experimental prototype for the Twin Mustang.

After several years of working the big engines at home, Dad got what he considered his big break when he got a job as a union carpenter. He could then afford to collect more aircraft and parts, which continued to sell at scrap-metal prices. With Dad at work, there came the day my sisters and I couldn't resist exploring his collection in the hangar. Mainly, the shop was filled with large aircraft engines. Most of the engines were piston engines from World War II bombers and fighters. However, he also had a few jet engines, which were still a new thing then. He had several fuselages in the building including a Corsair, a C-46 cargo plane cockpit, a BT-13 trainer, and one XP-82 fuselage. The building was also stuffed with countless aircraft parts, including landing gear, gunsights, propellers, canopies, instrument panels and other items.

With all the stuff packed in it, the hangar was dark and spooky. There were a few windows, which had their light mostly blocked by the XP-82 fuselage. Not all the lights worked, and those that did were often shaded by an instrument panel, flight control surface, or other item hanging by baling wire from dark wood rafters. In the shop area, Dad had a fluorescent light over his workbench, but otherwise the whole downstairs was very dark. Despite the darkness, I felt brave with my older sisters in the lead. One sister could reach the many light switches on the black and gray switch box and find the few that worked. With the lights on, we headed to the far side of the building to play airliner in the C-46 cockpit. Most of the way we'd slip through the narrow gaps between engines and cockpits, but sometimes we had to climb over a big engine or crawl under one that was mounted on a big stand. In the C-46 cockpit, we discovered knobs, switches, and control levers all over the place, so there was something for everyone. Still, we fought over whose turn it was to sit in the pilot seats. Near the cockpit was a gun turret from a B-24 bomber. One by one we climbed in and played. Fortunately, the turret was missing its guns.

Realizing my father was the one man behind all this, I developed a mystique about him early in life. Who is this big man, and where, as his little boy, will I fit in as I get bigger? Nearly six feet tall, Dad was a handsome, fit, and trim man of medium build. He had a thick head of black hair that kept him looking young despite some wrinkles lining his forehead and other wrinkles around his eyes. During the summer months, he'd bring home the added features of a deep tan speckled with particles of sawdust clinging to the sticky oils the sweat of his hard labor left on the skin around his leathery neck. When Dad wasn't at work, he was almost always at home. On occasion, part of Saturday was spent in the city chasing down leads on more aircraft or parts. Sports, hunting, fishing and other male-type outings were things he never participated in. A near-exclusive commitment, airplanes were his life.

Mom was a traditional homemaker and was also a devoted volunteer at St. Helen Catholic Church and its elementary school. Named Margaret after her own mother, she went by Peggy instead. She was always pleasant and easygoing, and often had the AM radio in the kitchen tuned to classical music. Her favorite radio program was *Adventures in Good Music*, broadcast with syndicated host Karl Haas. Mom became immersed in music in the soothing half-hour, during which we knew without ever being told to just let her be. The introduction to the show was the second movement from Beethoven's Pathétique Sonata, and was played on the piano by Haas himself. If there was ever a piece of music my sisters and I had etched fondly in our brains forever, that was it.

With five kids to keep dressed, Mom was always sewing something, and at times seemed to have her own factory going making dresses for my four sisters. She was very good at that, and by the mid-1960s it was common for her to be a 4-H teacher mentoring a dozen or more young girls on dressmaking. The house was filled with pleasant sounds of Mom and the girls working together on their projects with happy light chatter. Occasionally, I would overhear a girl suddenly upset upon discovering she made a bad mistake on her partially finished dress. Mom to the rescue, she was always calm and sweet in reassuring her student the mistake was okay. Then Mom would help and show how to carefully remove the wrong stitching without damaging the fabric. Soon the young girl was happily on her way making good progress. I really admired Mom in those moments and greatly appreciated her being so sweet and helpful with her 4-H girls.

When Mom wasn't teaching 4-H, cooking, doing laundry, or volunteering at church, she was a bookworm who got Dad to take us to the Burton Library every Friday night so she could stock up on her next week's supply. Altogether, she provided the foundation for a stable atmosphere that kept things pretty normal, considering the unusual situation that Dad's hobby put us in.

During the early years, Dad tinkered with his planes often, but overall spent much of his time at home doing the things you'd expect a family man to do. Fixing the car, mowing the grass, painting the house and other domestic chores kept him busy. With five kids and very little money, almost everything we owned was used. We never got a new car or even a new bike. Since the toys and bikes were used, they always needed fixing. When part of the frame on one bike came apart, Dad welded it back together. When a support for the axle on the wagon broke, he fixed it by making a new support with a salvaged piece of steel. When I got my first bike at the local firehouse auction, one tire was shot. Quickly, Dad put a new tube and tire on it. It still wasn't a very good bike, since it had no fenders, no chain guard, no training wheels, and no kickstand. Yet, when I got it and Dad fixed it good enough for me to ride, I was happier than ever.

Dad had an amazing talent as an improviser. This enabled him to create things from a wide variety of surplus hardware and parts. Of the many things he made, our favorite was a go-cart we affectionately called "the racer." For the drive train on the racer, he used parts of a self-propelled lawnmower. The frame and front end of the racer were homemade from a combination of airplane parts, car parts, and welded steel tubing. The steering wheel was actually a pilot's control wheel from a C-82 cargo plane.

Walter and Peggy Soplata together at an airshow in 1954. During more than 60 years of marriage, she stayed ever devoted beside her husband to whom it was said she came first and airplanes were a close second. There were times I had trouble seeing things in that order.

Dad's mechanical aptitude was incredibly evident when it came to his hobby. To put large aircraft together, you'd normally need a crane. He couldn't afford one, so what he used instead was the homemade boom tractor. Dad made the tractor from a 1936 Chevy car combined with an old Studebaker truck. When finished, the rig had three transmissions. Two were for pulling power, and the third transmission took power from a power takeoff shaft (PTO) to spin a homemade winch. The winch itself was made from a big truck axle on which the steel rim from a truck tire was the spool for the winch cable. The back of the tractor featured a boom about 30 feet long that could be raised or lowered as needed for lifting big and heavy objects. The tractor was also useful for towing the planes as he moved them around occasionally to make room for more. With both of the driving transmissions in low gear, Dad showed me how very slow the tractor would go while also having incredible power. Needing a new path to drive through the woods, he had me watch from a safe distance as he used the tractor and a heavy log chain to yank big trees out of the ground. I was impressed! And just for fun, he once showed me how putting both transmissions in reverse caused the tractor to move forward.

Initially, Dad kept his favorite aircraft right next to our house. On the lawn in full

Chimney sits on east side of our home in this winter wonderland photograph. All of our living space was on the second floor. The picture window left of the chimney is for our kitchen/dining room. Our house dog Curly often sat on the porch roof below this window to enjoy the outdoors. Window just right of chimney is for living room and windows at corner of building and further right facing north are for sunroom. All the windows on the chimney side of house are the ones we kept a lookout from when we knew Dad was hauling an airplane home.

view of the kitchen window, he parked his pride and joy Cleveland National Air Race champion Corsair. On the other side of the house, the F-82 continued to sit where I viewed its assembly from the sun room. Just west of the house, there was a thin tree line that ran north and south. This tree line separated our house and yard from about fifteen acres of land that ran west, which we commonly called "the field." Dad kept two aircraft in the field. One of these was a complete single-engine BT-15 trainer, and the other was a giant Fairchild C-82 Packet cargo plane fuselage.

The C-82 fuselage made a unique and roomy clubhouse my sisters and I played in. Mom set up a table and chairs for us to play games on inside the C-82, where we sometimes took refuge from the rain. It was built of very thin aluminum skin, and it seemed that when inside its enormous interior during a soft rain you could hear every drop of rain softly echo a slightly different musical note from hitting the varied shape and structure of the C-82. Though the C-82 and the BT were then the only two aircraft located in the field, in the coming years they would gain a lot of company. Dad soon filled the C-82 with airplane parts and electronics, which put an end to the clubhouse years his children enjoyed inside it.

An unwelcome event shaped Dad's future plans. His mother didn't sell him the last fifteen acres he wanted. Instead, she sold the property as housing lots to make more money. Twelve houses were then built on the land that Dad envisioned being his airfield. While our neighbors were all very nice, their presence represented a shattered dream. No flying to or from this location would ever happen in the future. Like all the airplanes currently on the property, all future additions would have to be dismantled

Late 1950s at home with Mom posing by a jet engine and its nearby components. Giant C-82 Packet fuselage looms large behind the tree line. Dad is ahead of his time here, trying to scrap some early jet engines already obsolete at a time when jet airliner service is just beginning. Certainly an unusual setting for a home and family, and much more is coming.

and towed down the highway. Like it or not, Dad's mother defined much of his airplane future for him.

A wonderful place to live, Newbury's hilly landscape, lakes, winding roads, and abundant forests made it a beautiful country setting. It was located in the snowbelt close to Lake Erie, and the winters were especially fun for kids as the deep snow and hills made for ideal sledding. There was plenty to do, our neighbors seemed to enjoy the rural setting as much as we did, and no one seemed to mind that one resident liked to collect and tow old airplanes to his property.

We had a variety of entertainments available in the region, and Dad's favorite thing was to take us to airshows. Occasionally, we did go to Geauga Lake and Euclid Beach amusement parks for some non-airplane entertainment. We never missed the local Geauga County Fair or Chardon Maple Festival. When going to see a movie, our choices were few. We could watch airplane movies and that was it. Fortunately, Hollywood did produce a significant number of airplane movies in the 1950s and '60s. Our favorites included comedies involving airplanes, like *Those Magnificent Men and Their Flying Machines*. We also got to see another comedy, *It's a Mad, Mad, Mad, Mad World*, only because Dad heard about a scene in which Mickey Rooney and Buddy Hackett fly a large Twin Beech through a highway billboard. *Flight of the Phoenix* was an epic film for us. Starring actor and aviator Jimmy Stewart, the movie was centered on the quest for survival after an oil company cargo plane crashed far from civilization on an Arabian desert. The badly disabled C-82 cargo plane featured in the film was exactly like our own.

2

Airplane Siblings

One evening as suppertime came and went, we wondered why Dad was late getting home from work. We talked of various theories like a flat tire or his old car breaking down. I noticed his trailer was gone that day and had my suspicions. Soon we saw Dad's old 1952 blue Chevy sedan towing the trailer loaded with a big blue airplane wing. My sisters and I chased the car and trailer out into the field, where he parked next to the C-82.

"What's that?" one of my sisters asked.

"I bought a Corsair, and this is one of the wings," Dad answered, looking happy. I looked at his small homemade trailer and was amazed he could haul the big wing on it. It looked like more airplane wing was hanging off the trailer than riding on it. Little did I know in my next dozen years with him, this would become a routine experience, even after he built a much larger trailer.

I went back into the house, where Mom was busy keeping our late dinner warm. She looked upset. Corsairs are sometimes referred to as bent-wing birds due to the shape of their wings, and those words fit perfectly—Mom was bent. After about 15 minutes, Dad came inside and sat in his usual spot at the head of the small rectangular table we all squeezed around and ate from in our tiny kitchen. As Mom paced the kitchen, she wasted little time letting him know how she felt about the Corsair. She was furious. She didn't rant and rave, but she didn't have to. Seldom having a lot to say, Mom still communicated her extreme displeasure. With stern looks that could kill and some muffled sentences perhaps intended to avoid a major eruption in front of her children, she got her point across. Finally, she spelled it out.

"We *just paid off* the thousand-dollar loan you took out to buy the F-82, and now you bring home another Corsair ... without even telling me! Where's the money coming from?" Mom's eyes shot rays of fire at Dad. For four years we hurried once a month to the bank in Chardon to make a payment on that loan. The minute Dad drove home with his paycheck, it was off to the races before the bank closed.

Though Dad's carpenter job had improved our standard of living somewhat, money was still tight. Several construction companies Dad worked for went out of business. When he found a good company to work for, even those quit building houses during the long winters with endless ice and heavy lake-effect snow. As our crate-lumber home also suggested, we got by on a shoestring budget. The old Chevy Dad used to trailer the Corsair wing with was a hundred-dollar clunker he had bought a few years earlier in 1958. The car was quite rusty from the snowy Ohio winters spent driving on salt-covered roads. As kids we liked it a lot, even though it was a squeeze to get us all in. For Mom, it met her one requirement. She felt a two-door vehicle was safer for her children than a four-door. She was that easy for him to please.

When I began first grade in 1959, I soon realized my status was often below that of the other kids in my class. From the red boots that Mom handed down from my sisters, to the dingy and frayed winter coat she got me at a rummage sale, I sometimes felt like the boy version of a rag doll. Accessories like new metal lunchboxes were items the other kids had, and even my Crayons were nubby hand-me-downs. Money didn't explain all of this, as my sisters recently reminded me of a story I almost forgot from sixty years ago.

I was not yet in school when a thunderstorm hit as my older sisters walked the half-mile home from the school bus stop. As lightning hit nearby, one of them feared the metal lunchboxes would make them a target for the next lightning strike. So they dropped their new lunchboxes beside the road and ran home. After the storm passed, they went back to retrieve their lunchboxes, and all of them were gone. Upon hearing that news, Dad told the family he wasn't buying any more lunchboxes.

I had just started second grade when Dad surprised Mom and the rest of us by showing up with the Corsair wing. In that rural area of Ohio, where it rained a lot, many kids came from homes located on gravel roads like us. Because of that, my red girl boots frequently reminded me that money was tight, so I could understand Mom's anger about the money Dad spent on another Corsair. After Mom finished venting her displeasure, things calmed down. Dad didn't even attempt to fight back or argue. That got my attention. Young as I was, I knew he was short-tempered and could explode without warning, like the early rocket failures NASA was shooting off back then. But never at Mom. Dad was always calm with her. This event had her more upset at him than any I can remember. Yet he kept his cool, stayed quiet and let Mom have her say.

Dad even conceded he should have told her about the plane ahead of time. That got my attention too. He wasn't known to admit error about anything. And as I would find out, this wasn't the start of a new trend. But he promised Mom he'd never buy without her permission again. Then he got to the bottom line. The plane was worth more in scrap metal than the $200 he paid for it. Thus, he hadn't "wasted a dime." If we really needed the money back, he could always junk the plane. Still, she laid down the law. "No more surprises," she said, pointing her finger at him.

Dad found the Corsair at an airport east of Cleveland, where it was considered an eyesore. There was actually very little wrong with the plane, but its appearance looked bad. The Corsair was a top Navy fighter plane in World War II, but a significant amount of its wing and tail surfaces were covered with fabric. This Corsair continued flying into the 1950s with the Navy Reserve at Akron. But after its retirement, a few years of sitting outside in the weather caused its fabric to become rotten and torn, making the plane look ugly. The airport manager wanted the Corsair off the property and sold it to Dad for $200, which in 1960 is about what the plane was worth. As a Navy fighter designed to fly from aircraft carriers, the plane had wings that folded up just outboard of the main landing gear. The outboard section of wing on the trailer was one of these folding sections. The next day, Dad hauled the other outboard wing.

Dad decided to use a simple method to haul the rest of the plane down the highway to our home. He planned to borrow a big flatbed truck and attach the tailwheel to the truck bed in order to tow the plane backward on its landing gear. The method was risky because even with the outboard wings removed, the remaining center wing was more

2. Airplane Siblings

than twice as wide as a pickup truck. Still, Dad towed his other Corsair home this way and didn't have a problem.

I was watching Saturday morning cartoons when I heard the loud sound of a truck laboring up the hill east of our house. I raced across our second-story living room to the windows and saw the big flatbed truck cresting the hill. As I continued looking down from my perch, I was wowed by the incredible sight unfolding before me. On the narrow dirt road lined by tall weeds, the big truck moved slowly with the Corsair's tail riding high on the truck bed. Tail first, the Corsair rode backward behind the truck with its wide landing gear cutting a path through the tall weeds until it entered our wide dirt driveway. No doubt Dad put on quite a show for people on the highway. Without a problem, Dad and his new Corsair were home.

Except for all the torn fabric, the Corsair appeared in good condition. The metal exterior of the plane was perfect with no dents or holes anywhere. The blue paint and associated Navy markings showed some weathering. The wings had familiar paint scratches where they sloped down steeply. I suspected other kids had discovered this Corsair's excellent sliding-board qualities, just as we had. The Corsair's paint scheme had us all puzzled. On the engine cowling, two giant white zeros were painted on both sides of the engine. Zeros? Both numbers? It just seemed odd. But who were we to question the U.S. Navy? Instead, we took the hint. From then on, we all referred to this Corsair as "Zero Zero." Dad owned this plane for many years before we learned the double zeros designated this Corsair as flown by the Navy Air Reserve Squadron Commander at Akron.

Goodyear FG-1D Corsair Zero Zero exactly the way Dad towed it home. Fabric holes visible in tail section and outboard wings (not shown) resulted in its sale as an eyesore. C-82 Packet fuselage beside Zero Zero is the earliest production C-82 remaining.

Dad was instantly proud of Zero Zero. Carefully standing atop his creaky wooden stepladder as it wobbled on the soft and weedy ground, he used a long screwdriver to twist and undo numerous quick-release fasteners. He was then able to remove assorted metal panels to inspect behind the Corsair's engine. To his delight, everything was in place and no corrosion was evident. Even with my untrained eye, I could sense the plane was in excellent condition. "She's a beauty!" Dad concluded. Later, he invited me into the cockpit.

Climbing into the high cockpit of a Corsair is a bit of a trick for an adult. With Dad helping me from his ladder, I hopped in. Everywhere I looked, the cockpit was loaded with control levers, switches, and instruments. It still had the things that told you this was a military fighter plane, like the gunsight mounted directly under the windshield. Down on the left side of the cockpit near the throttle and other engine controls, the bomb release levers were still there. Some planes Dad purchased had their cockpits badly vandalized, so the excellent condition of Zero Zero's cockpit was impressive.

Among Mom's complaints, she could not understand why Dad needed another Corsair. He in fact had a partial fuselage of a third Corsair in storage near the C-46 cockpit we played in. When asked to explain getting Zero Zero, Dad reminded Mom that his first Corsair was totally different and uniquely rare. As she was aware, it had won the 1947 Thompson Trophy Race in the Cleveland National Air Races, racing as number 74.

As an F2G, Corsair 74 was indeed rare and very different from Zero Zero. The major

Winter of 1965 with me standing by bottom prop blade of Goodyear F2G race Corsair 74 that won the Thompson Trophy Race at the Cleveland National Air Races in 1947. Shadow of Dad shooting photograph in lower left. He was always a man who cast a long shadow in a wide variety of ways.

reason 74 won the National Air Races was its enormous 28-cylinder, 4,360-cubic-inch engine. Only ten F2Gs were built. Despite their small numbers, they would gain wide air-race fame as "Super Corsairs." Originally designed for Navy service, F2Gs were fitted with the giant engine to make a hotrod breed of Corsair that could climb quickly to intercept and shoot down Japanese Kamikaze planes. World War II ended before any of the F2Gs saw combat, so a Navy production contract for over 400 of them was canceled. Dad's ownership of one of these rare Corsairs already became a signature issue that would define his collection. He collected old airplanes, and like the rare XP-82 and F-82 Twin Mustangs, his racing champ F2G Corsair was among the rarest of the rare. Dad's addition of some extraordinarily rare aircraft and other items to his small but growing collection would continue. More importantly, that one carpenter with such limited resources would continue to grow a collection of such aircraft would make Walter Soplata as incredibly rare and unique as the airplanes he would save.

Not our plane, but race F2G Corsair 57 sits derelict nearby in Chardon, Ohio, in the early 1960s. It also raced at Cleveland, but this photograph shows how rotted fabric on wings and tail quickly made Corsairs eyesores that often got junked. #57 was eventually restored back to flight status in the late 1990s.

3

Sky King

During breakfast on a Friday in the early fall of 1961, Dad told me that after school he wanted me to pump up the trailer tires. As usual, both trailer tires were flat. After school, I did exactly as he asked and used our old and rusty tire hand pump. It took forever for me to pump up the two big tires, but I got it done. When Dad came home, I proudly reported my job was complete.

"What are you going to do with all that wood?" I asked as I pointed to a pile of scrap wood loaded in the clunker Ford station wagon that had replaced the blue Chevy.

"I'm using the wood on my trip," he answered. Then he asked me to keep quiet, explaining he had not cleared this trip with Mom. We both headed to the house, where Mom had supper waiting. As we ate, Dad approached Mom about his desire to drive to an airport near Pittsburgh to take a look at an old plane. "What kind of plane is it?" she asked.

"It's an old Cessna Bobcat like they use on TV re-runs of *Sky King*."

"Sky King's Bobcat?" I asked excitedly with wide-eyed wonder. Dad explained it was the same model, but not Sky King's actual plane, smiling his approval of my enthusiasm. In the original *Sky King* episodes from the early days of TV, Western hero Sky King didn't ride a white horse. Instead, he flew his Bobcat named "Songbird" from the show's Flying Crown Ranch to help the local sheriff defend the west from bank robbers and other bad guys. An airplane that was blunt and stubby with two round engines and a big cabin for pilots and passengers, the Bobcat represented what was soon considered the classic look of the old passenger planes built in the 1930s and '40s. In the newer *Sky King* episodes, the plane flown was a modern twin-engine Cessna 310. The newer Cessna was sleek and slender with a pointy shape that made it look fast. But none of that mattered to me. The *Sky King* TV series began with a Bobcat, and we might be getting one!

I always watched *Sky King* when it aired on our black-and-white TV and was fascinated to watch Sky use the Songbird to fight crime. In his speedy plane, Sky and his petite niece, Penny, could beat the sheriff to the scene where villains were up to no good, stealing horses or hiding the loot from a bank robbery. Whatever the bad guys were doing, it was just plain wrong, which matched perfectly with the days of black-and-white TV then. No matter what bad deed was unfolding, Sky would land in a field or on a dusty road in the barren west and foil the crime.

Sometimes the bad guys got the upper hand on Sky. Then it was up to young Penny to save her uncle with her quick wits. Near the end of one episode, *The Golden Burro*, a bad guy has Sky at gunpoint as he escorts Sky toward the Bobcat. As they approach the tail of the Bobcat with Sky holding his hands up, Penny is in the pilot seat with the plane's engines running at idle. As the engines gallop, sounding like a pair of Harleys stopped at a red light, Penny looks back and realizes the situation. Then she pushes the throttles forward, causing the propellers to blast a blinding storm of sand into the eyes of the bad guy, giving Uncle Sky exactly the help he needs.

"The man only wants a hundred bucks for the Bobcat," Dad said to Mom. "Heck, the engines and props are worth a lot more than that," he added, giving her his sales pitch. She asked why the owner was selling it and Dad explained it had a wooden wing that did not pass FAA inspection. It was too costly for the owner to fix the wing, so he decided to junk the plane. Next, Mom asked where the money would come from. Dad replied he just cashed his weekly $125 paycheck, and if the bills could be put off until next week, he could pay for the plane with that check. Mom agreed the bills could wait, easily giving Dad the go-ahead to buy the Bobcat. After the Corsair uproar, I was surprised she approved so easily. Now Dad had Mom figured out. She didn't mind him spending money on buying old airplanes; she just didn't want to find out about it after the fact.

Then, after supper, Dad drove the car out into the field and hooked up the trailer. "Can I go on the trip?" I'd been dying to ask, but waited until now.

"Not this time," Dad answered. He explained the engines were really heavy and Mom would probably not want me around while he was working to get them off the plane and onto his trailer. "But maybe next time," he added as he finished preparations for this trip.

Early the next morning, Dad left for Pennsylvania. As usual, my sisters and I watched Saturday morning cartoons until *Sky King* came on. I watched the show intently. While I always enjoyed it, today I was really fascinated. I could just imagine myself in that Bobcat pilot seat playing cops and robbers the Sky King way.

Actor Kirby Grant plays Western hero *Sky King* with this Cessna T-50 Bobcat, later replaced by a Cessna 310 in the 1950s cops-and-robbers TV show. *Sky King* inspired many children to become pilots, including some who became astronauts (courtesy Ron Mueke at www.skyking.com).

While Dad was on his trip, my sisters and I spent the afternoon mostly outside. The day was as beautiful as they get in the early fall in

Ohio. Most of the leaves were still in the trees and had all changed color to scenic reds, browns, and yellows. The sun was bright as ever and the temperature was perfect. But this day was extra special. Dad was getting an airplane just like the one on TV. As we played outside and rode our bikes around the neighborhood, we told everyone we saw that we were getting a plane just like Sky King's airplane. The news made the neighbors seem as excited as we were. Just before dark, Dad came down the dirt road with the old Ford and trailer. He had both Bobcat engines on the trailer with their shiny aluminum propellers. The round radial engines were bigger than I expected, and the little trailer sagged under the heavy load.

"Are you just getting the engines or the whole plane?" Mom asked.

"I'm getting the whole plane," Dad answered. He then told us how it was in really nice shape and looked ready to fly until he took the engines off. He also told us about the Ford's engine overheating while towing the engines up a big hill. That made Mom worry, but Dad assured her the engines were the heaviest load. Still, he promised to visit a radiator shop before the next hauling trip. She had plenty of other reasons to worry about the car.

The Ford wagon was rusted far worse than the Chevy, it used a lot of oil, the heater didn't work, and the passenger door popped open sometimes when Dad made a left turn. It had been built over a decade before car seatbelts were mandatory, and none of us, or I should say almost none of us, needed Darwin to tell us to hang on when Dad made a left turn in the Ford. The Chevy was actually a much better car, except its primitive automatic transmission kept breaking. Dad bought the terribly rusted Ford exactly because it was stick-shift and only cost a hundred bucks.

With a little convincing, Mom agreed I could go on the next trip. On Friday night, she helped me pack. Dad and I left early Saturday morning while it was still dark, since he wanted to get a lot done. The morning sun eventually rose in our face to announce what would be a perfect blue-sky day, and as we headed for Pittsburgh, I left Ohio for the first time.

At the airport, I was able to see and understand an odd situation Dad mentioned. There were no big hangar doors because the airport was being converted into a shopping center. A new cement block wall now stood where the giant hangar doors once were. Entering the hangar through a small side door, I finally got my anxiously awaited view of the Bobcat.

A little surprised by its big size, I liked the plane immediately. I could tell it had been well kept. When I climbed into the cabin I was totally impressed with the stylish civilian interior. I later learned many Bobcats were drab military. Talk about a clubhouse! I couldn't wait to have this in the backyard. There were two pilot seats side by side and a big bench seat for passengers behind the pilot seats. Most of the instruments were installed, and the cockpit was nicer than any plane Dad owned. There was going to be lots of Sky King playtime in this plane!

Wasting little time, Dad put me to work. The plane had a lot of fairings, or thin curved panels of aluminum covering the joints where the wings and tail attached to the fuselage. Many screws were located along the edges of all the fairings, and my first task was to remove the screws. For a long time, I had wanted to play with Dad's big metal toolbox, which I had been forbidden to touch prior to this. Now I had free rein of it and felt like I was big stuff. But I quickly learned that play and work were not the same thing.

Dad went inside the plane cabin to work and left me on my own to take out the screws. I tried the first screw and it wouldn't budge. I tried the next one and it was stuck just as bad. Then I tried a few more. Eventually I found some that I could turn. But even the ones I could turn required a lot of strength. I didn't realize that aircraft screws and bolts are either self-locking or safety wired. For the self-locking type, a binding material is put in the threads so screws and bolts won't come loose from vibration when aircraft fly. For a kid age 8, it definitely posed a problem. As I looked the plane over, I became worried. This plane had rows of screws that looked a mile long. I crept along at a snail's pace, taking out what I could.

Before long, Dad came out and saw the struggle I was having. He decided to help loosen the ones I couldn't turn. To my surprise, he had a tough time with some of them. He realized I wasn't strong enough, so he went around the plane and loosened all the screws for me. He then showed me how to hold the screwdriver better. Soon, I was making good progress, and the sound of screws going "ding" echoed in the hangar as they landed in a coffee can on the bare concrete floor.

As we took it apart, I felt sad. The more we took it apart, the more obvious it became that it couldn't fly. Dad was a hard worker who got things done quickly, which made the Bobcat look sadder almost by the minute. While I was turning screws on the outside, he took all the seats out of the cabin in no time. Out came the interior panels and fuselage gas tank next. Before long, Dad was finished disconnecting all the control cables, wires, fuel lines, and other items in the area where the wing attached to the fuselage. He even had most of the wing mounting bolts removed. Unfortunately, there was no crane or lift to hold the fuselage up while removing the wing. I would now get my first of many looks at the genius inside the man who was my father.

To separate the wing from the fuselage, he backed the trailer under the front of the fuselage. Then he slowly retracted the Bobcat's landing gear. Normally in flight, the landing gear was retracted and extended by jackscrews rotated with a bicycle-type chain turned by an electric motor. To retract the landing gear, Dad moved the chain by hand until the fuselage descended onto the trailer.

Now it was time to lower the wing. Dad let the partially retracted landing gear hold the front of the wing, while our spare car tire, wood blocks, and a jack held up the rear. He removed the last of the wing bolts and then further retracted the landing gear. Sure enough, the wing lowered while separating from the fuselage. After using the jack several times to take more blocks out from under the back of the wing, we finally had the wing resting on the hangar floor. He made it all look so easy. My airplane dad was Superman.

By using jacks, planks on roller pipes, and a winch, we were able to pull the fuselage forward to get it completely on the trailer. Dad and I felt really proud—briefly. Dad looked at the hangar's garage door, which was now the only big door remaining in the building. Then he looked back at the big bulky Bobcat fuselage on the trailer. "Gosh, I hope it's not too high," he said, sounding worried. The way it looked to me, I had my doubts. Dad quickly tied the fuselage down on the trailer and then slowly drove the Ford toward the door. As he suspected, the top of the Bobcat fuselage was too high.

"I can't believe it," Dad said, dismayed. "I don't know how the heck we're gonna get the fuselage off the trailer, drag it outside, and get it back on the trailer." We both walked around the trailer for a few moments. I could tell it was going to be dark soon and I was getting a little scared. I missed Mom and just wished I was home. I began to wonder if coming with Dad was a good idea. "Maybe I can take the wheels off the trailer and tow it out riding on the brake drums," Dad said. With a flashlight, we looked inside the trailer's Model-A Ford wheel hubs. Because that old type of hub was prone to collect and hold rainwater, the wheel lugs were caked in very heavy rust. Dad figured the wheel lugs were so rusted they'd snap and break if we tried to remove them. That also meant we had no way to change a bad tire if one of the old tires let go.

Quickly, Dad measured for height and realized we just needed to come down a few inches. We then let most of the air out of both trailer tires. That was enough to get us under the door and out the building. As I pumped the tires back up, Dad used wood blocks and more tie-downs to secure the load. After adding a taillight far behind the trailer to where the tail of the long fuselage eventually ended, we then headed home.

We didn't get real far when we realized something was very wrong. When Dad got out of town and hit the open road reaching a speed of about 50 mph, the trailer and car started to swerve. I snapped around and looked back. What I saw in the red glow of the Ford's taillights frightened me. The Bobcat fuselage was swaying wildly left and right. Dad jumped on the brakes and everything straightened out after a moment. As soon as he could, he pulled off the road.

We got out and looked things over closely with a flashlight, but couldn't find anything wrong. The trailer hitch, tires, and tie-downs were all fine. Dad went to the tail of the fuselage and pushed it left and right really hard. When the fuselage moved, the trailer moved with it as if the two were welded together. Since the load wasn't loose

Sky King–type Cessna T-50 Bobcat we hauled in October 1961. This trip begins the trend of too much airplane on too little trailer. Rust has visibly eaten away the 1952 Ford behind the rear wheel. Passenger door ajar as usual, which later resulted in Grandmother Murray almost falling out. School bus in background will soon make the epic 600-mile trip hauling the F7U Cutlass fighter jet from Boston.

and nothing else seemed wrong, Dad was baffled. "I guess we've got too much airplane on this small trailer," he shrugged his shoulders. I felt anxious as we got back in. In the middle of nowhere at night with a car that wouldn't drive straight, my young boy mind felt like we were a million miles from home.

As Dad accelerated, the car and trailer drove fine at first. I felt good that we were moving again. But as soon as he got up to about 50 mph again, the swaying came back. Dad slammed on the brakes and again we were okay. Since he figured there was nothing else he could do, he kept on driving. With a little trial and error, he finally figured out a speed at which he could maintain control. Since the Ford's speedometer was broken, we never knew our exact speed, but Dad was good at estimating his speed from experience. At what seemed like a snail's pace, we pressed on. Soon, cars started lining up behind us. Before long, we heard horns blowing. Dad pulled over and let the cars go by. As soon as we cleared the road, the cars roared by, with some laying on their horn as they passed. We continued to pull off the road about every five miles or so when Dad found a good place to do so. We were about halfway home when I suddenly noticed bright red flashing lights behind us.

"Oh no, the cops got us now!" Dad said as he pulled off the road. I was terrified. I knew we didn't rob a bank or steal the plane. But I was still panicked about going to jail like bad guys on TV. Dad got out of the car and so did I. The policeman asked for Dad's driver's license and vehicle registration. As I stood frozen with fear, the policeman smiled at me and said, "Hey, young man, looks like your father got a big toy airplane for you!" With that, he quickly calmed much of my fear.

"We didn't steal the airplane. Daddy paid a hundred dollars for it," I told the policeman. He assured me he wasn't worried about that, and said he just wanted to make sure everything was okay.

Cessna T-50 Bobcat on takeoff roll piloted by my longtime friend Rick Rice in 1983 (courtesy Rick Rice).

"What kind of airplane is it, son?" he asked.

"It's a Bobcat, just like Sky King flies on TV," I answered proudly. He turned to Dad for confirmation and Dad explained it was the exact same model as King's plane. The policeman knew of the TV show and seemed impressed, while also a bit amused, that we were hauling one down the highway. He led us around the car and trailer with his big flashlight, making an inspection of everything, including the Bobcat tie-downs. Dad made a point of showing how he nailed many wood blocks to tightly cage and secure the fuselage steel tubing to the trailer. The policeman only had one complaint, and that was about a crudely wrapped airplane cable serving as the safety chain for the trailer.

"That's probably just as good, but the law says you need a safety chain," the policeman stated.

"Yes sir, I'll have a safety chain next time," Dad replied. With this being my first airplane hauling adventure of countless more to follow, getting pulled over by the police was something Dad and I would have many opportunities to get used to. Compared to the ordeal he would soon face with many police, this event was a snoozer. I would be forever thankful that I would miss what was coming next.

4

Scraping By

"That should be long enough," Dad said while peeking through a clear spot on a frosted sunroom window to look down at the Ford. Though it was bitter cold on this Saturday morning in January, I could see frost and snow melting from the hood of the car. It should have melted from Dad's warming up the car, but the Ford wouldn't start in cold weather without some help. So he borrowed an electric heater we used in the house, and slid it under the car to warm the engine up. It was robbing Peter to pay Paul.

The house was freezing! On cold days like this, we were doing good to get the temperature in our house to 60. Except in the attic, the house had no insulation. For heat, we used an old coal furnace down in Dad's shop, and a potbelly coal stove upstairs. Mostly that combination worked okay, but when bitter cold hit, the house stayed cold. Luckily, Dad found a tall and narrow electric space heater at a rummage sale for a buck, and on really cold days, that old brown heater was helping heat the house when not doing duty under the Ford.

As I watched from upstairs, Dad got the Ford started. Besides the sound of the motor starting, another telltale sign told me it was running. The Ford puffed a cloud of blue smoke on startup. I felt dismal as I looked on. Round airplane motors were supposed to smoke during start—car engines were not. "Do I have to go?" I asked Mom for about the 10th time. I knew I had to ask while Dad was out of the house or somewhere he couldn't hear. He was a father I knew when not to question.

"Your father says you're going, so that means you're going," Mom answered. Reluctantly, I put on my dingy brown rummage-sale coat. I hated the coat so much the first day Mom tried to send me to school wearing it I purposely missed the school bus. But on this frigid day, the coat did its job of keeping me warm. Next, I did what I detested even more. I put on the red girl's boots I still had. What mattered more, I would soon realize the red rubber boots had little if any insulation. Finally, I put on the blue knitted mittens and hat my mother made.

Out the living room door, I headed down the unheated staircase of creaking oak steps that were mud-stained and worn. Reaching the cement at the bottom of the staircase, you had three options. A left turn took you into the hangar. A right turn took you inside the furnace room. I took the third option, straight ahead, opened the door and walked into a frigid blast of arctic-type air. Almost immediately, the sound of brittle snow and ice crunching under my boots told me this wasn't the day to play outside and have a snowball fight. Much too cold for that.

At the car, Dad was clearing frost and ice from the windshield in his own unusual way. The ultimate penny pincher, he didn't own a windshield scraper. Instead, he was using a narrow aluminum panel from the F-82 Twin Mustang. Winter after winter, he'd use that thing. It didn't do a good job and he'd scrape forever while that chunk of aluminum made a shrieking sound that could split ears better than ice. But as insignificant as this single endeavor was, it would hint a lot about the future and how a single word, *unconventional*, would continually define my father. But right now I was too young and too *cold* to be analytical.

Dad and I got in the car, and when my bottom hit the brown vinyl seat cover, a rude chill to my backside suggested I was sitting on an iceberg. Though the motor had been running for a while, more bad news was that car's heater still didn't work. The ice-cold interior of the car had frost on the inside of the windows as a result. More *unconventional* on the way. In the car, Dad grabbed an old cloth diaper that was bound into the shape of a sack, with a drawstring choking the diaper into a neck-like shape to prevent the contents, a few pounds of salt, from spilling out. Until now, the salt-sack diaper had been kept warm in the house. With the heat it retained, Dad was able to rub the windows with the salt sack and remove the frost.

Riding along as Dad drove on this bitterly cold Saturday, I had a lot on my mind. To start with, I was miserable. Certainly before the day was over, I figured I was going to freeze to death. And when I thought about why I was in this situation, things didn't add up. My father was a man who could singlehandedly take apart big airplanes and put them back together. He could build his own homemade equipment like the powerful boom tractor that could lift heavy airplane engines one day and rip large trees out of the ground the next. He could build our home using lumber from airplane engine crates. Even as a youngster I'd been impressed seeing my Superman father do so many things. But now, here we were into our second winter with the dreadful '52 Ford, and he had never *attempted* to fix the car's heater.

"My toes hurt," I told Dad after about 30 minutes on the road. I knew that pain well. The frequent snowstorms we got in that part of Ohio made boundless winter wonderlands that my sisters and I seldom missed the opportunity to play in. Whether we made snowmen, rode sleds down the many hills, had snowball fights, built ice forts, whatever, we all knew the pain you eventually get in your toes and fingers from playing in the cold. Nobody had to tell us when it was time to go inside.

In the house, my sisters and I would quickly shed our boots, coats, hats, and mittens. Then we'd form a circle around the black potbelly stove that was perched in the walkway between the living room and kitchen. Mom kept the coal fire well stoked, and always had more coal ready to go that was stored in an old five-gallon paint bucket nearby. With the cast iron top of the stove virtually red hot, the stove provided quick relief to frosted fingers. For fun, we'd take turns shaking our icy mittens above the cast iron top. Little clumps of snow and ice would fall onto the stove and instantly sizzle, pop, and steam like crazy. Years before anyone outside of MIT spoke the word *microwave*, we knew how to nuke the cold. But on the highway with the Siberian Ford taking me farther away from that potbelly stove, I was worried. Over and over I'd wiggle my toes, as I'd been taught that movement was one way to fight off frostbite and keep your blood flowing. "We're almost there. Maybe we'll find a place to go in and warm up," Dad said.

We pulled into a small parking lot at an airport. Nobody flying today as we observed snow-covered planes parked here and there. All but one of the planes were small private planes. A snow-covered stretch of land with a few weeds protruding up through the snow suggested the runway was a grass strip. Dad had me wait in the car while he got out and walked up to a country farmhouse nearby. At the front door, he talked to a man for a few moments and then came back. "Let's go take a look," he said to me as he opened the door and motioned for me to come along.

As we crunched our way through the ankle-deep snow, my rubber boots felt like concrete. After walking about a hundred yards or so, we came to the one big plane on the airport. It had one big round motor up front and seats for two pilots, one behind the other. Most of the plane was in a dull aluminum finish. The engine cowling and wingtips were painted bright orange. Dad said the plane was a T-28. I hardly knew one plane from another then, but later found it was a military training plane used mostly by the Air Force and Navy. This one had been sold surplus by the Air Force and now had a civilian FAA N-number. Unfortunately, the plane had been banged up in an accident. Both propeller blades were bent back, the nose landing gear was broken off, and the front canopy had a big hole knocked in it. We were told later the pilot had engine failure and landed at this airport. The airport was too small for the T-28, but the pilot had no other options. He ran out of runway before getting the plane stopped. Dad looked the plane over for about ten minutes before we headed back to the car. Forever tap dancing and wiggling my toes, I dreaded that we had a long, cold drive to get home. As we drove on, I fought the preoccupation with my freezing feet by listening to Dad rattle on about his predicament. "The guy wants $400 for the plane," he said.

"Are you gonna buy it?" I asked.

"There's no way right now. I've got no money." He then spoke of how he'd been out of work for over a month and it would be a few more months before he'd be called back. He went on talking about his frustration that he couldn't go to the aircraft boneyards in Arizona while there was still some time to save airplanes. "Right now, I can't even afford to drive to Arizona, let alone buy anything there," he said sadly. He talked on about being tied down here in Ohio with five kids and how he could not even afford a good car. He paused for a moment to rub the salt diaper against the windshield to clear some fog. "If only I didn't have such a large a family. I'm trapped now." As Dad drove while continuing his familiar spiel, my mind drifted back to stories and photographs he shared with me about the Arizona boneyards.

Arizona, Arizona, Arizona—the airplane land of milk and honey. Ever since he bought an old school bus two years earlier in 1960, he talked about the place a lot. Originally, he got the bus just to go there. He planned to make a camper out of it and, like legends of old, go west. But nothing became of those plans. His dismal financial situation, worsened by the burden of having a large family, made an Arizona trip about as far-fetched as President Kennedy's speech wanting Americans to go the moon.

More than once, I got to see what made him obsessed with going there. Dad collected books, magazines, newspaper articles, and almost anything else that related to airplanes. He had many articles and photographs of the aircraft boneyards he talked of so much. Some pictures were incredible. The pictures showed why America played such a decisive role in the victory of World War II. In aviation alone, our nation's industrial might enabled us to produce over 300,000 airplanes. Likewise, American factories cranked out record numbers of jeeps, trucks, tanks and ships. We simply overwhelmed our opponents by using every kind of factory to make war materials. As one example, the Goodyear tire factory in Akron ended up building warplanes, including Dad's Corsairs.

After the war, our military had an incredibly huge surplus of equipment, especially warplanes. Like the scrap yard where Dad previously worked in Cleveland, elsewhere in America large furnaces were still busy melting down old warplanes to recycle the metals. Of all the places doing this, the volume of recycling being done in Arizona was enormous. At Arizona boneyards like Litchfield Park, the pictures Dad collected told the story. As far as the eye could see, the desert was lined with untold thousands of warplanes stretching for miles and miles.

"Look what they're doing there," Dad said as he pointed to some photos in a scrapbook he was thumbing through as he sat on our worn sofa. The edges of the sofa cushions were badly worn, which prompted Mom to do her best, using a brown bedspread to conceal the wear. As Dad motioned to me, I joined him on the sofa.

"Look what they're doing to that poor TBM," Dad said as he pointed to a photo sequence showing the demise of a Navy TBM Avenger torpedo plane. As a crane holds up the big plane by its tail, the front of the plane is being slowly lowered into a giant vat of molten aluminum. In several time-elapsed photos, the plane is dipped lower and lower until eventually it was all gone. "Makes me want to cry," Dad said. Anguished, he repeated over and over his no-money-for-saving-airplanes blues. He told how the planes were still being sold cheap at their scrap metal value, which made his situation hurt even more. He didn't need a lot of money, but he needed more than he had. No credit cards in those days. You either had the money to go on a trip like that or you didn't go.

As I looked on, he continued thumbing through the scrapbook. Page after page showed pictures of doomed planes in the desert awaiting their trip to the furnace. Then, Dad flipped to a picture that hit home. Again, as far as you could see were rows of planes, but these were ones I knew. Corsairs, just like in my backyard. Several years later, those pictures came to mind when an ex-Navy mechanic visited our place. He told us something about Zero Zero that made us stop in our tracks. He remembered this distinctly numbered Corsair very well. Zero Zero, he told us, was supposed to go to Arizona. On the day of its scheduled flight from the Akron Naval Air Station, they couldn't get the engine to run properly. They had so much trouble with the engine they wanted to change it. "Stupid Navy," the mechanic said. He then told how the Navy took away their spare engines before all the Corsairs were flown to the boneyard. "That's how this Corsair got stranded in Ohio," he finished.

"Well, I could care less if she's got a bad engine. If that's what kept her from going to the furnace, that's fine with me—she's safe here now," Dad said lovingly as his hand gently caressed the front of the wing. "Smart bird, I'm telling you. She knew what was up."

Finally home from our frigid trip in the Ford, I quickly had my frozen feet adoring and all but touching the potbelly stove. I couldn't care less about Arizona, except Dad had mentioned the place was really hot.

With bills to be paid, it was during this same winter that Dad had me working with him in his shop. With the days of scrapping aircraft engines in his shop long over, Dad turned to something else. Through one of his old scrap yard contacts, he began to work scrap metal again. For many years, Dad and a man named Mike had been good friends. They stuck together as friends since the days when they worked side-by-side using cutting torches on surplus airplane engines at the scrap yard. Since that time, things had changed a lot. Mike stayed in the scrap metal business, working his way up, while Dad went off to be a carpenter. By the time I met Mike, he owned and ran what had become a large industrial magnesium plant.

About six feet tall, Mike had a trim and solid build, and with his handsome and chiseled European facial features, he had a bit of a Robert De Niro tough-guy look about him. By Dad's description of how he rose to take over the plant, Mike would also pass the test for being a tough and go-getter kind of guy. Above all, Dad respected Mike as a man who climbed the company ladder by working hard.

I can't say I liked going to the magnesium plant. It was noisy, filthy, and blazing hot with thick gray smoke billowing out its vast open doors from the giant vats of molten metal, and I didn't see how anyone could work there. But somehow they did, as a dozen or more men tended to the furnaces. Some would add scrap magnesium to some furnaces while other men drained the molten metal from other furnaces and formed them into shiny ingots.

Mike, of course, was nested in the front office now. Seeing him was always a treat. Like I was his own kid, he always greeted me with a big smile. With little delay, he'd reach in his desk drawer and then toss coins at me with one hand while pointing the way to the soda and candy bar machines with the other. When I came back with a drink and chocolate bar, he'd shut Dad up and then ask me to tell him any new jokes from school. I always made sure I had a few good jokes ready to tell him and he would laugh his butt off each time.

With the big airplane engines mostly gone, Mike had to buy all sorts of scrap to get magnesium for his plant. Among the big lots of scrap he'd bid on and buy, some electrical and aluminum scrap would be mixed in with the magnesium scrap he needed. He explained to Dad that this other scrap was more of a nuisance than anything else. Leading us out behind the plant, he pointed out several huge stacks of electrical cabinets and other items in the scrap yard while telling Dad, "Take all you want, it would cost me a lot more to clean it than it's worth." Then Dad and I would drag the electrical cabinets and other stuff to the old Ford and trailer, loading all that we could get aboard.

Back home in Dad's shop, we began to work the electrical cabinets to separate the copper, aluminum and steel from each other. We did the same with large electric motors. It was tedious, hard, and dirty work. Dad taught me a lot about the motors and other electrical items, so I found that interesting. Still, processing scrap metal was nasty work. Yet Dad seemed totally at home working scrap metal, and as I would see, the junkman roots his earlier scrap metal job planted would grow deeper and influence much of his life to come. We were of totally different minds here. I didn't like the scrap metal work, but realized it helped pay the bills. Still, like hauling the Bobcat, I found Dad a lot easier to be with when we were working. Hard at work is where I saw his best moods. As we both sat on old wood carpenter benches working the scrap metal, he told a lot of his stories.

As he often did, he told stories of the rough times during the Great Depression. Relating those times to what we were doing now, he told story after story about how people were so poor then that finding any kind of scrap metal was like winning a prize. The story that got me the most was the one of how people would pick through big city trash dumps looking for old light bulbs. Once finding a bulb, they would pry off and salvage the small piece of brass that was soldered to the tip where the bulb screwed in. To this day, many light bulbs are still made with that tiny piece of brass. Thus, I could easily visualize what Dad was saying. People during the Depression were truly *desperate.*

Finally, Dad hauled a load of scrap metal to a dealer in Cleveland. He walked away with around $200 in cash. Even in 1962, that wasn't a lot of money, but fortunately we didn't have many bills. No house payment, no car payment, and no such thing as cable

TV back then. My parents' bills were limited to property tax once a year, a phone bill, and what Dad called "the light bill." Unlike homes today, we didn't have electrical appliances like a clothes dryer, dishwasher, or air conditioner. Even our coal furnace didn't have an electric blower. Coal furnaces were installed in basements so the heat would rise through the furnace ducts to warm the rooms above. So our living expenses were quite low. Money went a lot further then, with a new car typically costing about $2,000. And far short of even thinking about a new car, my parents were frugal in so many ways that it didn't take much money to stay afloat. When I wore a hole through the bottom of my shoes, Mom bought some glue-on soles to keep the old shoes going. And when my belt eventually got too short for a growing boy, Mom simply punched an extra hole in the leather to extend it further.

While I found the scrap metal work depressing, Dad was diversified in his endeavors, with some being more encouraging. Though the old school bus Dad planned to use as a camper for his Arizona trip never turned into that, he found a good use for the bus. The previous summer, he bid on a stockpile of B-25 bomber parts from a military depot in Columbus. Few World War II era aircraft were kept in the active military through the 1950s, but the B-25 was a big exception. Hundreds of them found new life after the war as multi-engine pilot and navigator training planes. Eventually, by 1960, most Air Force B-25s had taken their final flight to an Arizona boneyard. The Air Force sold off all the spare parts as well.

With the bus stripped of every seat except the one for the driver, Dad packed the entire bus all the way to the ceiling with the B-25 parts he won on the bid. Though the bus did a good job of hauling the big load, Dad was in great danger. An old splintered sheet of plywood jammed behind the driver seat was the only thing separating him from the tons of boxes loaded behind him. If he'd had an accident or hit the brakes too hard on the 150-mile trip, he likely would have been crushed to death by the shifting cargo. He hauled the parts on a Friday to avoid missing more than one day from his carpenter job.

That meant a busy weekend for the rest of us. Luckily, the Saturday morning weather was nice as the dirt parking area on the north side of our house became a sea of cardboard boxes by mid-morning. Dad was chipper as could be going through the myriad of boxes with all of us pitching in. To his amazement, all the parts were either new or freshly overhauled. Since I seldom saw anything new on our property, the scene was astonishing. The parts were spotless. Glass windshields and Plexiglas windows glistening with perfection were devoid of the typical cracks and fading we were accustomed to seeing in similar items on the planes Dad owned. And no matter what each part was, all were professionally packed to the point you felt like an intruder to dare open a box.

Before that summer ended, Dad hauled two more busloads of B-25 parts home. By the time he was done, his poor shop was stuffed up to its tall ceiling. And like other things he collected, I wondered what he planned to do with it all. When money got extra tight that winter, I got my answer. While working the scrap metal as a laid-off carpenter, Dad also began to advertise his B-25 parts in *Trade-A-Plane*, a yellow paper airplane shopper. Fortunately, a number of civilians were operating some of the bombers to haul cargo, fight forest fires, and perform other roles. Thus, the ads in *Trade-A-Plane* turned out to be a bonanza.

Dad got a lot of orders. In particular, we found that B-25 owners disliked the multi-pane windshield the planes originally came with. When they found out that Dad had dozens of new one-piece windshields, they went nuts. Suddenly we were in the parts and shipping business. Ever the scrounger, Dad had a collection of crates from bathtubs, sinks, toilets, and other household items he hauled home before getting laid off from his carpenter job. After packing the orders of B-25 parts into the crates, we'd haul them in the old Ford wagon to the local trucking company. I don't know how much Dad charged for the parts, but I know the markup was great. I remember helping him pack one crate, which he said was an order for over $300. Considering that each busload of parts cost him barely $100, Dad was making a killing. Despite what seemed like an enormous profit to me, he set a great example being honest and fair.

"Several of these people have called to tell me I'm selling the stuff too cheap!" he chuckled. They told him they couldn't believe he wasn't charging more, once they saw how new everything was. He was happy with his big profits, and if buyers were happy about getting a good deal, that was fine. "There's no point in me being greedy," he emphasized, and set a good example for me. The money could not have come at a better time. Mom and Dad were able to pay off some bills, and I finally got my first new pair of black boots made for a boy.

There also occurred a sign that timing is perhaps everything. While at the trucking company unloading a crate of B-25 parts from the Ford one night, the entire tailgate fell off and hit the ground with a thud. Rust and gravity had won another battle with the car. The tailgate had been giving Dad fits when he opened and closed it. Now we knew why. With some money in his pocket, Dad finally set out to find a better set of wheels. Needless to say, I was thrilled about that. What I didn't know was that he had some other shopping in mind.

5

The Banana Bus

Dad had been gone for over a week now getting a Navy jet fighter plane known as an F7U Cutlass, and we were all terribly worried. Never before had he been gone overnight, let alone a whole week. The house seemed empty without him. He was truly the man of the house whose commanding presence gave our family a strong sense of security. Now we felt anxious, as it seemed he was never coming back.

As the days went by, I kept hoping that after school I'd find him back at home. Instead, Mom would get a phone call every night, and each time it was the same story. He was having lots of problems. Finally, he told her he was heading home and expected to arrive sometime that night. Dad used the same old school bus to go on this trip that he used to haul the B-25 parts the previous summer. By now, I knew the bus well, and that it had a unique sound due to some custom exhaust pipe work Dad did. On those previous hauling trips, I would always play out in the yard until I could hear the telltale sound of the bus making its way on the narrow gravel road. This evening I roamed the yard and played outside well into the night as I waited to hear that sound. Eventually, the phone rang. Dad called to report that he was having more problems and would not be home tonight. As I went to bed, I didn't know what to think.

The next morning started off bright and sunny with a late winter frost blanketing the neighborhood. I was up about five minutes when, even with the windows closed, I could hear it. "Hey, listen, I hear the bus!" I yelled. A few of my sisters doubted me. One suggested I was hearing a garbage truck. Mom walked to the big windows on the east side of our second-story living room and looked down the long gravel road from which Dad always appeared when towing a plane home. She commented, "Garbage trucks are never out this early."

Quickly, we were all staring out the windows looking for signs of the bus. Mom opened a window to hear better. Without a doubt now, something was heading our way, laboring with a heavy load. I was certain this was it. The sound grew really loud as the vehicle climbed up the hill. Finally, it came into view, and at first nothing looked amiss. Then we could not believe our eyes. "Look, look, look!" everybody started yelling. "Oh, my gosh!" Mom exclaimed.

I started for the door, but Mom hollered, "Stay inside until he's done driving."

"What happened to the bus?" someone yelled.

"It looks awful!" said another.

"What on Earth has he done this time?" Mom said. She sounded a little stunned and amused all at the same time. Dad slowly parked the bus alongside the house, and as Mom gave the go-ahead, I dashed noisily down the wood stairs and out onto the

5. The Banana Bus

Photograph Dad took of a Navy F7U Cutlass in Cleveland in 1956. Due to safety problems and other issues, F7Us were taken out of service a few years later. I doubt Dad would have guessed his bid of $200 on a military scrap sale would win him a Cutlass in 1962.

driveway. The bus and its cargo created an unbelievable sight. There was a huge jet airplane crammed inside the bus. Unfortunately, it didn't exactly fit. The entire back wall and rear door of the bus were missing. The jet stuck out about ten feet past the rear bumper. In addition to being too long, the jet was too high and too wide to squeeze inside the bus. Thus, the back half of the roof and the side of the bus were split in two places kind of like a split banana peel.

As I stood in the driveway in a daze, I wondered why Dad was taking so long to get out of the bus. I went to the side door of the bus and looked inside. Almost in my face was the dull silver round shape of a jet plane blocking entry into the bus. Then I heard a grunting and scuffling sound up near the bus ceiling. I leaned in the door and looked up and back where I heard the noise. I spotted Dad spread-eagle on top of the plane behind the cockpit. There he was, working his way through the small gap between the top of the fuselage and the ceiling of the bus to get out. Being a typical school bus, it had no door on the driver side, so this was the only way out. Dad looked tired and haggard as he struggled to get out of the bus. His clothes were filthy dirty and he hadn't shaved in a couple of days.

Still, after working his way down to the steps of the bus, he cracked a smile on his weary face. "I didn't think I'd *ever* get home! I've been on the dang road without any sleep for over 40 hours!" He slowly headed to the house and up the stairs, where Mom gave him a big hug. She offered to cook breakfast, but Dad was too tired to stay up. Instead, he went to bed, where Mom took breakfast to him.

Soon it was time to head to school, so my sisters and I left the house and headed to the bus stop. The Newbury School bus was right on time, and even though this bus was getting a little old, it looked like a million bucks compared to what I'd just seen. The school day started off in the usual way. We said the Pledge of Allegiance, and then had show and tell. Since I was in the third grade, the topics were mostly limited to a new toy that someone got or maybe a new baby brother that was just born. I was dying for someone to say, "Hey, Wally, what's new at your house?"

"Oh, nothing much—my father just came home with a jet fighter plane crammed inside a school bus." Fortunately, it wasn't my turn today. The time would soon come for me to share my news. I'd always had some trouble concentrating in school, but today was beyond compare. I didn't hear a word the teacher said. All I could think about was the bus with the jet plane stuffed inside. I wanted to get home and hear all about it. But I also knew Dad was sleeping. So even if I were home, it wouldn't make any difference. The day dragged on forever, and as it did, I wondered what the trip must have been like. I also reflected on the things about the jet I already knew.

About a month earlier, Dad saw the jet listed for sale in a government scrap metal bid at South Weymouth Naval Air Station near Boston. On a bit of a whim, he decided to bid $200 for the plane. One day he picked up the mail and was shocked to find he was the highest bidder. Mom didn't know what to think, but Dad was excited. To get himself prepared, he dug through his book and magazine collection looking for everything he could find about the plane. As he read about the F7U Cutlass, he got more excited. But he also found reason to worry.

Though the jet was a fighter plane, it was a big fighter. It was also very heavy. Largely a result of being sturdy enough to handle Navy carrier landings, the Cutlass fighter weighed more than many World War II bombers. Dad hadn't realized this until *after* he won the bid for the plane. Quickly, he found himself having second thoughts. But now it was too late. He owned it, and the Navy expected him to pick it up within 30 days.

The more he read, the more concerned he got. The Cutlass was by far heavier than any plane he had ever hauled. Also, the 600-mile trip to Boston was at least three times farther than any trip he had ever made. Having hauled most planes 50 miles or less, the thought of hauling something all the way from Boston troubled him a lot. In addition to the problem with the distance, Dad didn't have and couldn't afford a truck. As more details about the Cutlass became known, Mom wasn't happy. But she accepted the fact that Dad won the bid and was now required by the government to get the thing. With the 30-day clock ticking, he started his preparations right away.

He hooked the small trailer we hauled the Bobcat with to a '57 Chevy Suburban he'd recently purchased and went to a truck salvage yard in Cleveland. When he came home, he had a big and long frame from a junked delivery truck loaded on top of his old trailer. Quickly he went to work on the truck frame to convert it into a new heavy-duty trailer. He removed the front axle, then cut and welded the frame to make a hitch. Next, he mounted two long wood beams on the frame like runners on a big boat trailer. After the installation of taillights and wires, the old truck frame was now a sturdy and big two-wheel trailer.

Next, he started working on the old bus. It had been off the road for a while and needed some brake work, a trailer hitch, and some other minor repairs. Using his torch and some scrap steel, he made a trailer hitch in a few hours. The rapid speed with which Dad got all these things done suggested he had a fairly exact plan in mind. But for the rest of us, what he was about to do was far beyond anything we imagined.

5. The Banana Bus

Since he had used the bus to haul the B-25 parts, the idea that he would go on another hauling trip with it didn't seem out of the ordinary. As he made his preparations to leave, things were pretty much business as usual. When he left for Boston early on a Sunday morning, he only expected to be gone a few days. But now, with him back at home more than a week later, the incredible sight of the huge jet inside the bus made it easy to see that Dad's trip had been far more difficult than he'd expected.

None of us knew what to think about Dad's latest airplane adventure. I was still in a bit of a daze as it just seemed unbelievable. At age eight I still wasn't sure what to think of this man who was my father. One thing for sure, I would never view him as boring! He was up by the time I got home, but he was still very tired. I wanted to know all about the trip, but he wanted to wait until all of us were together before he began his tale. Mom cooked an early supper, and as we gathered and ate, Dad got started.

"Never do that again," he said, sounding a bit shaken. "Didn't think I'd ever make it home." Wondering if he meant the old bus gave him trouble, I asked if the bus ran okay.

"Sure, it ran fine," Dad responded with a proud smile. "Ran like a clock the whole trip."

"Yeah, until the alarm went off," one of my sisters wisecracked. We all laughed, including Dad. He was used to us by now. Between five kids, someone often had a funny comment to add to whatever was being said. Dad proudly explained how the old bus handled the long trip well and only burned a quart of oil. By the time he got to Boston, it was late Sunday night. He found a truck stop to park at and went to sleep in the back of the bus with the pillows, blankets, and cushions Mom packed for him. The bus had no heat, but fortunately the Boston weather was mild that March night. The next morning, he arrived at the Navy base. The guards at the gate gave him a pass and let him right in.

"Things are going great, I thought," Dad told us. "Then I went to the disposal yard and all heck broke loose," he said wearily. He met the civilians running the disposal yard and told them he was there to get the Cutlass as he showed them his paperwork. Then they had a few unexpected questions.

"Do you have a check for the performance bond?" one of the men asked.

"What bond?" Dad replied. They showed him some papers that required him to put up a $10,000 bond to guarantee that he would *destroy* the plane. Dad was stunned. He purchased the jet for the purpose of displaying it in his airplane collection, so the idea of destroying it was a complete surprise. Dad was unaware the military made a recent change in its policy for selling aircraft. In the past, some people bought surplus military planes and sold them to foreign governments. Fearing the planes could later be used against the United States, the government decided it would no longer sell combat planes to civilians—unless they were destroyed. Of course, the other problem with the $10,000 performance bond was the $10,000 part. Dad barely had enough money with him for food and gas. Just coming up with the $200 to pay for the plane broke the family bank. And there was more trouble.

"Do you have your insurance policy available?" the disposal man asked.

"What insurance?" Dad answered, getting a bad feeling. The disposal man explained that accident insurance was required in case he or one of his workers got hurt.

"But I don't have any workers," Dad said. "I'm here by myself."

"Then what salvage company do you work for?" the man asked, sounding puzzled.

"I'm a carpenter. I haul planes as a hobby," Dad answered. "I'm doing this totally on my own." The civilian told Dad that without the performance bond and insurance policy he could not let him do anything. He said he would need to discuss the matter with some Navy officers before anything could be done. He did give Dad permission to go out and look the plane over.

When Dad got to the plane, he was shocked by its size. Quickly, he began to measure and study it. Before long, a group of men arrived in several Navy vehicles. Just the size of the group made Dad feel uneasy. As he looked the men over, he saw a mix of Navy officers in their dress uniforms as well as some enlisted men. Dad couldn't help notice the officer uniforms. The black coats, braid, insignia, ribbons, and most notably—*wings*. Some of these officers are Navy pilots, Dad realized. He looked at their shoes, which were so spotless and shiny "you could eat off of them," he told us.

In early 1962, the civilians running the disposal yard at Boston's South Weymouth Naval Air Station call in the Navy leadership to question Dad about his plan to haul an F7U Cutlass fuselage using the 1945 White Motor Company school bus in the background.

"Are you the man here to get the Cutlass?" one of the officers asked.

"Yes, sir, I bought it on this bid," Dad said, as he showed him his papers. "Doesn't say anything about a $10,000 performance bond."

"Well, it must be a mistake," the officer answered. "We'll need to straighten it out before we can let you take the plane. And what about insurance for your workers? You don't have that either?"

"No, I don't have any workers. I'm here by myself," Dad answered, feeling very uneasy with the direction the conversation was going.

"No one else is coming?" the officer asked, clearly puzzled. "Well then, who's going to bring your truck?"

Dad was really on the spot now. He knew the answer to the officer's question, but he also knew what the answer would sound like. Sure, he'd love to have cruised in with a big eighteen-wheel flatbed, and he understood the Navy sort of expected him to show up with one. But short on money, the bus was all he had. Fearing he could be locked up as a crazy lunatic, Dad simply answered, "I don't have a truck—I'm going to put the fuselage in this bus and put the wings on that trailer."

"Do what!" the officer exclaimed. "I thought the bus was your camper. You're, you're not going to do … uh … gee, did you guys hear that?" he said, turning to the others. As Dad told this part of the story, his expression was haunting. Young as I was, I could tell my otherwise strong father had been worried sick. As he continued the story, he told us he figured the Navy guys were either going to throw him off the base or maybe even lock him up. For some reason Dad wasn't even sure of, he took his airplane photo album on the trip and suddenly figured his only hope was to show the Navy officers some photos of the Corsairs and other planes he had saved.

"Two Corsairs?" The senior officer sounded impressed. Dad explained how his rare F2G Corsair won the 1947 Cleveland National Air Races and would probably have been scrapped if he hadn't saved it. Then he showed pictures of his Zero Zero Corsair and the F-82 Twin Mustang, telling how these planes would have been scrapped if not for him. Then, he told how many types of military planes were now almost extinct as the military scrapped them with little or no thought of keeping some for museums. Like all the other planes now gone, he told them, "The Cutlass jet will die the same as the others" unless he got it home—somehow.

"Well, it sure is an interesting collection you've got," the officer said. He sounded supportive, but expressed concern there was likely no way around the new regulation requiring the jet to be destroyed. Then he explained that he'd have to go back to his office and see if the issues could be resolved somehow.

"I scored points with those pictures," Dad told us. He described it as like a miracle he took the photo album with him since the Navy men didn't believe a thing he said until he showed them the photos of his Corsairs and Twin Mustang. While he still wasn't allowed to do anything, he at least felt relieved the senior officer appeared willing to try to work things out. "I was just happy they didn't lock me up and throw the key away!" Dad grinned.

Before long, the people running the disposal yard let Dad know that their commander gave approval for him to work on the Cutlass, but he was not allowed to remove anything from the base yet. It was great news, Dad thought. He figured it would take about two days to get the plane apart, and by then everything else would hopefully be taken care of.

Being a large fighter, it was powered by two jet engines with afterburners, one of many jet innovations pioneered with the Cutlass. As he continued to study the plane, he debated whether to remove the internally mounted engines or leave them in the fuselage. Removing the engines would bring down the weight of the fuselage, but wouldn't make it any smaller. Also, it would mean another trip to Boston to get the engines. And it would be a lot of work to remove them. While studying the airframe, Dad found that the wings were made to come off at the fuselage. That made him glad, since it meant he wouldn't have to use the torch to cut anything. The rear fuselage came off where the afterburners were, and since there was no tail section on the odd-shaped plane, that was it. The disassembly looked fairly simple.

Dad had been working on the plane for several hours when a staff car pulled up. Several officers got out, and Dad could tell that these guys were a bit more senior than the first group. The most senior officer held the rank of commander.

"I hear you plan to put this plane in a museum," the commander said.

"Well, it's not officially a museum, but I do have a collection of planes I let the public see for free," Dad answered. He got his photo album out again and gave this officer the Corsair pitch.

"Great airplane, that Corsair. I'm glad you saved a couple," the commander nodded his approval of the pictures. Dad explained how the performance bond and insurance requirement caught him by surprise. He showed the officer all his bid paperwork, which made no mention of these requirements. "I'm not sure what's going on here, but maybe we can work something out," the commander said, sounding positive and friendly. "What I do know for sure is that we must demilitarize the plane so it can never fly again."

"What if I just damage the airframe so it can't fly but could still be displayed in my collection?" Dad asked.

"What do you mean?" asked the commander.

Dad then led the commander to the nose gear wheel well. "I'll cut the longerons here and here," Dad pointed to the structural parts of the forward fuselage. Then, going back to the wing where he had removed some access panels, he pointed inside to the heavy wing spar structure. "Here, I'll cut sections out of the wing spar with my torch." Dad elaborated that besides cutting these structural areas and removing metal, the extreme heat of his torch would ruin the precise heat treatment manufactured into the remaining metals. "After I cut and damage these areas, the plane can never fly again," Dad told him, while telling of his airplane mechanic's license in order to sound credible. He was certain the plane would still be plenty strong to hold together on the ground for static display purposes.

The commander paused for a bit, then said, "If the structure is ruined so it can't ever fly again, I suppose we could call it demilitarized." He gestured that this could be a reasonable compromise. "It certainly won't be anything you'll want to display if we make you cut it into small pieces," he added, seeming to agree that the book answer was too severe. Then he moved away and talked it over with the other Navy personnel for a while. When he came back, he told Dad he would accept Dad's plan to damage the plane's structure. He added that his Navy mechanics would need to inspect the plane and concur that it was no longer capable of restoration for flight before the plane could be removed.

"I understand," Dad replied.

5. The Banana Bus

"You know I'm really sticking my neck out over this. But if you're planning to display the jet to the public, I'll agree to it," the commander said.

"Thank you, sir, I promise she'll get a good home!" Dad answered. He was really excited. The Navy red tape, rules and regulations had seemed impossible to overcome. But now it was beginning to appear he was going to be able to save the jet after all. Yet more good news, the commander offered Dad housing on base. He became aware Dad was living in the bus and kindly insisted there was no need for that. Finally, he offered the support of Navy mechanics and equipment to disassemble the plane.

"That's okay, I can do it," Dad reassured the commander.

"I'm sure you can," the officer smiled. "But I'll bet we've got a few guys on this base that need something to do," he added as he looked around at the others, who nodded in agreement. "Whatever you need to get the job done—let me know." Then he and his staff got in their car and left. Before long, some Navy vehicles arrived with about a dozen enlisted men. The guys all seemed willing and ready to help. With all the equipment the men had available, Dad figured he'd be on the road home in a day or two.

"I would never have guessed I'd still be with those guys a week later," Dad told us. Getting the wings off the plane turned out to be a major ordeal. When the plane was built, large pins were used to attach the wings to the fuselage. As Dad and the Navy mechanics soon discovered, the pins were put in with a very tight fit. When they tried to get them out, the pins wouldn't budge. As each thing they tried failed, the Navy

Dad gets the okay to proceed with his plan to save the Cutlass. Left to right: CPO Jacobs, CDR Mellblom, Walter Soplata, LCDR Kuhns, LCDR Miller.

mechanics went back to their shop to get more and more tools. They used all kinds of jacks, drivers, hammers, and penetrating oil, but nothing seemed to work. Finally, after they tried heating the fittings with a torch and wiggling the wings with a crane, the pins slowly began to come out when pressed with a hydraulic jack. Dad was impressed by how hard the Navy mechanics worked to help him.

During the disassembly process, the commander came by to visit once a day to see how it was going. Each time he came, he brought more people with him to see the man from Ohio who was going to save the Cutlass. The commander was always friendly and even joked with Dad after a few days. "You've gotten more work out of these men than we have. Maybe we should commission you as an officer!" the commander laughed.

As Dad spent more and more time with the mechanics, he learned some history about the Cutlass, since a few of the men had worked on the fighters back when they were still flying. The mechanics informed Dad that the Cutlass, unlike most military planes, wasn't retired due to being obsolete. Instead, the planes were taken out of service due to a poor safety record, especially on aircraft carriers.

Perhaps too forward-thinking for the Stone Age days of the early jets, the Chance Vought engineers who designed the Cutlass were out there on the edge of the frontier—way out. Lacking a tail, the somewhat bat-shaped plane was by definition unconventional. The lack of a tail forced the Cutlass designers to use one control surface instead of tail-mounted "elevator" controls to raise and lower the nose of the plane and "ailerons" on the wing to control roll. They created an "ailevon" behind the wing on each side to do everything. A simple innovation, it would seem; however, it came with a price. Most planes use "flaps" that lower at the back of the wing to get more lift at slow speeds for takeoff and landing. For the Cutlass, the presence of the ailevons on its wing, combined with the lack of a tail, ruled out the use of wing flaps.

Without any flaps, the only way to get a Cutlass airborne on a short carrier deck was to catapult the jet in a steep nose-up attitude that put the wing at a high angle to the wind. Properly termed, engineers and pilots call this "angle of attack," or simply AOA. To get the high AOA needed for carrier takeoffs, the Cutlass had a very long nose landing gear. Unfortunately, the gear was so long that its leverage caused structural problems. On some carrier landings, the long nose gear would collapse, causing the cockpit to slam down, which resulted in severe and sometimes fatal injuries to the pilot.

Additionally, early jet engines weren't known for being powerful or reliable. In particular, the engines used in the Cutlass had numerous development problems, some of which caused them to be de-rated to far less thrust than originally expected. Though the plane had two engines and was the first jet to use afterburners, it still ended up being so underpowered that it needed both engines to fly a landing approach to a carrier. As a result of that problem, it gained the nickname "Gutless Cutlass."

When flying it from land bases, the pilots actually liked many things about the jet. It was known for being very maneuverable and great for aerobatics. But operating from carriers became a different story. Accidents at sea claimed a number of Navy pilots, resulting in yet more bad names like "Ensign Eliminator" and "Widow Maker." By today's standards the jet would never have been produced. Back then, though engineers were learning rapidly, the Cutlass and other early jets were virtual experiments. Like the early NASA rockets that were prone to blow up, early jet planes had a lot of problems, which made crashes a lot more common than today. Of the pilots who flew the Cutlass, the most famous had to be astronaut Wally Schirra. In his pre–NASA days, while serving as a Navy test pilot, Schirra was well known for his expertise in flight testing the Cutlass and teaching other pilots the finer points of flying it.

While the Cutlass greatly advanced the frontier of jet fighter planes, in just a few years 25 pilots paid for that advancement with their lives. Due to the jet's poor safety record, the Navy finally gave up on the Cutlass. Dad was told the plane he got just happened to be in Boston on a trip from another base when the grounding order came. Since it couldn't be flown anywhere, the Navy decided to sell it for scrap after the plane had sat on the base for several years. Another thing Dad found out was that in the few years since the last Cutlass flew, most had already been junked. Many that were on aircraft carriers were said to have been pushed overboard into the sea. Thus, much like the World War II planes, the Cutlass jets were quickly destroyed almost to extinction.

When Dad and his Navy crew finally got the wings removed, it was time to load the fuselage into the bus. Some of the mechanics tried to talk Dad into removing the engines to make the fuselage lighter. But being weary from removing the wings, he decided to go for it and haul the fuselage, engines and all. To prepare the bus for loading, Dad used his torch and removed the last foot of the bus body, making the back completely open. As a crane held the fuselage in the air, Dad backed the bus to slide the fuselage inside the bus. This worked well for a while. Then, the fuselage hung up and wouldn't go in anymore. The men looked everywhere to see what was caught. They determined that the roof of the bus was not quite high enough for the middle section of

Navy crane holds the Cutlass fuselage for loading. Bulging right wall of school bus peeling open results in Navy personnel calling it the "Banana Bus."

the fuselage to fit. Thus, Dad got his torch and cut a slot in the middle of the roof on the rear half of the bus. They got the fuselage in a little further, but it got stuck again. Then, one of the Navy guys had an idea.

As Dad sat in the driver's seat of the bus, the Navy guys parked a big truck in front of him and set the brakes. Then Dad held the brakes on the bus as another man drove a bulldozer up behind the jet and pushed it the rest of the way into the bus. "I was scared to death," Dad told us. He quickly realized there was no way the dozer driver could see him as the dozer pushed the nose of the jet forward toward the bus's dashboard. And there was no way anyone could hear him yell if need be. With the loud sound of the bulldozer and all the metal scraping, popping, and screeching, the noise was deafening. As Dad watched the nose come further and further forward toward him, he worried it might cock to one side and crush him. As the jet's nose came far enough forward to block his path to the bus door on the right, Dad realized he had no chance of escape if anything went wrong. Despite the slot Dad cut in the roof of the bus, the fuselage was still too big. As the bulldozer forced the fuselage the rest of the way into the bus, the right wall of the bus split away from the floor aft of the rear wheels. As a result, it was the Navy men who quickly nicknamed the bus the "banana bus" since it was big, yellow, and had split apart at its seams.

Dad stands on his new homemade trailer behind the Cutlass fuselage. This trailer soon becomes Walter's airplane-hauling workhorse. On this trip it rides behind the school bus under the overhang of the Cutlass fuselage. A torched-off corner of the bus displays the license tag for the epic road trip home.

After the bus was loaded, Dad attached the bus license plate to the back of the jet and was ready to go. The plan to put the wings on the trailer was obviously too optimistic. He'd have to come back for them later. While the bus carried the full weight of the fuselage, about ten feet of the jet hung out over the trailer. As he prepared to leave, the commander and other Navy staff came by to see him off and wish him good luck. Dad was touched by the sincerity of their sendoff and good wishes, but also heard rumors that no one expected him to make it. One enlisted guy even told him the sailors on base were making bets. Dad asked the sailor, "What do the guys think the odds are for me making it?"

"Oh, nobody's betting you'll make it. They're just betting how far you'll get," the sailor answered. "The highest bet right now is 50 miles."

6

Walter the Conqueror

Despite finishing the long ordeal of getting the Cutlass disassembled and loaded in the bus, the truth was that Dad's problems were just beginning. "Took forty hours to get home," he told us. "I don't know how I ever stayed awake that long." We began to ask him questions about why it took so long. Did he have to go slow because of the load, did he have flat tires, or were there other problems? He said no to all of our questions speculating about the delay.

"No, I would have gotten home a lot quicker if the police hadn't kept stopping me," said Dad.

"Did you have to go jail?" someone asked. Our eyes got big and we looked at each other, afraid Dad had been in jail with bank robbers and other bad guys like on TV.

"No, no, not arrested like that," said Mom, realizing what we were thinking.

"No, I didn't have to go to jail," Dad assured us. He told how he kept getting stopped by the police because of the bus and the load he was hauling. Mostly, they stopped him because of the sight the bus made with the jet stuffed inside. Then, when they looked the bus over, they didn't like what they saw. They pointed out problems like bald tires, a missing windshield wiper on the right side, and lights that weren't working.

Dad responded to their concerns by telling a sob story how he was simply trying to save an airplane for public display at his home in Ohio where his wife and five children were waiting. He told them of being down to his last forty dollars and not able to afford paying much of a fine. He promised to drive very carefully the rest of the way if they would just let him go. Some cops were hard to persuade, while others let him go easily. One cop informed Dad that he was the talk of the police radio and admitted making the stop because he wanted to see for himself. He quickly let Dad go. After being stopped and let go a number of times, Dad figured he might make it home okay without much trouble after all. Then, he was cruising the New York State Thruway when a state trooper pulled him over.

"He had to be the meanest cop in the whole state of New York," Dad said as a worried look of reliving the event showed on his face. "I figured I was done." The trooper made Dad follow him to a truck weigh station a few miles down the road. When they got there, Dad had to drive the bus on the scales for a few minutes. Then, after the bus was off the scales, the trooper did all the vehicle safety checks on the bus, walking around while pausing now and then to write all over his clipboard. He inspected and measured everything. "I could tell he was fuming," Dad said.

"Look at this thing," the trooper barked. He listed all the bad tires and lights the other cops noticed, but then went further to what Dad knew were more serious problems. "Your load is too wide, too long, and you've got too much weight on a single axle," the trooper said tersely. "This bus is impounded and ain't going anywhere except maybe the junkyard!" he growled. The trooper had Dad get in the back of the patrol car and then drove him to the Highway Patrol station. When they got to the station, Dad could hear everyone talking about the guy with a jet in a school bus as the trooper took him to a waiting area. Dad realized none of them knew he was the guy, so he kept his mouth shut. The trooper told Dad to stay put while he went away to do some figuring. It took a while, but finally the trooper came back.

"Well, here it is," the trooper spoke sternly. "Your fines come to $750, the bus is condemned, and will not be permitted on the highway." He explained that Dad would have to remove the jet from the bus and "come back with a *real* truck" that could pass inspection and be within weight limits. If anything was still oversized, he would have to get a permit. Dad once more told his sob story that he only had forty dollars, he didn't have any type of truck available, and was unemployed with a wife and five kids waiting in Ohio.

The fuming trooper then turned Dad over to the station chief. The chief turned out to be a much nicer guy and was even curious about the type of jet the Cutlass was. Dad answered the chief's questions and told him about his airplane collection that the Cutlass would become part of. The chief appeared impressed by that and was also understanding about Dad's financial situation. Then he got to the bottom line. "If you don't move this thing out of here, I don't know what the hell we'll do with it." Then he made an offer. The chief would drop all the fines and let him go, but Dad was prohibited from driving on the New York Thruway. Dad easily agreed. "We'll call ahead for the police to watch for you, but only monitor and leave you alone if possible. But if we catch you on the Thruway, we'll put you under arrest—understand?" Dad nodded. He finished by telling Dad he couldn't offer any help upon reaching Pennsylvania. "When you leave New York, you're back on your own."

After getting off the New York State Thruway, Dad proceeded west on two-lane roads. He soon found himself navigating steep mountainous roads. "The mountain roads were terrible!" Dad said, as his looks told of reliving another nightmare. He told of crawling up the steep and narrow winding roads in low gear wondering the whole way if the bus would make it. Then, going down the other side of each mountain was even worse. He had to ride the brakes for miles going downhill, even using low gear. He could smell the brakes burning every time he went down a long hill, wondering how long they would last. "If that drive shaft broke, there'd been no way those brakes would have held without the help of the transmission," he explained. "Yep, the Cutlass would have flown one more flight—right off the side of a mountain!" Dad laughed a bit. "And none of the Navy guys thought I'd make it." Dad said, turning upbeat. "I should have bet with those guys—I'd have all their money!" he laughed hard.

For his return to Boston to get the wings, Dad made his first haul with the Chevy Suburban. Behind the Suburban was the new homemade trailer. The Navy guys were really excited when he returned. They were all glad, yet surprised that he actually got the bus home. They had a good time listening to all the police stories, and everyone wanted to see the pictures Dad took. Some of the pictures even made it into the base newspaper.

While the wings were large, they did fold in half because the Cutlass was a carrier-based jet fighter. The ability to fold the wings allowed each one to fit onto the trailer without any further disassembly. Unfortunately, they were still large enough that only one would fit on the trailer at a time. On the first trip, Dad brought home the right wing. Compared to the ordeal with the bus, the trip to get the wing was uneventful, or a "milk run," as he described it. In the process, he discovered something that would greatly influence the years to follow. The Suburban and the new homemade trailer made an excellent airplane hauling combination.

Walter the Conqueror stands ready to begin the 600-mile trip home from Boston. He was told the highest bet made by a Navy sailor was that he'd make it 50 miles.

7

Heavy Metal

Like a number of young boys growing up in the early '60s, I had a collection of plastic model airplanes. They weren't assembled very well, as I still had to learn how to keep the glue off my fingers. As a result, I often left permanent fingerprints on everything my sticky paws touched. The FBI would have no trouble identifying the models as mine. I had a lot of fun building the models, and Dad seemed proud that his only son was destined to have airplane blood flowing in his young veins. With the arrival of the Cutlass jet, it was time to put the models away. Dad was putting me to work on the real thing.

At the time we got the Cutlass, the Bobcat was still disassembled, so I didn't have any experience putting a real airplane back together. With the right wing of the jet home, it was time to start putting the Cutlass back in one piece. Most of the other aircraft Dad got required little reassembly. The two Corsairs and the BT were towed home with only their outboard wings removed. Also, they were relatively small. The only other aircraft Dad put completely together was the F-82 Twin Mustang. The F-82 wasn't nearly as heavy as the Cutlass, and Dad also had the boom tractor available when he reassembled that plane. Now the boom tractor was broken, and fixing it would be an enormous project. So Dad retired the tractor and planned to make a new and improved one in the future.

Without the boom tractor, getting the jet out of the bus and putting it back together was going to be a big challenge. I was very curious to see how Dad was going to do it. More airplane genius was on the way. He started the project by using his torch to cut more of the bus body away in order to expose the fuselage area where the wings attach. The vehicle I often played bus driver in was now looking really sad. Next, Dad used the Suburban to park the trailer loaded with the right wing in the correct spot. With a bit of maneuvering, he had the wing attach fittings as close as possible to the corresponding fuselage fittings. Our job now was to bring the wing and fuselage together enough to install the big attachment pins. The trailer and wing sat several feet lower than the bus. Dad decided the best way to match the height was to jack the trailer.

Dad showed me how to put the jack under the trailer axle, set the valve, put in the handle and pump the jack up. The jack piston only had about six inches of travel. So when the jack could go up no further, I set wood blocks under the axle next to the jack and then let the jack down. I then pushed the jack piston down, set jack higher up on new blocks, reset the valve and started jacking again. This became a repetitive process, and to keep the trailer level, I had to move back and forth from the left wheel to the right. In about an hour I had both trailer wheels about a foot off the ground. Then she

1957 Chevy Suburban and new trailer up on blocks hold right wing in position for its reattachment to the Cutlass fuselage. Wing folded vertical in its aircraft carrier parking configuration is exactly how both wings were towed home.

saw me. Mom stepped out of the house, saw me under the jacked-up trailer, and had a fit.

"Wally, get out of there, get out!" she yelled at me. I was shocked, as Mom seldom yelled about anything. I wondered what I'd done wrong, but soon realized someone else was in trouble. She chased Dad down and chewed him out bad. "How dare you have our son under that trailer!" she hollered. "He'll get killed if your damn trailer falls on him under there! If you want to kill yourself with your airplanes, that's fine, but you're not going to risk killing the children!" she got right in his face.

"But I'm watching him," Dad answered sheepishly.

"I don't give a damn who's watching him, he's only eight years old!" Mom stood her ground. With that, my job of jacking the trailer was over. Actually, I was kind of glad, since the jack, block, jack routine was already getting old. With the jack being hard to pump due to the heavy weight of the entire right wing and trailer, my skinny arms were wearing out. Dad worked a lot faster than I did, and soon the trailer was high enough for the wing to be reattached to the fuselage. Still, there was a problem. The wing and the fuselage were separated horizontally by a foot or so.

Fortunately, Dad had a pair of World War II bomb winches. We used one to winch the Bobcat fuselage forward on the trailer, and on another trip to winch the Bobcat wing. So I was well familiar with them. The winches were designed to snap into the top of a bomber above the bomb bay. Each winch had two cables with hooks to keep each bomb level as it was lifted up. A pair of hand cranks operated the winch. For us, the winches got a lot of use for many years to come. For assembling the Cutlass, they proved very effective.

Hydraulic jack on a stack of cement blocks in center of photograph, plus a vertical wood post behind the trailer tire, support the wing as the trailer heads down a ramp. Trailer must be removed to install the dreadfully heavy right main landing gear visible, but not fully extended behind the trailer. Star insignia of forward fuselage is visible through bus windows in photograph.

Dad hooked one end of the winch to the wing fitting on the other side of the fuselage and then hooked the winch cables to the wing. Soon I was cranking away as he closely watched the alignment of the wing fittings. They came together nicely, like putting the fingers of both your hands between each other at the fingertips and then sliding together more and more. We had to get the fit correct both vertically and horizontally. We'd jack one part of the wing and block it. Then we'd winch a little. Then we'd jack somewhere else and block, repeating the process. Finally, the fittings were meshed well enough for Dad to slide a big bolt into the wing fitting.

"Not going anywhere now!" he said proudly. We weren't done, but clearly our doubts were eased and we both felt confident. However, the last part of the alignment took forever. To get the original pins back in meant the fittings had to be aligned perfectly. The pins were solid steel, about two inches thick, and really heavy. It took us hours of tweaking the precise fit using the winch and jacks before the first pin finally went in. Then the others went in more easily after more tweaking. Eventually we got the terribly heavy landing gear installed. We towed the trailer away, and the Cutlass was starting to stand on its own feet.

Confident as ever, Dad soon went to Boston to haul the left wing home. Now there were no unknowns. The Suburban and trailer proved they could haul the right wing folded up, and the left wing was no different. For this trip, Dad took more pictures to show the Navy guys how we reattached the right wing. They marveled at the pictures and gave Dad their most recent base newspaper featuring the Cutlass story. Before long, the Navy crew lifted the wing with a crane and loaded it on the trailer. Soon after, he had it all tied down and was ready to head home.

Everybody came to see him off and Dad felt really sad. All the Navy people had been so nice and bent over backwards to help him. He realized he would never see them again. They asked him to mail more pictures, and they promised to send more base newspapers.

Close-up look behind Cutlass shows trailer used for Bobcat in front of folding "hangar doors." Located behind these big doors are many engines, plus *Lucky Gallon* race Corsair fuselage with its engine, and left fuselage of XP-82 Twin Mustang. Also home to the C-46 cockpit we played in as kids. Railing at top of hangar is another location our dog Curly enjoyed being outdoors on the large flat roof. Visitors were always amused seeing our dog on the roof.

8

The Mother-In-Law

Up, up, up, straight up in a vertical climb, airshow star Bill Adams pilots his red and white 450-Stearman biplane into a full-throttle "hammerhead stall." The airshow plane's billowing smoke trail tells that the plane is losing *all* of its speed despite the ear-splitting noise of the powerful engine's propeller clawing at the sky. A young woman hooked to a brace appears to be standing on the top wing fearlessly extending her arms straight out. Just as it looks like the plane has come to a complete stop, the nose kicks over and the plane pivots, making a tight U-turn. Exactly on cue, legendary airshow announcer Bill Sweet reacts,

"Oh-oh-oh-oooooh—don't do-uh-uh that!" Sweet hollers on the booming PA system that has to compete with the piercing propeller noise from the Stearman. The big biplane then dives straight down with its white smoke trail telling of its rapid acceleration. Plunging at the earth, Adams pulls the biplane out of the dive at the last moment. Now the Stearman is flying just a few feet above the ground while the lady wing-walker waves both arms at the crowd.

"Bet a lot of you gentlemen would pay fifty bucks to get your mother-in-law up there standing on that wing!" Sweet yells, getting the crowd fired up.

"Now, there's an idea!" Dad says as we both laugh with the giant crowd. Dad never got his mother-in-law to wing-walk on a Stearman biplane in an airshow. He never got her in any airplane, for that matter. But of the things he did do, hauling a big Navy fighter jet to the family home in a junked school bus didn't exactly blow her skirt up, either.

Of all my grandparents, my maternal grandmother, Margaret Murray, would be the only one I'd get to know well. And though knowing her would prove to be a great joy for me, Dad as her son-in-law would have a different experience. In general, they got along, but every now and then a bitter conflict would erupt that would bring to bear the family impact of Dad's growing airplane collection.

For my father, the conflicts with his mother-in-law would prove to be yet another bitter pill to swallow. On his side of the family, things didn't go well. His parents came to America as Czech immigrants in the early 1920s, and they were still poor years later when the Great Depression made things worse. Though his mother, Agnes, died when I was one year old, and I obviously don't remember her, I sure heard a lot about her. Like the way she forced Dad to hand over his paychecks to her. Everyone seemed to have a story about her strong will and overbearing ways. An impeccable home decorator and neat-freak, she was well known for being talented in music, art, and many other areas. But of all her many talents, she was best known for getting people to do what she wanted and how she wanted. If anyone got in her way, she'd raise so much fuss they'd forever

Mom and I pose with the Cutlass, showing its tall nose landing gear. Dad's sheet metal repairs included covering the canopy with scrap sheet metal. I later made my first jet plane emergency egress jumping from the tall cockpit upon discovering a giant wasp nest when I slid the canopy forward to close it.

regret having crossed her path. Either because of her temperament or for a combination of reasons, her first husband, Adolf, left her and their two boys in 1931. Dad was only eight when he last saw his father, and while he never talked about it much, it was evident he was deeply scarred by his father's abandoning him and his family.

His mother thus ran the house and raised him and his older brother George. Later she remarried and had another son, Chuck. In her second marriage, she continued to wear the pants in the family by managing the home, a chicken-raising business, a housing development, and everything else she could think of. Thus, many years after her death, few things got Dad going like stories about his mother. Of all the things he remembered her for, he complained most about her being a workaholic who expected everyone else to be one. My early observation was that this trait had certainly been passed on.

Dad was a bit distant from his two brothers, especially from his older brother George. Dad had a lot of wild stories about George, most of which involved fearless escapades behind the wheel of a car. As Dad told it, George tended to be the prankster and bully who relished every opportunity to cause havoc in young Walter's life. After serving in the Army in World War II, George came home as a war hero. This made Dad jealous of his brother, since the military had disqualified Dad from serving in the big war due to a stutter in his speech. And while I was well aware my father stuttered, I was totally oblivious to the social insecurities that problem could affect him with. For war hero George, his veteran's preference helped him get into the carpenter's union in Cleveland. A few years after becoming established in the union, George helped get his

8. The Mother-In-Law

brother Walter into the same union. It was not common for Dad to express gratitude to others. But despite the conflicts he had with his older brother, Dad remained forever thankful to George for this good deed.

Eventually, George grew tired of the harsh winters in the Cleveland area, especially with the heavy lake effect snow from Lake Erie pounding the Geauga County area where Newbury township was located. Having enjoyed tropical climates during his Army service in the Philippines, George packed up his family and moved to Florida. After that, though both brothers would live for decades to come, Walter and George never saw each other again. My older sisters last saw Uncle George when they were just a few years old. My only meeting with him would take place in 1979 during a short stay I had in Florida.

Dad's half-brother Chuck was ten years younger. Tall and handsome with brown hair, Chuck was clearly the most refined of the three, and spent a career as a structural engineer after graduating from Miami University in Oxford, Ohio. Tasting success early as a teen, Chuck was the star player on the Newbury High School championship basketball team. Articulate in speech and gifted with a natural poise and other talents you'd expect from a professional engineer, Chuck was in a league far different from his two older brothers. Though I always knew him to be warm and personable, it was obvious that Dad carried a chip on his shoulder in regards to Chuck's status as a college graduate who enjoyed his white-collar success. I was so aware of this issue early in my school years that it made me wonder: If I ever got the chance to go to college, how would my father react?

On my mother's side of the family, I never got to know her father since he passed away when I was three. But her mother, Grandma Murray, was definitely alive and well. Thus, she would be the one grandparent my sisters and I would come to know best, and she became a huge influence in our family. In a reciprocal kind of way, my sisters and I were her only grandchildren. Mom's only sibling, John-D, and his wife Gerry were unable to have children. I didn't realize it then, but looking back, it was as if Grandma Murray took it upon herself to make up for the other grandparents my sisters and I didn't have. In that role, she was the first person I knew who had a bigger-than-life presence about her.

Her ability to smoothly run the spectrum from being sweet and sensitive to harsh as a military drill sergeant caught my attention right away. She could holler at me for leaving the fridge door open one minute and be the sweetest old lady the next. She was a big woman and when she did raise her voice, it was like the room shook. To her, being tough and being Irish were synonymous—and both were virtues. One day, a thief in Cleveland made the mistake of trying to rob her. Not only did she hold onto her purse, but she knocked the guy to the sidewalk and then beat him with her umbrella. Eventually, the would-be robber scrambled to his feet and fled.

Even though she could sound and act tough, I never feared her. Above all else, she was a loving grandmother who, if need be, would step in front of a speeding train to save me or my sisters. But in Dad's case, I discovered at an early age he was afraid of someone that I was not. To Dad, Grandma Murray was the complaining, bellyaching, thorn in the side "you ain't good enough for my daughter" mother-in-law. To Grandma Murray, my father was the odd, planes-on-the-brain son-in-law whose idea of providing for his family was to have two junk cars on cement blocks instead of just one.

Grandma Murray spent her whole life living on the east side of Cleveland. During most of the years I knew her, she worked in Higbee's Department Store in downtown Cleveland. She didn't drive or own a car, but instead took the bus everyplace, since bus routes conveniently passed right in front of her apartment on Miles Avenue. About once a month, we would pile into the car on a Friday evening and go into town to pick her up for the weekend. I really enjoyed the car rides as we made the transition from the rolling hills of the countryside to the bustling streets of the big city. It was about a 45-minute drive to her apartment, so my sisters and I had plenty of time to enjoy the scenery, tell jokes, ask Mom a million questions, and just laugh while singing silly songs.

While my sisters and I were always thrilled to see Grandma Murray, there was no doubt that for Dad, she could be a pain. First of all, she wanted to make sure that we five kids got what we needed. When she was around, it was kind of like being in a kid's union and she was Grandma Hoffa. Until we switched from coal to oil heat, the house was typically cold in the winter, causing Grandma Murray to complain constantly. Seeing the extensive wear on our sofa, she'd complain and needle him that he needed to do better. Whether it was pressure from her, or of our parents' own choosing, we did make a trip to a local used furniture store and upgraded many items while using Dad's trailer to haul the nice furniture home.

Grandma Murray's greatest bellyache was with Dad's cars. Of the series of old clunker cars we went through, the '52 Ford station wagon we hauled the Bobcat with was the worst. From the outside it looked okay—if it was dirty. But when you washed the dirt off its white paint, you realized how rusted it was. It was rusted through so badly that there were holes in the floorboard, and the only thing under the floor mat—was highway. To me, having holes in the floor was kind of scary. Dad at times, however, thought it was funny. One time we were driving Grandma Murray home at night and Dad was going kind of fast.

"Slow down, Walter, you're driving too fast," Grandma Murray said sharply.

"No, I'm not. Look here, I'm going zero," Dad answered as he pointed at the broken speedometer.

"I can see the speedometer is broke, but you're still going too damn fast, Walter! Next thing you know the brakes will quit. Everything else is broken on this lousy clunker, so how will you stop this damn thing if the brakes quit?" Grandma Murray gave Dad her mean look.

"I'll just stick my feet out like Fred Flintstone," Dad replied as he lifted his floor mat so Grandma Murray could see the rusted hole in the floor. As he held the mat up, you could see the night highway flashing by, lit up from the headlights of other cars, and you could also hear the roar of the street noise sounding raw as it entered the car.

"Damn it, Walter! Your junk car's got a damn hole in the floor! I can't believe you drive your family around in a piece of junk like this. You need to buy your family a good car, for crying out loud!" As bad as the rust was, the Ford still had the problem with the right door popping open sometimes during a left turn. The car had no seat belts, and the front seat was covered with a really slick brown vinyl. More than once I thought Mom was a goner. Dad would make a left turn, the door would pop open, and Mom would be grabbing anything and everything. She always hung on, but it made you wonder about the next time. She didn't get stern with Dad very often, but after a few close calls, she really got after him about the door problem.

As I looked on, Dad put some new door latches on the car and thought the problem was fixed. But as luck would have it, Grandma Murray was riding up front when Dad took a sharp left turn, and sure enough, the right door suddenly popped open. Now I thought Grandma Murray was a goner. Mom was in the middle between Dad and Grandma Murray. Frantically, Mom grabbed her mother and fought hard to keep the two of them from flying out into the street. I was afraid for a moment they'd both be ejected from the car. They managed to stay in, but Dad might as well have pushed them out. He was a dead duck now. "Damn it, Walter!" Grandma Murray screamed. "This damn junk car of yours is gonna get somebody killed already! How many times do I have to tell you that you need to get your family a good car?" Everybody was silent for a while as Dad and Grandma Murray both stewed.

During most visits, Grandma Murray stayed for the weekend. But by the early sixties, she had enough seniority at Higbee's to get a couple of weeks off during the summer. The first time Mom suggested that Grandma Murray spend a full week with us, Dad really cringed. But while he dreaded the idea, he didn't resist. Dad was always quick to say that Mom never asked for much. Also, ever since the second Corsair uproar, she never again objected to Dad's airplane collecting. So when she did suggest something like having her mother over for a week, Dad knew better than to argue with his very tolerant and accommodating wife.

The first time we picked her up for her vacation, my sisters and I were really thrilled. I just couldn't believe she'd be with us a whole week! In contrast, Dad was pretty subdued. When we got to her apartment, she had some surprises for us. Besides having her suitcase and personal things packed to go, she had several shopping bags full of wrapped packages. Additionally, she had some kind of new table that was all folded up. Soon we had all the things loaded in the old Ford and were headed home.

When we got home, she had us open the packages. I was hoping toys would be in those bags. But mostly they were packed with new clothes of the correct child size for each of us. The big table turned out to be a Ping-Pong table, and with it came a package of paddles and balls along with the table net. In addition to that, she got us a new charcoal grill. In no time at all, we were in the yard under a big shade tree playing game after game of Ping-Pong while cooking hot dogs and marshmallows on the new grill!

As I expected, having her with us for a week turned out to be very special. On the weekend visits, we rarely got far from the house. But now, we had all the time in the world to be with her and take her on a tour of the country setting we lived and played in. She went on walks with us through the woods on a dirt path that had once been a railroad track. In the many years since the railroad had been there, nature reclaimed and closed in on much of the path, with tall trees making it well shaded and perfect for a summer stroll. Another path in the woods took us to Restful Lake, where Grandma Murray sat on the beach to watch us swim.

As for Dad and his mother-in-law, I think the first week-long visit, as well as those in years to follow, actually helped him and her learn to appreciate each other and get along better. Seeing Dad come home from work all dirty and worn out made her appreciate how hard he worked at his carpenter job. She was always telling him to rest and relax. "You're gonna have a heart attack if you don't slow down, Walter. Take it easy already," she'd say, sounding genuinely concerned. Though it didn't sound like a lot on the surface, Dad appreciated that once in a while, Grandma Murray did appear to acknowledge that he was a hard worker. In many ways, it frustrated him that he worked hard his whole life and rarely got any recognition for it. In contrast to the father figures he was raised under, he reasoned that he'd done pretty well for himself and his family.

Like so many men of my grandparents' era, Dad's father, his stepfather, and Mom's father all drank a lot. And they certainly weren't alone. It was during Mom and Dad's childhood that Prohibition was the law of the land. Hindered by alcohol, the father figures Dad knew had trouble keeping their jobs. When they did earn a paycheck, a good chunk of it went to the local taverns. To help pay the bills, Dad's mother actually forced him to drop out of school after eighth grade and take a job. When he did so, she took his paychecks and he rarely saw any of the money he earned. As an adult, Dad never touched a drop of alcohol. He continued working hard both on the job and at home. Though he did spend some of his carpenter wages buying old airplanes, he considered each a wise investment for the future. "Better than money in the bank," Dad frequently stated to Grandma Murray and other adults who well knew exactly what Dad was saying.

In addition to learning to avoid alcohol, another childhood experience that dramatically shaped Dad's outlook on life was the stock market crash of 1929, and the bank failures that followed. He was six years old when that happened, and therefore spent most of his childhood in the Great Depression. Again and again, my sisters and I heard the never-ending stories about the Depression, and we knew them all by heart. We heard how nobody had any money in Dad's family. How his mother had to run the bill collectors off all the time. How the power company man kept threatening to turn the electricity off. How they put kerosene in the radiator of the Model A Ford because they didn't have money for antifreeze. How they patched holes in tires by inserting chunks of rubber cut from scrap tires. How they never went to the 10-cent movie show or anywhere else. And how on top of all that, they often weren't sure where their next meal was coming from.

As a result of the Depression, Dad didn't see much security in having money in the bank. Instead, having tangible assets on your property that you could touch and feel—*that* was security. Thus, Dad was absolute in his conviction that he had managed his meager income and lifestyle quite well. His land and house were paid for, and in his backyard he had a growing collection of airplanes that no bank failure could ever take away. He didn't drink, but instead worked hard and put food on the table. Now all he wanted from Grandma Murray and others was a little respect. If they couldn't give him that, then he at least didn't want to catch any grief about collecting airplanes.

I never saw her show any curiosity about Dad's planes until one day. It was a weekday on her vacation when she asked me to show her the planes. I was about 10 or 11. Dad was at work, so I found it interesting that in his absence, she wanted me to give the tour. Mostly, she wanted me to tell her the identity of each plane and in some cases wanted to know how we hauled them home. Additionally, she wanted me to show her which plane won the Cleveland Air Races. During that evening we were sitting around the living room when Grandma Murray surprised me again. "Walter, you've got some rare airplanes out there," she said to Dad, sounding impressed. Every head turned.

"Yeah, some of them are very rare," Dad answered, seeming a little stunned.

"And your son here, you should be real proud. He's so young to know so much about airplanes. He told me everything," she said as she smiled warmly at me. Then Dad started to talk, and he blew it. He started grilling her about the details of the planes. Encouraged that she finally acknowledged there was some value in his airplane collection, he had to make sure that his little boy hadn't left any important details out.

"Well, did he tell you about Cook Cleland's Corsair, and…"

8. The Mother-In-Law

"Yes, he did," Grandma Murray interrupted.

"And that it won the 1947 Thompson Trophy Race, and that..." Dad tried to continue only to be interrupted again.

"Yes, yes," she answered as she nodded.

"And about the Twin Mustang? There's only a few left, and..."

"Yes, yes, he told me all that, Walter!" Grandma Murray nodded more strongly.

"Yeah, but he probably forgot to tell you that there are only three of those..."

"NO, NO, Walter, he didn't forget to tell me a damn thing!" Grandma Murray's voice grew louder. "Now look, Walter, you have some valuable airplanes and your son has told me all about them, so I don't need to hear anymore!" she cut Dad off.

"But..." Dad tried to keep going.

"I TOLD YOU, WALTER, I don't need to hear another word about your damn airplanes!"

With that, Dad gave up. In his deep-set eyes, I saw a wounded look appear. I'd seen that look before, and at times it could be a little haunting. Clearly, Grandma Murray's rejection got under his skin in another way, and he couldn't stand it. He'd put up with grief from her all these years about his airplanes. Now she acts interested, and his young son gets to tell the whole story. I wasn't surprised that Dad didn't trust me to get the details right. But I knew that I knew my stuff. After hearing him tell the same stories to visitors over and over again, there was no way I could ever forget. Still, Dad later got me outside where Grandma Murray wasn't around and grilled me for every detail about everything I told her. After about ten minutes of nonstop interrogation, his attitude finally softened. Something changed. I think it dawned on him for the first time ever,

Dad's rare F-82E Twin Mustang was not made by joining two P-51 Mustangs together, as is often suggested. Instead it is a totally different airplane, both longer and larger than two joined P-51s would be. Here it sits next to race Corsair 74 at far left. I greatly enjoyed taking my Grandmother Murray on a tour of these and the other planes as a young boy (courtesy Jason McKeon).

that maybe his little boy was paying attention and did know something about airplanes after all.

From this and other experiences, I always felt that Grandma Murray was the one person I could count on for encouragement. She seemed impressed by the things I did when no one else noticed. We had an old wood Adirondack lawn chair that was her favorite. One armrest on the chair was terribly cracked and splintered. We often had short scraps of new boards Dad's construction company discarded, but Dad scavenged. So I took one of those boards and made a new armrest for her, cutting and sanding the curved shape to match the original. While I was proud of the job I'd done, I didn't think it was a big deal. Yet Grandma Murray noticed it and acted like I was a wood-carving genius for being able to shape wood like that while still being about ten years old.

As I got older, I built a few tree houses, a lot of model airplanes, a battery charger, and an air compressor, and I took on more and more repair work, especially on the Suburban that we were always asking to do far more than it was designed for. No matter what it was that I did, Grandma Murray was always full of compliments. In contrast, Dad was generally mum. When one or more of my sisters got an occasional straight-A report card, it was Grandma Murray who made a big deal about how smart they were. I was the slacker in school, so no compliments for me in that regard was exactly as it should be. With Mom generally being the quiet type, I found Grandma Murray to be a sweet and encouraging grandmother who was truly a joy to be around. She filled a giant void in my life then. I later began to say during my adult years that in the lifespan of a child, she gave me a lifetime of joy.

9

Wild Cargo

"Look, look, Wally, you're missing it!" Dad called out as I stood in the kitchen getting a snack. It was a statement I probably heard hundreds of times during my growing years. What I was missing was another flying scene from an airplane movie on TV. Nothing could glue Dad to the TV like a good old airplane movie. In 1964, watching TV was simple. We only got three TV channels, which made it easy to keep track of what was on. TV shows were black-and-white then, and remote control was something that NASA did. Still, people got addicted to TV, and Dad was not immune. He carefully read the TV listings to see what airplane movies were on during the week. Since there were no recording options like today, Dad had one chance to see each airplane movie listed. When a good airplane movie was on the schedule, nothing else happened in our house.

On this day we were watching *Thirty Seconds Over Tokyo*, which told the story of the daring Doolittle Raiders making America's first bombing raid on the Japanese mainland using B-25 bombers during World War II. Just a few months after Japan's surprise attack on Pearl Harbor got us into the war, such a raid was unthinkable. America had no bombers capable of flying the long distance to Japan. And the Japanese knew it. But Jimmy Doolittle was long known for doing the unthinkable.

Considered by many aviation historians to be perhaps the most prolific aviation pioneer, he was incredibly innovative and successful both as a civilian and as a military officer. Among his many aviation breakthroughs, he demonstrated the first-ever "blind flying" instrument landing that allowed aircraft to land in low visibility weather. As an executive at Shell Oil, he was a mover and shaker, developing the first high-octane aviation gasoline. Racing with this fuel, Doolittle and others set ever-increasing speed records in an age when many people thought it would be fatal just for a human to travel past a certain speed. Using speed to shrink the world, he was the first to fly coast to coast in less than a day. In aerobatics, he was the first pilot to perform an outside loop.

Yet far more than the lucky stunt pilot some people assumed him to be, Doolittle earned one of the first doctorates in aeronautical engineering at MIT. He was no stunt pilot, but instead a methodical aeronautics innovator, professional race pilot and test pilot, as well as an incredible leader. After developing a secret plan and secretly training Army pilots to fly B-25s from the aircraft carrier deck of the USS *Hornet*, Doolittle commanded the lead plane of this group of 16 B-25s that bombed Japan.

"If only I could find a B-25, I'd have a *bomber* to add to my collection!" Dad said as we watched the movie. Not long after viewing the movie, the inevitable happened. A visitor came to see Dad's planes and had a tip. "There's a B-25 in Cincinnati that made a gear-up belly landing a year ago," said the visitor. He then said it was going to be cut up for scrap. Get scrapped! To Dad, the thought was unbearable. Quickly, Dad was on the phone. Like a private detective, he tracked down who was going to scrap the B-25. Then, like a mother pleading for her son's life, he convinced the man to sell him the B-25 instead of scrapping it. The agreed price was $500.

Coincidental with the availability of the B-25, awareness was spreading in the aviation press that World War II airplanes were getting scarce. One new magazine, *Air Classics*, was almost exclusively devoted to aviation heritage, with an intense focus on World War II aircraft. As the aviation press documented the trend toward extinction of these aircraft, concern to save them grew. So even if Dad had to damage the B-25 to haul it down the highway, he knew it was an airplane he somehow had to save.

To Dad's delight, there were several groups doing what they could to save some of the rare aircraft, with the best known of these being the Confederate Air Force, or simply "CAF," in Texas. They have since changed their name to Commemorative Air Force. Though this group would blossom tremendously in the coming years, back in 1964 they were still small. Also, Dad had some concerns about the CAF. First, he noted they were only interested in fighter planes at that time. He knew of no organization making an effort to save bombers or transport planes. Also, with the CAF, they were dedicated to restoring and flying most of their aircraft. Another collector named Ed Maloney was doing a fabulous job of saving planes out in California, but he also became involved in restoring and flying the planes in the ever-growing museum he founded. This created a concern with Dad that would grow stronger with time. He simply felt that some aircraft were too rare and historic to risk losing in a plane crash.

Since Dad's planes were not flyable and thus had to be hauled down the highway, the size of each aircraft was a big concern. While hauling the Cutlass gave him an increased sense of confidence, he was still in awe of the huge size of a bomber, and he still didn't have a real truck. Although he was working more steadily as a carpenter now, he knew he could not afford to buy airplanes and a truck. So to start with, he figured he'd bring home what he could with the Suburban and trailer.

By far, the B-25 exceeded the size of anything we had previously hauled with the trailer. After first using the trailer for the Cutlass wings, Dad upgraded it by replacing its two long wood runners with a 6 × 14-foot hardwood trailer bed. A new wood bed a few years later would make it wider. The biggest plane hauled on the trailer with its new wood bed was a wrecked Skyraider prop plane we got on a scrap bid from Grosse Ile Naval Air Station near Detroit in 1963. We also hauled a complete T-28A, and sections of some jets including an F-84 Thunderstreak fighter and a T-33 T-Bird trainer.

But compared to the B-25, those planes were small. As a result, it appeared likely that the B-25 would have to be dismantled and possibly cut into small sections. This didn't bother Dad too much because the B-25 was about to be scrapped and had already been damaged by the wheels-up landing. No matter what damage we'd cause by hauling it, the plane would be far better off with us than going to the scrap furnace. Despite Dad's hope he would not have to cut the plane, a nagging problem was that none of the information he could find in his book collection showed how the bomber was built. So he had no idea how to haul it.

On a clear crisp September dawn the next Saturday, we hit the road for Cincinnati. On the first trip, Dad took me and three of my sisters. It was about a 250-mile drive to Cincinnati, so for us this was a big adventure. I enjoyed the company of my sisters, and though the drive seemed long, we passed the time easily by playing games and singing songs like "100 Bottles of Beer on the Wall." The Suburban had no radio, so if we wanted music, we had to make up our own.

The Suburban was cramped with the five of us on board. Besides having our snacks, drinks, books, blankets, and other personal items, there was all of Dad's equipment. Inside the Suburban we had toolboxes, a stepladder, cables, chains, two bomb winches, a few jacks and assorted wood blocks. That was just to work on the plane. In addition, Dad even packed some spare parts for the Suburban, plus several spare tires. So it wasn't exactly a limousine ride we were having. But except for resting our feet on rusty metal toolboxes, jacks and other stuff, we were comfy.

As we approached Cincinnati from the northeast, we enjoyed the scenery as we weaved our way past long-established neighborhoods shadowed with trees that were sporting their brilliant fall colors. A sense of discovery grabbed me as we took in the sights of a big city none of us had ever been to before. Finally, we crested a hill from which we could see Lunken Airport up ahead. Dad could hardly contain his excitement when he first spotted his new prize. "Look, look, there she is, there's our B-25!" he pointed while turning around to see if the rest of us were looking.

"Watch where you're driving!" one sister said. We knew well that when driving within five miles of an airport, Dad was watching everything except the road. After checking in with a fixed base operator handling the B-25 sale, Dad got permission to drive onto the airport. As we pulled up next to the B-25 parked in a remote area of the airport, my initial impression of the plane was good. Despite the belly landing we had heard about, the bomber was now standing on its landing gear and was basically intact.

Even before beginning my tour of the plane, I was first fascinated by the airport itself. Since it was a blue-sky day with perfect weather, the weekend fliers were out in force. Though I eventually visited many airports over the years, none seemed as busy and lively as Lunken Airport was at that time. My knowledge of light aircraft was limited, but I recognized Cessnas, Pipers, Navions, and ex-military AT-6 "Texan" trainers. You name it, they were flying it.

Of course, Dad was like a kid with a big new toy and was quickly all over the plane, inside and out. For me, I knew I had to get my exploring done fast, because the moment Dad was done looking, it was work time and he'd be barking orders. As I roamed around the old bomber, I was fascinated by its unusual condition. As expected, the belly landing had severely damaged the plane by ripping much of the aluminum sheet metal from the bottom of the fuselage. From watching war movies with Dad, I expected the propeller blades to be bent and curled, but oddly only the prop on the left engine showed this kind of damage. Finally, on the copilot side of the forward fuselage, someone had painted in big black letters:

KEEP OFF
WILD CARGO

The words were painted crudely with a brush, which, like painting a car, is something you just don't do to an airplane, unless you are a Soplata. I could only wonder what the warning meant. Most of the bomber was in its bare aluminum finish except for the engine nacelles and the bombardier nose, which were black.

After checking the exterior, I figured it was time to catch up with Dad on the inside. Two hatches used to enter the B-25 are both located in the belly. One is for the forward fuselage and another is used for the aft fuselage. Due to the gear-up landing, both hatches were missing. Back at the rear of the plane, I noticed a small barrel located by the aft hatch. I went to the barrel, climbed up and easily got into the tail section.

Inside the plane, there was plenty of room to stand up and walk around. It was a bit dark in the rear fuselage because the place where big curving waste-gunner windows should be was covered over with aluminum. On the right side behind the window area was a round open hole where an escape hatch was supposed to be located. This one was missing. In the very back was the tail-gunner position. As I moved toward the tail, the fuselage became very small, and even though I was still a boy, I had to get down on all fours to crawl all the way back.

After checking out the tail, I went forward and found the solution to getting in the cockpit. The forward and aft sections of the fuselage were separated by the center section of the wing that passed through the fuselage. Inside the fuselage, the wing structure was located up near the top to make room for the bomb bay located under the wing. Despite the wing's location, there was still a small crawl space between the top of the wing and the ceiling of the fuselage. This enabled crewmembers (very skinny ones) to move the length of the bomber in flight. As a kid, I could easily make it.

A small ladder was installed to get you up to the top of the wing, so up I went. Right away I wondered how any adult could crawl through the space since it was cramped even for me. As I made my way forward, I discovered a large round hole in the bottom of the crawl space that went down into the bomb bay. Since the bomb doors were open, it went about 10 feet right down to the concrete. The hole was easy to avoid, and soon I was in the forward fuselage. Now the tough part. There was about a four-foot drop to the cockpit floor, and the idea of going headfirst wasn't very appealing. The obvious choice was to turn around and go feet first. It wasn't easy to turn around in the small crawl space, and I wondered again how grown men managed to maneuver around in there during flight.

The B-25 cockpit was actually a split-level arrangement. On the bottom floor was the opening for the hatch that we were missing. The second level had the actual cockpit with the pilot and copilot seats. But right now I didn't care about that. Where was Dad? I knew he was in the cockpit a few moments ago, but now he was gone.

"Where are you?" I called.

"Up here," he yelled back. I was confused. Somehow Dad was in the bombardier nose up in front of the cockpit and was completely out of sight.

"How'd you get there?" I asked.

"Through the tunnel," Dad replied.

"What tunnel?" I thought. Then I saw it. Against the left wall of the fuselage and in front of the belly hatch was a small tunnel. It ran under the cockpit floor and up to the nose. Like the people who were gunners in the tail or who climbed over the wing, bombardiers were skinny people, or else they were people who got stuck a lot. I crawled into the tunnel, which was about ten feet long. As I got about halfway through the tunnel, I nearly got claustrophobic since the tunnel was so small. When I got in the nose, I could see I'd made a mistake.

"There isn't enough room for both of us, so just wait a minute and I'll be out," Dad said. Still, to get out I had to decide whether to go backwards through the tunnel on all fours or wrestle with Dad in the small bombardier nose to get turned around. Figuring it was better to back out than to end up tangled up with Dad in a confined space, I put it in reverse and backed out.

9. Wild Cargo 63

B-25 *Wild Cargo* at Lunken Airport in Cincinnati in September 1964. I'm sitting above the cockpit on the edge of one of the bomber's many escape hatch openings. Dad's first bomber presents many challenges for us and the six-cylinder Chevy Suburban.

Once back in the cockpit area, I climbed up to the second level and got into the pilot seat. It wasn't a pretty sight. Figuring the plane was getting scrapped, vandals had stripped out a lot of the instruments and other parts. Still, the pilot's control wheel was there, as were all the throttle, propeller, fuel-mixture, and other engine control levers the old planes were known for. How anyone could keep all those levers properly adjusted in flight was beyond me. Also of great interest were the pilot seats. They were made of thick armored steel. Since bombers got shot at a lot, a little protection was built in.

"What do you think?" Dad asked as he joined me in the cockpit.

"It's pretty big," I said, and then added, "I wonder why they bellied it in."

"Me, too. The landing gear looks okay, so I really can't tell," Dad seemed puzzled. We speculated on a few possible causes, but it was really time for us to get to work. I got the tools and equipment out of the Suburban that I had learned Dad would want. I was already the one packing it at home with all his favorite stuff. We seemed ready to handle any major disaster from a nuke power plant meltdown to a hurricane recovery or oil tanker spill. As I put the toolboxes, winches, cables, chains, and blocks near the bomber, I could tell Dad's excitement was growing.

"I just can't believe it," he said, sounding very enthusiastic. "They made this plane to be hauled down the highway." Then he showed me how all the major sections were bolted together. The forward fuselage could be unbolted in front of the wing, as could the aft fuselage behind the wing. The outboard wings unbolted just beyond the engines, and the engine nacelles unbolted right behind the wing. Dad was jubilant: "Boy, is this thing made for hauling." He explained his long-range plan was to eventually haul the center wing section on the trailer lengthwise. That said, he believed the Suburban and trailer could haul every section of the plane! Just 30 minutes ago that seemed impossible. "And I won't have to cut or destroy anything!" he joyfully concluded.

Even I knew this was great news. If a major part of the aircraft structure was cut, the plane was very hard to put back together. Also, the potential to restore the aircraft to flying condition became doubtful. Dad forever mourned a mistake he made with his first Twin Mustang, the prototype XP-82. To haul the plane home, he used a torch to cut the midpoint of the wing between the plane's two fuselages. Later, he discovered the plane could be disassembled in a way that required no cutting. He often told of how sick he felt over making that mistake. For every other plane that followed the XP-82 disaster, Dad studied the airframe very carefully before making a decision to cut any part of it.

Dad decided to start with the small stuff, including all the flight controls, the tail section and various doors. He told a few of my sisters to help him with the landing gear doors and bomb bay doors. My assignment was to remove fairing screws from the tail. I again crawled on all fours through the narrow part of the rear fuselage to get on top of the tail section. The only problem now was the height. It was about ten feet down to the concrete and the stabilizer got narrow as I carefully crawled toward either of the twin rudders. Until now I didn't know I was afraid of heights. All of Dad's other planes were relatively low to the ground. I wondered, "Pilots aren't scared of heights, are they?" I tried to stay near the middle of the stabilizer, and I was very careful when I had to get near the edge. Before long I had screws going ding-ding into a small can I had.

Around noon, we got takeout food from a small restaurant at the airport terminal. Most places we hauled airplanes from didn't serve food, so this was a nice convenience. Even though it was just burgers and fries, this was still a treat, since we almost never ate out except when helping Dad haul a plane. As we continued to work on the B-25, we started having visitors stop to see what was happening to the old bomber. "What are you going to do with it?" was the question we got most.

"We're saving it to put in our museum," Dad answered. The visitors were delighted. Many had heard the rumor the plane was about to be scrapped. Realizing we came to save it, they were thrilled. Some offered to help work on it, but Dad turned them down, fearing they'd get hurt and he'd be sued. Others offered us airplane rides, and Dad turned them down, too. I didn't mind that he was turning down free help, but plane rides? I wanted to fly so bad I could taste it!

Perhaps it was all because of the environment I was in or just my own yearnings, I guess I'll never really know. But already as a boy, I'd spent a fair amount of time looking up at the sky and simply wondering—what's it like up there? Some days it would start with shadows moving across the ground on sunny days with scattered clouds being pushed by strong winds. I'd be in our second-story kitchen looking out the big picture window and spot the shadow of a cloud scooting along the lush green grass on the long yard that ran east of our house. With the wood-framed screen door slamming behind me, I'd run down the old wood stairs and out into the yard.

Then, after finding a good viewing spot away from the trees, I'd stop and gaze at the sky. Gawking with wide-eyed wonder, I'd take in the scene of the frothy white popcorn-shaped clouds drifting by while floating in the stunning blue. As I'd pick one cloud and stare, I could see it slowly change its shape as if some invisible giant hand was churning the brilliant white cotton candy aloft. With the same joy that my sisters and I would share when spotting a wild rabbit in the woods, I'd simply stand there totally delighted by the lively scene above. And just as we'd often chase the elusive rabbit, I wanted to go up in a plane and chase the clouds the same way. But back in Cincinnati, there were wrenches to turn. My eager yearnings to touch the sky would have to wait, and wait, and wait.

By mid-afternoon, things were looking good. As Dad held the landing gear doors, we kids took turns pushing the bolts out. We did the same with the bomb bay doors, except it took all kids on deck to help Dad with the large doors. To remove the flight controls, Dad parked the trailer under each wing, and we stood on the trailer to remove the ailerons and flaps. Then, he parked the trailer under the tail section so we could remove the twin rudders, vertical stabilizers, and elevators. Finally, Dad had all the mounting bolts out for the horizontal stabilizer. Again, as we stood on the trailer, it took all hands to lift and remove the bomber's stabilizer.

I could tell Dad felt good about the progress we'd made, but he was concerned about the tremendous amount of disassembly work remaining. We perhaps had hundreds of bolts to remove, and many were in tight spaces that were hard to get to. Like the Bobcat, the vast majority of the bolts were hard to turn due to the binding material on the nuts. So combining the tight workspace with the binding material, wrenches had to be applied several times just to make one revolution unscrewing each nut. As a result, we worked a few more hours turning bolts on the plane after having our trailer loaded for this trip. Finally, it was getting late, so we packed up the tools and headed home.

It was a long drive home that night, and many others would follow. I wondered how Dad did it. He got up around 4 A.M., drove over five hours down, worked harder than everyone all day long, and then drove home. My sisters and I slept most of the way home while maneuvering in the crowded Suburban to get comfortable. We eventually got home about midnight.

The next school day couldn't come quick enough for me. I was so anxious to see my good friend Rick and tell him all about the B-25. He also shared some of my enthusiasm about airplanes, and he had also recently seen the movie *Thirty Seconds over Tokyo*. "No way!" Rick responded when I told him the news. He couldn't believe we were hauling something as big as a B-25. In a way, neither could I.

10

The Flying Zoo

The next Saturday, we returned to Cincinnati to get the B-25's outboard wings. Compared to the rest of the bomber, the outboard wings weren't too big and looked like they'd be easy to unbolt and remove. Just outboard of the engines, it was clear where the outboard wings came off. A large number of bolts with 9/16" heads formed a long row on both the top and bottom of the wing. Most planes would have a fairing covering such attachment bolts, but not the B-25. The bolts were right there in the open, suggesting that in World War II there wasn't much time for cosmetics. Since the bolts went straight into the wing from the outside, we figured you unscrew the bolts and bingo, off comes the wing. It looked so easy, Dad planned to get both outboard wings removed and loaded on this trip. Dad and I got on top of the wing, and I watched as he began to spin a bolt out with a speed handle. He turned the bolt and we both expected it to rise above the wing as it threaded its way out. But it didn't rise at all, it just turned and turned. He tried another bolt and then another, and they all behaved the same.

"Don't tell me they didn't put self-holding nuts inside the wing!" Dad said, sensing a nightmare job ahead. We both got off the plane and quickly Dad was on his stepladder under the wing. An access panel led to an oil cooler located inside the wing joint. As I handed him tools, Dad soon had the panel off. With a flashlight he looked around the oil cooler and spotted the nuts screwed onto the wing bolts. "Lousy damn engineers," Dad said. "How the hell are we supposed to get a wrench in there?" He sent me up the ladder to take a look. As I peeked around the oil cooler air ducts, I could tell we had a problem—a big problem. What baffled us most was how anyone ever installed the nuts. Even with special tools, it just looked impossible for anyone to put nuts on dozens and dozens of bolts. We couldn't even see a lot of the nuts, let alone get a wrench on them.

Dad quickly got the oil cooler removed, which resulted in thick black oil bleeding from the cooler and the oil lines in the wing. The access we gained inside the wing by removing the cooler was small, but we took what we got. With me holding the nuts, I could reach inside the wing, Dad spun the bolts out from the outside. For the nuts I could reach, I sometimes had trouble holding the wrench when Dad put the torque to bolts. Each time he'd call "ready," I'd just cringe. I tried my best to get the wrench against some metal so it would hold by itself. Still, when Dad put the muscle to it, I often got my fingers and hands mashed between the wrench and piece of wing structure. We made good progress with the nuts I could reach, but eventually could go no further.

Still needing more access, Dad cut the rivets that held the air ducts for the oil cooler. With the air ducts removed, I was able to snake my skinny-boy head and shoulders through the oil cooler opening and get deeper inside the wing. Fearing I'd get stuck inside the jagged structure, I spent hours with my body contorted in the wing as I took my wrench from one nut to the next while Dad spun the last of the hard-to-reach bolts out. Altogether, it took us about four to five hours to get all the nuts removed.

We left about a dozen bolts in the top of the wing to hold it in place until we were ready to load. Dad positioned the trailer to get it exactly where he wanted it under the wing. From the bottom of the wing to the top of the trailer was a space of about five to six feet. With no lift or crane to use, Dad had to come up with some way to lower the wing. As usual, he had planned ahead. A few days before the trip, he went to a local sawmill and bought some long hardwood lumber. Now I knew why.

As a carpenter, he quickly made a pair of H-shaped wood frames and then had them erected to hold each end of the wing. We removed the last bolts, and just as planned, the wing rested nicely on the flat part of the two H-frames. A genius at making a hard job easy by constructing something cheap and simple, Dad connected the H-frames to the trailer in a way that would allow them to fold down to the trailer. Using our bomb winch to control the rate the H-frames folded, we gently lowered the wing to the trailer. I was totally wowed by his thinking.

It was late afternoon by the time we got the first wing loaded. Rather than go home, Dad decided we would keep working on the bomber and eventually spend the night. I knew we had a ton of work to do, so I wasn't surprised by his decision, which also meant sleeping at the airport in the Suburban. I hoped we'd go to a motel, but money was tight in those years. I don't know how many nights I slept in the Suburban on this and other

Kneeling above the right wing joint on B-25 *Wild Cargo*, I spin some bolts out. Dad's shadow looms large as he shoots this photo. As I view this photograph today, I feel no amount of film could capture the enormousness of his long shadow. Carpenter Dad's wood frames mounted to the front and rear of the trailer support the wing as we prepare to separate it from the plane.

hauling trips, but I'd guess about 15 or 20 times. It was never comfortable, but at the end of the very long days we usually worked, I was too tired to care where I crashed for the night.

Before calling it a day, we worked through the afternoon until dinnertime, when Dad sent me to get our hamburgers and fries. For his drink, Dad was a hot chocolate guy no matter where we went. A thermos bottle refill of hot chocolate or coffee on occasion was always top priority when he sent me or one of my sisters for food. The airport restaurant was small, but very good. Over a period of nearly two months, they got to know the Soplata kids and the thermos bottle of our father very well. We usually ate our takeout food beside the B-25 or in the Suburban. It was typically a quick meal and then back to work. Dad didn't like surprises taking a plane apart. The left wing had already spooked him a bit from the problem we had discovered removing the bolts.

Though we still had to remove the right outboard wing, we now knew exactly how to do it. But separating the forward fuselage and its cockpit from the center wing made Dad a bit anxious due to the complexity of that disassembly. Tackling this problem is where he chose to put in the extra hours we spent that Saturday. Of course, the cockpit was the nerve center of the airplane. The many control cables and electrical wires that it took just to operate the two engines and propellers all had to be disconnected. Then there were the airplane flight controls, including rudder, aileron, elevator and trim tabs, plus flaps and landing gear. Wheel brakes, hydraulic controls, lights, radios, on and on—everything had to be disconnected for the forward fuselage and its cockpit to be removed from the center wing.

Dad had no worries about removing the engines. He'd done enough of that on other aircraft. So this is where he put me to work. He instructed me on exactly what to do preparing for the removal of the two engines on a later trip. After showing and explaining the prep work I was to do on the engines, he went inside the B-25 to work the forward fuselage items that concerned him most.

As I worked outside, I was still fascinated with Lunken Airport. There was so much flying going on, and while it slowed down a bit at sunset, the place was still busy. Blue taxiway lights soon came on all around the airport, with some of them right near us. Combined with the red and green lights on the wingtips of the planes taxiing by, there was a new mystique about the airport on this calm and clear evening that simply gripped my sense of fascination.

I still had not been up in an airplane of any kind. Except for the many airplane movies we watched, I had no idea what flying was like, even in the daytime. Now in the dark, I really wondered. Since there are no roads for the headlights to shine on like a car, how can a pilot know where he is? Daytime pilots seemed brave enough, but nighttime pilots must really be something. Every time a plane taxied by, I envied the people in it. The planes were obviously in great condition and did what airplanes were supposed to do—they flew! Here I was, a dirty and grimy grease monkey in the sixth grade working on an old World War II bomber that had probably seen its last mission. Still, the old bomber had its own mystique, so while I envied the folks flying, I wasn't totally disappointed either.

Eventually it got too dark to work without a flashlight, so we were back together as I became Dad's official flashlight holder while he worked. We kept at it for another hour or so, and finally called it a night. We hadn't planned to spend the night in the first place, but luckily Mom somehow knew to pack blankets and pillows for us to sleep with in the

Suburban. I still didn't like the idea, but Dad explained we didn't have a minute to spare checking in and out of a motel anyway. October nights can get pretty cold in Ohio, but we lucked out and had a mild evening that was just a little cool. It seemed like I had just lain down when I heard Dad digging in the toolbox for wrenches.

At the crack of dawn, we were back at work taking out more bolts. We made good progress, and before long I could tell Dad wasn't worried anymore. As we took more and more bolts out, he whistled and hummed old big band Glenn Miller–type tunes. The tunes weren't anything new as Dad often made his own music while working on something or driving the Suburban. I didn't think the tunes were anything great, but if Dad was humming them, at least I knew he was relaxed and confident.

When the airport restaurant opened, Dad sent me off to get a breakfast takeout order and to freshen up his thermos bottle of coffee. Being really hungry, I was glad to go, but I was also a little embarrassed. Since we didn't plan to spend the night, we didn't bring any extra clothes along, and mine were really dirty now with black grime going down both legs. Fortunately, there were only a few other customers there, so I made a quick dash in and out.

As we worked through the morning and into the afternoon, more visitors came to look. Usually the conversation was very casual. But one man said something that got our attention. He told of being at the airport when the plane landed gear-up. As he explained it, there was a man with a wild animal show that hauled his animals in the B-25. He was coming to Cincinnati to put on the show with alligators, big snakes, apes, turtles, you name it; the guy had the plane filled with cages full of wild animals. "That's why it's got 'WILD CARGO' painted on the side," he said.

"Why did it land gear-up?" Dad asked. The man told us the right engine quit, and after the loss of the hydraulic pump from the dead engine, the pilot could not get the landing gear down. From research done many years later, it seemed odd that a camera crew just happened to be at the airport as the stricken B-25 orbited overhead. A crew member parachuted out of the plane, and a photo of that made the local news. In a story published in 2016 about this B-25, it was suggested the gear-up landing was staged to drum up publicity for the animal show. B-25s weren't worth much in 1963, so to sacrifice this plane in a publicity stunt was not beyond reason.

After we made another uneventful trip to repeat the outboard wing removal process on the right wing, we returned on our fourth trip to Cincinnati to get the rear fuselage section. We still had a ton of disassembly work to do. In addition to the many bolts to be removed, the rear fuselage also had a bunch of control cables, trim tab cables, and electrical wire bundles to disconnect.

Dad went to work in the bomb bay and I worked in the rear fuselage. To disconnect a wire bundle in the back of the plane, I followed the bundle along the ceiling looking for a cannon plug. If I couldn't find a plug, the wires might have to be cut. Suddenly, WHAM! The breath was knocked out of me, and the worst pain of my life shot through my body. I gasped and moaned, struggling to get my breath back. When I tried to breathe, I sensed nothing but intense pain. I wanted to yell, but I couldn't. While preoccupied looking up at the wires running along the ceiling, I had stepped into the square hole where the bottom hatch had been removed. The trip to the concrete was quick. My thigh hit a metal barrel on the way down, and from the horrible pain just below my hip, I thought my leg was broken.

"What happened, what happened?" Dad hollered as he ran over to see if I was injured. It seemed like forever, but I was soon breathing okay again. Dad carefully checked me over, and luckily I didn't have any broken bones, just a lot of pain. After about 30 minutes of resting in the Suburban, I was feeling better and was back at work. I sure learned an unforgettable lesson about paying attention to where my feet are when in or on an airplane. We had a good laugh later when one of my sisters said: "At least the plane wasn't flying when you did *that*!"

11

The Little Six That Could

The hauling trips to Cincinnati provided an opportunity to spend time with Dad in a unique kind of way. Behind the wheel of the Suburban, he was pinned down. Not to say he wasn't home much; he was actually home a lot. But even at home, he was always busy. There were always things to build storage shelves for, things to move, things to paint, or things like a new plane to reassemble. Leisurely chats while sitting on the sofa didn't happen. In our home, leisure itself was a dirty word. In Dad's work-ethic world, any hint of relaxing or having fun was usually met with a disgusted frown.

His reputation as a hard worker came in second place just slightly behind his reputed enthusiasm for airplanes. A lot of factors shaped his powerful work ethic early in his life. Growing up during the Great Depression, he was raised in a period when almost everyone was poor. As Dad told it, a man enduring the Depression was considered lucky if he could feed his family by working like a dog for almost no pay. Those who had jobs were under enormous pressure to perform. If the boss didn't think you were working hard enough and fast enough, he'd gladly give your job to one of the thousands waiting in line.

Dad got the message. And as the head of our family, his work ethic, combined with a miser mentality, influenced nearly every aspect of the way we were raised. It was as if the Great Depression never ended. We wasted nothing, learned to work at an early age, and got by on the bare minimum comforts of life. Activities like attending a baseball game, going camping, or spending time and money on a vacation were things other families did. In Dad's workaholic world, there was simply no time to waste on playing or being idle. Thus, it seemed the only place he could really sit still was behind the wheel of the Suburban on a long hauling trip.

Fortunately, his carpenter job had improved, and as the hours on the highway passed, Dad's commentary on life was in a rare upbeat state. By the time he bought the B-25, he'd been working as a carpenter for Go Go Construction Company for well over a year. While the work was hard, Dad really liked the company. He had worked for other companies that went under, but this one impressed him as being stable. Though the foreman was very demanding and pushed the men hard, Dad's strong work ethic made him feel right at home. Owned by two brothers, Tony and Danny, the company seemed well managed. The brothers knew the business, used good building materials, appreciated quality workmanship, and had a booming business.

While Dad would talk at length about his carpenter job and the cast of characters he worked with, his nonstop dialogue about life covered a wide range of other topics. An avid reader of the newspaper, he often rambled on about world events. Of all the things happening, few topics got him on his political soapbox more than the commies. Since the Russians now had nukes and were establishing footholds in places like Cuba, Dad was convinced that unless we were vigilant, they'd take over America someday. Certainly, he wasn't alone in his fears. With the Cuban Missile Crisis just two years in the past, the nerves of many Americans were still on edge. As a result, he was very pro-military. Strategic Air Command (SAC) was at the height of its power, and Dad expressed comfort in SAC's huge arsenal of B-47, B-52, and B-58 nuclear-armed bombers. There was no doubt that we were the good guys, and SAC's bombers would make the commies think twice about messing with the good old USA.

Dad's only gripe with the military was the way they treated airplanes when they were through with them. In addition to scrapping the World War II planes to near extinction, the military continued to do the same with planes currently being retired. In fact, things had gotten worse. As he discovered with the Cutlass, you could no longer buy an ex-military plane in one piece. The idea that you had to cut it up into small chunks to demilitarize it was borderline sacrilegious to an airplane fanatic like Dad. The fact that old military planes were being destroyed and discarded like yesterday's trash gave him all the more satisfaction that we were saving the B-25. And not until we'd made our first few trips did we realize how close it had come to being scrapped.

Since we first saw the B-25, we noticed that someone had removed the panel below the right main fuel tank and cut a big hole in the rubber fuel bladder. That seemed strange. If someone wanted to salvage or steal the tank, why destroy it? A local airport man visiting us one day explained the mystery. "You saved the B-25 just in time," he said. He told of being at the airport when a junkyard crew was getting ready to take apart the B-25 with cutting torches. They used knives to slash open that fuel tank to make sure the torches wouldn't blow the plane up. Before they could cut open the other fuel tanks, they were told to quit because the plane was sold to some airplane collector.

The story of how perilously close *Wild Cargo* came to being destroyed gave us a chill. After hearing that, we were very proud of Dad for saving the plane. As we drove down the now-familiar road to Cincinnati during the remaining trips, you could just see the satisfaction on his face. Still, the drive was long, and Dad was determined to haul all he could on each trip. On this trip we were en route to get the bomber's engines. Though each was big and heavy, Dad figured he could save a trip by hauling both of the engines together.

When we arrived at the Lunken Airport, we found the B-25 parked on the grass near the terminal building. The towing of the plane to this location was done after Dad accepted an offer made by the airport manager. The manager felt it would be safer to have it within close watch of the airport staff in case climbers or vandals would try to take advantage of its vulnerable condition, half disassembled now. As the B-25 sat parked on the grass, all that was left was the forward fuselage, center wing, and both engines.

Although much of the plane was gone now, it still sat nicely on its landing gear. This was an important consideration for loading our trailer, since we still had no access to a crane. To ensure the plane would sit level on its own gear, we had to make sure we dismantled the bomber in the right sequence. For example, had we removed the engines before now, the weight of the rear fuselage would have caused the plane to rock back on its tail. Instead, by removing the rear fuselage first, and saving the engines for later, we avoided that problem.

With the plane parked near the terminal, we were getting a lot more visitors and a lot more offers for free airplane rides. I about had a fit. I wanted to fly so badly! Now maybe, just maybe, after years of dreaming of flying, I might actually get my first airplane ride. But like before, Dad declined all offers. I sort of understood, but was still terribly disappointed that I was missing many opportunities to fly. Being around airplanes so much made my desire to fly grow stronger all the time. Yet Dad was holding me back. I dropped several hints about the great deal it would be to get a free plane ride in one of the modern Piper or Cessna light planes. I wasn't surprised that he said no, but I didn't like the way he did it.

"I'm not interested in modern light planes," Dad scoffed, like I was nuts to want a ride in one. He often made derogatory comments about how he viewed these modern airplanes as "aluminum tin cans that sound like lawnmowers." In contrast, he was endeared to the classic look of the older planes with stylish and artistic contours. The old planes were often powered by the manly-sounding radial engines that he was a giant fan of. Adding to their appeal, the big round engines also wore cowlings matching the majestic shapes designed into the rest of the plane. Modern light planes had none of these features, so he dismissed them entirely.

We finally got everything on the left engine disconnected except for the top two engine mount bolts. He then backed the trailer under the engine and jacked the trailer slightly until it was snug with the engine. He finally removed those last two engine mount bolts, the engine settled nicely on the trailer, and we were loaded. I only had one concern after loading the first engine. I could tell it was heavy. The sag in the hardwood planks of the trailer bed, plus the look of the trailer springs, told me the engine was very heavy. Considering the old delivery truck frame and springs were probably designed for hauling hotdog buns, the B-25 engine was a bit much. Still, Dad planned to haul both engines in one load.

After repeating the removal process on the right side, we got the other engine loaded. Right away I could tell the trailer was really hurting. The trailer springs were bowed so much that I got down and had to take a look underneath. I reported to Dad that the springs were so bowed the trailer frame was sitting on the axle. Dad got down in the grass to look for himself. "Looks just like the old bus did," he said. I knew what that meant, and it was his story about the bus that caused me to look under the trailer now. When the Navy guys put the heavy Cutlass with its two engines inside the bus, Dad had the same problem of the springs sagging. To fix that, he jacked the bus frame and put wood blocks between the axle and the frame. Otherwise, he was afraid the bus springs would break. "We can't afford to break a trailer spring so we'll have to do the same thing here," Dad concluded. We then jacked the trailer frame and put wood blocks between the axle and the frame. Using some baling wire and nails, we secured the blocks so they wouldn't fall out when we hit bumps on the road. After tying down the engines and packing our things, we headed home.

As Dad drove away from the airport, there was another sign we were heavy. The Suburban didn't want to go. Even in first gear, when Dad let the clutch out, he had to rev the motor a lot and slip the clutch to get us going. As he'd slowly gain enough speed to shift to second and third gear, you could tell the poor engine was laboring really hard. Pickups and Suburbans then had virtually no soundproofing, but in a way that was good. Through sound you were really in touch with the vehicle. Nobody except hotrodders had engine tachometers, but we didn't need one. Just by the sound of the

I'm making faces at Dad the camera guy after we have the two Wright Cyclone R-2600 engines from *Wild Cargo* loaded. The trailer and Suburban are strained by the weight of both engines riding together. Winter is coming, so hauling the heavy engines one at a time for a fulltime carpenter is out of the question.

engine and whine of the transmission, you could tell exactly how the Suburban was doing.

It was unfortunate that we didn't have a real truck to haul the B-25 with, but even worse, the Suburban we had wasn't a powerful version. Modeled after the half-ton Chevy pickup, the Suburban was powered by a straight-six engine with a three-speed transmission that shifted on the steering column. Today, people wouldn't pull a jet-ski to the lake with a vehicle like that. With the heavy engines on the trailer, we'd eventually get our speed up and could cruise about 50 to 60 mph with the gas pedal to the floor. At least that's how fast I guessed we were going. Like the old white Ford, the Suburban's speedometer didn't work.

As we made our way home, it seemed the Suburban was handling the heavy load okay—for a while. After driving for about an hour, the transmission did something strange. Without any warning, it abruptly popped out of gear.

"What on earth!" Dad exclaimed as he quickly came off the gas to keep the engine from over-speeding. As we coasted along for a few moments, both of us stared at the gearshift and almost couldn't believe what we saw. As if a ghost had moved it, the gearshift jumped up all by itself from third gear into neutral. "Come on, baby, don't act up on me now," Dad said as he pushed the clutch down and re-engaged the transmission. Fortunately, he got it back in gear again, and as we motored along everything seemed fine. But soon it popped out of gear again. After that, I became the gearshift holder.

On past trips I enjoyed the drive home, as I could usually climb in the back seat and take a nap. It didn't take long for my arm to get tired of holding the shifter. As my arm got tired, I tried to guess just how hard I needed to hold the thing. I figured that if I pulled too hard, there was a chance I'd be doing more damage to the transmission. If I didn't hold it hard enough, I worried it would pop out of gear again. The other thing that bothered me was that I had to continue sitting right next to Dad.

Transmission problem or not, this was a routine issue when sitting in the front seat. The Suburban's front seat originally included a narrow folding seat located next to the right door in order for people using the rear seats to get in and out. Shortly after buying the Suburban, Dad decided the folding seat interfered too much when loading his carpenter tools. Thus, he removed it. That left the remaining front seat just wide enough for the driver and one other person, who now had to sit in the middle of the Suburban next to the driver. Year after year we drove it like that. If Mom was up there, people who saw us on the highway likely figured Mom and Dad were on a hot date. That was fine for them, but for me it was embarrassing.

While the transmission problem and the heavy load had us concerned, at least the trailer was balanced well with this load and there was no swaying. We'd had all we could stand of that while towing the long rear fuselage, which had swayed badly the whole way home. Once we got on Interstate 71 at Columbus, we made good time. There was no interstate highway between Columbus and Cincinnati then in 1964. As with the earlier return trips, our speed on the interstate was significantly less than the other traffic. Fortunately, in those days few vehicles were on the interstate after 9 p.m., and those who were on the road easily got around us.

While we were making good progress, I still had one more worry. "Do you think we'll make it up the hill on 306?" I asked Dad, referring to a long steep hill on Route 306 about 15 miles from home.

"I've been wondering the same thing," Dad said. He reminded me that second gear had handled every load so far, but we both knew this load was much heavier than any previous. We had to get off I-71 at the Medina exit in those days and then two-lane it the next 30 miles to the big hill. Leading up to the hill, the road had some sharp curves, so we could only go about 30 mph. When we rounded the last curve, Dad put the pedal to the metal. "You're almost home now, just one more hill, baby," Dad spoke warmly to the Suburban as he occasionally did. We got a little more speed and then started the climb. As we climbed the hill, our speed dropped off quickly. In a flash, Dad slammed the gearshift up the column into second gear. It was quickly obvious second gear was not going to hack it. I was nervous.

"I'm gonna have to use first," Dad said, sounding anxious. He had good reason to worry. The 1957 Suburban was made at a time when most stick shift transmissions didn't feature synchronization down to first gear. Unless the driver could match the gear speeds by some fancy gas petal and "double clutching" footwork, you couldn't get the transmission in first gear if the vehicle was moving. With the engine dying in second gear, Dad went for first gear and got nothing but the sound of grinding gears.

Anytime I sensed we were in trouble, I snapped my head to look at his body language. He was in a panic. His gearshift hand and both feet were busy with a flurry of activity. I could hear his left boot thumping on the bare steel floor every time he hurriedly mashed the clutch pedal down. Dad tried first gear again, but it just wouldn't go. Our remaining speed was dropping fast. In my mind an image flashed of the Suburban and trailer with the two heavy B-25 engines racing down the hill backwards into the darkness. I couldn't imagine the train wreck we'd be.

Dad worked the clutch and gas one more time with the shifter in neutral. With us barely rolling, he went for first gear and got it. It was clear the engine had the load, but even in first gear, it was barely running. For about ten seconds, I was on the edge of my seat, wondering whether the engine was going to hack it.

It reminded me of when I was younger and Mom used to read me the book, *The Little Engine That Could.* "I think I can—I think I can—I think I can," the little train engine continued repeating those words as it struggled climbing the big mountain with a trainload of toys and good food. Now, Dad and I desperately needed the Suburban's little six-cylinder engine to do the same thing. After a few tense moments, I could hear the engine pick up a little speed, and then a little more. "Yes, I think she's gonna do it!" Dad hollered. We still had a way to go, but unless something broke, I could tell we were going to make it. Finally, we crested the dreaded hill, and I could *feel* the train story Mom had read me over and over as a little boy.

When Monday morning came, Dad went back to his carpenter job, and I went to school. Now that we'd been hauling the bomber for five weekends, I felt amused listening to the other sixth-graders talk about their weekend. On the one hand, I envied them for being able to do the normal kid stuff that seemed so natural at that age. But on the other, I wouldn't have wanted to be anywhere else.

Back at home, Dad returned from his first day back at work and reported the Suburban's transmission continued to pop out of third gear. He had hoped it was just something related to pulling the heavy load of the bomber's engines. The drive to work proved him wrong. As a result, we gulped down supper and went transmission shopping.

Dad and I headed to the other side of Newbury to an auto salvage yard known as Hank's Junkyard. Hank and Dad had been good friends for many years. Hank was a tall, thin man who was easily old enough to be my grandfather. Every time we saw him, he had a bright smile on his face and was happy to see us. Typically, he'd ask Dad for an update on the latest addition to the airplane collection. Hank admired Dad for saving the planes he collected and always enjoyed our highway stories of towing them home. If anyone else was around, he'd introduce Dad as "the man who hauled the jet plane in the school bus." Dad explained that we were now hauling the B-25 with the Suburban, and Hank just smiled while slowly shaking his head in disbelief.

Dad explained the problem we had with the Suburban's transmission. Hank seemed as puzzled as we were, but quickly his concerned look changed to a big grin. "Walter, the Chevy boys didn't design that little transmission for hauling B-25 bombers!" Hank laughed. "I'm surprised you made it home at all with that little three-speed." With that, Hank pointed out where he had a few wrecked Chevy pickup trucks that for sure had what we needed. Soon Dad and I were on our way with a transmission Hank only charged $10 for. The one thing people didn't like about Hank's junkyard was that he also raised pigs. While most of the pigs were penned up, many also ran around the junk cars and trucks. Even though his prices were very low, the town joke was that you really paid through the nose at Hank's junkyard.

After replacing the Suburban's transmission one evening during the week, we were back on the road Saturday morning to get the forward fuselage. Fortunately, this turned out to be one of the easiest trips of all. Dad backed the trailer under the nose until it reached the nose landing gear. We put some pipe rollers and boards between the trailer and the plane. We then retracted the nose landing gear and backed the trailer all the way under the fuselage. We didn't have to worry about scratching the bottom of the B-25

11. The Little Six That Could

fuselage since it had already endured its gear-up landing. A few more hours of unbolting and we were done.

The next weekend we headed back to Cincinnati for the last time, and I had mixed feelings about it. With no disassembly left to do, I was glad most of the hard work was finished. On the other hand, I was a bit sad the whole event was almost over. I really enjoyed the adventure of hauling the B-25 and being on the flight line at Lunken Airport. Just seeing all the planes take off and land was a real boost. I didn't know when, but I was now sure that someday I was going to fly.

"This should be a real milk run compared to the other trips," Dad said as we drove I-71 southbound. All we had to do was load the center wing section. He made it sound easy, but I wasn't so sure. "Bet you're glad you won't have to do all that unbolting this time," he added.

"It will be nice not to get so dirty for once," I answered.

"There's nothing wrong with a working man getting dirty!" Dad said proudly. He was forever stuck on his blue-collar roots. A real man worked for a living and got his hands dirty doing so. As for the work ahead, there was one thing Dad was worried about with this trip: weight. Everything we hauled so far had been pretty light except the two engines. Dad knew from his engine-scrapping days how much the R-2600 engines weighed. And even counting them, there was a lot of weight not accounted for. An empty B-25 was supposed to weigh almost 20,000 pounds. But *Wild Cargo* was missing all of its guns and other military hardware except the steel armor pilot seats. So we just weren't sure.

There was one unmistakable sign the center wing was heavy when we secured it before leaving Lunken on the previous trip. Dad was afraid it would tip over and hurt

Forward fuselage and cockpit of *Wild Cargo* are finally free from the center section of wing and fuselage.

or kill someone if we left it sitting high on its landing gear. So we retracted each landing gear and used a jack to lower it close to the ground and set it on some sturdy wood frames Dad constructed. As we used his high-lift farm jack to lower the wing one side at a time, there was a lot of pressure on the jack handle, making it very hard to move. I had never worked the jack that hard before. One advantage of using Dad's simple equipment like this farm jack and his hand-powered bomb winch was you could feel what was going on. Even when moving a big section of airplane, there were few substitutes for the information provided by the human touch.

We figured it was too dangerous to try to jack the center wing high enough to load on the trailer. The risk that it would flip over if a jack or any blocks slipped was just too great a danger. So we resorted to another trick. We unhooked the trailer from the Suburban and jacked the trailer hitch until the back of the trailer bed was on the ground. Then we winched the trailer under the wing. It was a real slow process, but it worked. Perched about six feet in the air on the front of the trailer, I slowly cranked the old bomb winch. Meanwhile, Dad shifted the pipe rollers and boards while standing alert with his pry bar to keep things from getting caught. Every few feet that I winched, the trailer would start to pull to one side and get crooked. To straighten it out, Dad blocked one trailer tire so only the other tire could move, which forced the trailer to pivot. If that didn't always work, we'd move the winch cable to the side that needed to be pulled more. As a result, it took hours to get the center wing section onto the trailer, as one engine nacelle and then the bomb bay had to be supported with planks and rollers.

The bomb winch we used for this and so many other tasks wasn't designed to handle nearly the load we had it pulling now. To start with, it only had a ¼-inch steel cable. Like most of our equipment, the winch had seen better days, and the thin cable was badly frayed, with numerous broken steel strands. As we got more and more of the wing on the trailer, it got harder and harder to winch the heavy wing up the steep slope of the trailer. After a while, Dad and I began to worry about the cable breaking. Besides the obvious problem of getting the wing up on the trailer, he worried about a snapped cable whipping back and taking my head off. After thinking about it for a few moments, Dad decided to cover the cable with a blanket. That way, if it did snap and come loose, hopefully the blanket would keep the cable from whipping too much. Still, I was very worried as I cranked the winch. The winching process produced loud creaking and popping sounds, and the worst ones made me more and more gun-shy as cranking the winch began to require nearly all of my strength.

When we finally got the bomb bay up on the trailer, Dad decided to level the trailer and hitch it back to the Suburban. To do this, we jacked the section of wing sticking beyond the back of the trailer until the hitch came down low enough to reconnect. With the load level on the trailer now, winching became a lot easier, and we soon had the wing scooting forward at a good pace. Still, we had a problem. The center section of the wing was too long for the trailer. "We've got to get the bomb bay centered over the trailer's axle or this thing will sway like crazy," Dad said as he surveyed the load. He decided we had to get the wing as close to the back of the Suburban as possible. So I kept winching until he stopped me. We stepped back and I didn't like what I saw. "How will we turn corners?" I asked.

"I'll just turn real shallow," Dad answered.

"But when you have to make a sharp turn, the wing will smash the rear of the Suburban," I replied, still concerned. Dad wasn't worried about the Suburban. Never mind that it was the family car; to him it was expendable. The more we looked, he agreed the Suburban probably was going to get some big dents during turns. He said we'd fix it later if it got smashed. I already knew what "fix it later" meant. That was scheduled at the same time Hell would freeze over.

Just as it got dark, we hit the road. Even though we figured the load was balanced and wouldn't sway, it did. After a few miles, he figured that our max speed was about 50 mph. But it didn't matter. This load was so heavy that 50 mph was about all it seemed the Suburban would do. When we turned into our first service station and hit some dips in the road, an awful sound came from the rear of the Suburban. "Boom, pop, bang!" It sounded like a bulldozer was crushing the back of the Suburban. As I expected, the B-25 wing fittings were mauling the Suburban.

"Shoot, I'm busting everything back there," said Dad. The appearance of the center wing loaded on the trailer was more of a sight than anything else thus far. That, combined with the loud sound of the Suburban getting crushed, resulted in a good crowd of onlookers as we pulled up to the gas pumps. As we got out of the Suburban, we were barraged with "What kind of airplane you got there?" "Sure looks big!" "Where'd you get it?" Dad and I casually answered the questions like we did this all the time, because we did!

When I saw the back of the Suburban, it really upset me. One corner of the roof was mangled and crushed in. I didn't see how Dad could ever fix the damage and make the Suburban look right. The thought of our family having to ride around in it was quickly getting very depressing. Surprisingly, the bomber wing had no damage. The sturdy wing attachment fittings were covered with chips of paint, but otherwise, you couldn't tell they'd been chewing on the family car.

Center wing of B-25 *Wild Cargo*'s safe arrival home completes the stray-dog bomber's desperate journey to escape the scrapman's torch.

The trip home took forever. The Suburban drank a lot of gas pulling the heavy load, so we had to make more fuel stops than normal. Each stop generated more popping and crunching sounds as the wing and Suburban made contact turning corners. Otherwise, the night was almost uneventful. With a load that was too wide, too long, and too heavy, Dad and I expected we'd get to meet a few more police officers before the night was over. Not to be disappointed, red flashing lights lit up the rearview mirror. By now, even before Greenpeace was formed, Dad had his "I'm saving the world's endangered airplanes" pitch down to an art form. Most of the officers were just curious to know what they were looking at. One got out his tape measure and informed Dad he needed a permit for his oversize load. Dad also had his "Gee, I didn't think to measure it" routine down well, too, and as a result the officer let us go. Still, I had another worry.

"How are we going to make it up the 306 hill?" I asked.

"I've been thinking about that," he answered. After the near disaster towing the heavy engines, he had decided he would put the transmission in first gear at the bottom of the hill before beginning the climb up. "That way, I'll get the engine wound up in first gear and I won't have to shift gears on the hill." It sounded like a good idea to me. When we got there, he did exactly as planned. Sure enough, the Suburban handled the hill okay.

Shortly, we were home, and Dad cruised through the driveway out into the field. Under the light of the stars, he parked the trailer behind the cockpit section as if reuniting the two pieces of the plane. And with that, *Wild Cargo*, a stray dog of a B-25 once moments away from being put to sleep by the scrapman's torch, had been rescued and given a home.

B-25 *Wild Cargo* relaxing in the snow a few years later. Tail of P-47 we got from Earl Reinert is visible at far left (courtesy Jason McKeon).

12

Wings of the Night

I knew we had a lot of work ahead with the B-25 home. I was glad because it provided a needed sense of order in a home where I often didn't know what the heck was coming next. Into November of 1964, when we completed our last trip, Dad was determined to get the B-25 together before winter set in.

Fortunately, he had built another boom tractor the year before, and this one worked a lot better. Made from a 1942 Chevy flatbed truck, the new boom tractor Dad rigged together also included parts from four types of airplanes. His custom work began with his cutting torch removing the fenders and cab off the truck. Then he moved the rear axle forward and cut the frame off behind the axle. For lifting loads, he didn't rely solely on a winch like on the first tractor. Instead, he made a movable A-frame boom for raising and lowering objects. The boom was made from truck frame parts mounted on top of the landing gear struts from Dad's C-82. To raise the boom, a hydraulic system was used which included C-46 landing gear actuators, a Corsair hydraulic tank, and my least favorite aerobic workout device, a C-47 hydraulic hand pump.

Dad showed great innovation in building the tractor, but in its own crude way it helped define the direction his airplane collection was heading. The entire brake system on the Chevy truck frame was paralyzed by rust. But since three of the four rear tires did not hold air, the flat truck tires he drove on all but eliminated the need for brakes. Because the truck's radiator was shot, Dad ran the motor dry and limited engine run time to a few minutes. And though the new boom worked great, many of the bolts holding it together were of every size and length, depending on what he could scrounge together. Even then, many of the big bolts were never secured with nuts. They were simply inserted like pins through the jagged holes Dad's torch cut in the old truck frame and other vagabond steel components he slapped together. Fortunately, many of the bolts were extra long. As these bolts would gradually slide and migrate from their desired position, a few taps with Dad's carpenter hammer was always the fix.

Despite the countless hours of airplane related work the tractor endured in the years ahead, it also gave us a rare moment of mischievous fun. Its long gas tank was removed from behind the driver's seat during the truck-to-tractor conversion. Months later, we had a pile of stuff to burn late one evening, and on a whim, Dad decided to set the old gas tank on top of the pile. He lit the fire, and then we ran like crazy to hide behind the blue Chevy sedan retired on its perch atop four cement blocks. As the flames rose, Dad and I hid in the tall weeds and hilly area behind the blue Chevy, watching the fire through the car windows. Before long, the flames completely surrounded the gas tank. We waited and waited. Minutes passed and nothing happened. "Been years since I put gas in that tank," Dad said, disappointed. He explained how even the fuel vapors had probably long evaporated. "Looks like she's a dud."

We both stood up and walked a few feet from the car when, "Kaboom!" A big orange ball of fire briefly flashed around the gas tank, causing the long and slender tank to launch straight up like a missile heading for the moon. Dad and I jumped so wild with fright we both lost our balance on the sloping ground and fell down in the thick brush. After flying four to five stories high, the tank fell away from us off in the distance like in slow motion. After a brief moment, Dad and I erupted in hilarious laughter. Instantly, I met someone I'd never known. Dad laughed like crazy to the point of being near tears. He was suddenly my best pal, and we giggled uncontrollably as we rolled in the thick weedy brush. After getting up, we kept on laughing as we took turns acting out each other's cowardly-lion jumps and frightened expressions at the moment of blastoff. That will always be one of my favorite memories of being with my mostly stoic father.

The B-25 was the first large aircraft we used the new tractor for, and it handled most of the job well. With the center wing section still on the trailer, we used the tractor to pick up the cockpit section. After lowering the nose landing gear, we aligned the cockpit with the wing and bolted the two sections together. Next, we used the tractor to hold up each end of the center wing as we extended that side's main landing gear. We were then able to pull the weary trailer free, and *Wild Cargo* was standing on her own legs. The tractor was well suited for installing both engines, which made the B-25 look better yet.

Typically, we got a lot of rain in the fall, and the field could turn into a sea of mud at any time. As a result, Dad was in a hurry to get finished using the tractor on the B-25. Thanksgiving arrived with soil and weather conditions favorable for work. Starting early in the morning, we got busy installing the rear fuselage. Big and bulky as the rear fuselage was, the tractor lifted it easily. With some help from jacks and blocks, we soon had the bolt holes lined up and hurried the longeron nuts and bolts together. "Can rain all it wants to now," Dad said happily as he tightened the last longeron nut.

Still, we paid a price. Our uncles, aunts, cousins, and Grandma Murray all came to our home for the holiday. While my sisters were turned loose to visit, I had to stay with Dad until he was done. "What's wrong with you, Walter—having your kids working on your junk airplanes on a holiday when you're supposed to be with your family?" Grandma Murray scolded Dad as we entered the house, both of us very dirty. "It's Thanksgiving!" she emphasized as she pointed at the dinner table. The table was all set with the turkey and trimmings, and the food smelled great.

"I needed to get my new B-25 together while it's dry enough to work," he explained.

"Oh, nobody cares about your new damn airplane, Walter. Now sit down and have dinner with your family," she ordered. We had a wonderful dinner, and I enjoyed spending what little time was left of the holiday with my relatives. Despite Grandma Murray's objections, everyone seemed to enjoy hearing of the B-25 addition to the family. As the evening got late and all of them went home, Dad decided we'd work into the night on the B-25.

With each assembly, we initially put in the minimum number of bolts to hold the sections together, such as the longeron bolts. Dad was afraid a heavy snowfall or strong wind might cause the bomber to break apart without more structure bolted together. So he was in a rush to install more nuts and bolts. Unfortunately, the self-locking nuts were slow to install, requiring us a number of nights to do the job. This was nothing unusual, since Dad's daytime carpenter job often forced us to do our airplane work at night.

At night, I was ever the flashlight holder for Dad as he went about his work. Besides the B-25, we spent many evenings doing work such as installing cockpit instruments in the BT-15, the Zero Zero Corsair, Twin Mustang and other planes. As I stood on the wooden stepladder outside the Corsair cockpit or on the wings near other cockpits Dad was working in, my flashlight sometimes wandered. With me distracted and captivated by the night, Dad would call out flashlight aiming corrections. The fall air was cool and crisp in a way that matched perfectly with the crisp view of the vast and beautiful night sky abundant before us. Under the light of the moon and stars, the silhouettes of the World War II planes asserted a stunning presence. The dull tarnished aluminum of the Twin Mustang made it both subtle and majestic. With its two four-blade propellers set against the backdrop of the night sky, the long blades protruding upwards boldly split the sky while forming a stark contrast against the moon and stars. While the propellers had long been stilled, just a small amount of imagination allowed me to sense that at any moment their engines could roar to life. The night obscured and hid the small dents, faded paint, disconnected wires, and missing engine parts that guaranteed a quiet evening. Yet the night fueled my inspiration. By hiding what held the planes silent, the night allowed these eager-looking planes to fly wherever in the sky my imagination took them to soar.

13

Treasure Hunting

With B-25 *Wild Cargo* fully assembled on his property, Dad's search for aircraft and aviation artifacts went into overdrive. Several factors helped fuel his efforts. His carpenter job at Go Go Construction became so steady he now worked through the winter months and had not been laid off in several years. I was growing bigger and more able to help him haul stuff. Also, the combination of the Suburban and the trailer had clearly demonstrated its hauling capability with the B-25 *Wild Cargo*.

By the mid–1960s, World War II aircraft often fell into two categories. The flying category of aircraft had fortunately been well maintained in the two decades since the war. The other category included aircraft which were no longer flying and were either derelict or heading that way. Aircraft in flyable condition were increasing in value, while aircraft in poor condition were still being lost to the scrapman's torch. Besides being unable to afford a flyable warbird, Dad reasoned these aircraft were already saved. So he focused his search efforts on aircraft in marginal or deteriorating condition. His search criteria also included looking for aircraft parts and components.

Wings, fuselages, canopies, engines, landing gears, you name it, if it was an aircraft item from the World War II era or later, Dad collected it. In some cases, he was simply trying to find replacement parts for things missing on the aircraft he owned. But even if a wing or engine had no relationship to any of his aircraft, he'd still collect it if he could afford it. To find this kind of stuff, Dad and I began roaming airports, scrap yards, salvage yards, and military surplus stores.

I enjoyed visiting the airports and seeing all the planes based at each one. Yet it weighed on me to notice the vivid contrast between these aircraft and the ones in our back yard. The planes I watched taking off and landing were obviously in great condition, while even the planes tied down looked perfect and ready to fly. Returning home after each airport visit, I thought Dad's planes looked sad. And another major contrast sticking in my mind upon returning home came from something sticking to my feet.

Mud, mud, mud. At home, it was everywhere. From the rainy fall, through the snowmelt of winter, and on into each predictably cold and rainy spring, mud was almost as constant as the air we breathed. About five acres to the north and another five or so to the west all sloped uphill. So when it rained, our dirt driveway became a virtual riverbed for the runoff. Only a few times do I recall Dad spending some bucks for a load of gravel. So we dealt with a very muddy environment at home most of the year. At the airports, I appreciated their nicely paved parking lots, sidewalks, and parking ramps for airplanes. From our house, just getting to Dad's Suburban often required us to island hop a series of scrap boards or flat rocks to navigate the mud. One slip and you were a mess. As

I contrasted the modern airports Dad and I visited with the sea of mud we fought at home, something as simple as a nice slab of concrete caught my eye.

At most airports we visited, Dad knew some of the people who typically gave us a warm welcome. They always asked if he was hauling anything new, and an occasional grin accompanied the question of whether he hauled any new finds with the school bus. Dad enjoyed the notoriety of his unusual hauling methods, but more important to him, these people showed their appreciation for the aircraft he was saving. As though he were saving endangered wildlife, they admired him for pursuing an important cause, but it was also clear that saving the derelict aircraft was something they preferred someone else do. The men and an occasional lady would then trade the latest information about where they'd recently seen a World War II airplane, who owned it, and what shape it was in. A wonderful person Dad often visited was a man with an F8F Bearcat that was in the most immaculate condition of any aircraft I'd seen. His name was Bob Kucera.

Bob Kucera flew his Bearcat as a camera platform in an aerial photography firm he founded on the east side of Cleveland. Over the years, Dad and Kucera became good friends, and each visited the other regularly. Being the last propeller-driven fighter plane developed for the Navy and Marines, the Bearcat represented the latest and greatest. Powered by a later and more powerful version of the Pratt & Whitney R-2800 engine than the early R-2800 used on Dad's Zero Zero Corsair, the Bearcat had other features that made it a hot performer. These included drag-reducing aerodynamic innovations, a small size, and a very lightweight design. While the Bearcat proved to be a high-performance fighter, it was produced too late to see combat in World War II.

Kucera's Bearcat appeared perfect in every way. First, it was painted in glistening white and beige colors with stylish black stripes flowing back from nose to tail. Void of any military markings, this type of paint scheme was typical for civilian-owned fighter planes during the 1960s. The plane was so spotless Dad often commented, "You could eat off of it." Just like people bond to and pamper their horses, aviators often do the same with their airplanes. Without a doubt, Kucera's Bearcat was always well groomed.

The contrast between the condition of Kucera's pristine Bearcat and any of Dad's ratty planes coincidentally spilled over into the way each man appeared. Kucera's clothing, manner, and personality reflected an executive quality that would make him a natural fit chairing a shareholder meeting for a Fortune 500 firm. Tall and trim, he was typically wearing a white shirt and tie, if not a complete suit. A pilot from the World War II generation, Kucera wore a haircut that would easily pass a military inspection.

At the other end of the spectrum, Dad's rough and worn work boots, unkempt bushy black hair, picked and worn sweatshirt all made him the polar opposite of Kucera. Also wearing a beat-up dingy ball cap and dirty construction work trousers, Dad was the complete package for visiting the muddy and dreary scrap yards we would visit. Though this vivid contrast told that each man defined the bookends of lifestyle, I also observed how they nevertheless remained very good friends. I saw most of that as a reflection of Kucera's personality. Any other man with Kucera's corporate appearance would have intimidated Dad. But Kucera had a natural warmth that made people comfortable in his presence.

Still, in any other setting, I doubt that these two men would claim to know each other. The single thing that knocked down their lifestyle barriers and brought them together was their common love of airplanes. Clearly, Dad admired Kucera for actively flying such a gem of a Bearcat. On the other hand, Kucera stated repeatedly how he wanted Dad's high-powered F2G racing Corsair. He asked Dad to sell him the F2G almost every time we met, but Dad kindly refused.

Besides being spotless to perfection, Kucera's Bearcat was also unique. To facilitate the aerial photography work, he had a special compartment built in the rear fuselage behind the pilot seat. The compartment was fitted to hold special aerial cameras, and it also featured two extra seats. When he first offered to give us a ride in the back of the Bearcat I went nuts. Holy cow! A ride in the Bearcat—I just couldn't believe it! But each time, before I could mutter a sound, Dad started some excuse that there was a junkyard we needed to check out or some other place to go to. It was bad enough that Dad's planes didn't fly, but when he repeatedly turned down airplane rides from Bob Kucera, I began to suspect we'd never see eye to eye.

Visiting scrap yards was the most dismal aspect of Dad's hobby. Everything about these places was nasty. From the front office to the forklifts and trucks, and out into the scrap yard itself, *everything* including the dang fence was dilapidated and filthy dirty. Even the *mud* was disgustingly polluted and nasty. Yet for some reason I just couldn't figure, Dad pressed on with the scrap yard aspect of his scavenger hunt with tremendous zeal. When we eventually finished our search of the Cleveland area and got a few smashed and corroded aviation artifacts home, I figured we were done.

Wings: Right side of photograph shows two AD-5 Skyraider outboard wings flat on the ground next to the F-82E. These came in handy for an X-prototype Skyraider we later got that was missing its outboard wings. Lower left is a '55 Suburban even more rusted than our '57. We salvaged many parts from it, including the entire engine (courtesy Jason McKeon).

13. Treasure Hunting

Wow, was I wrong. With the wide-eyed wonder of an archaeologist, he went to the library to plan his next expeditions. Searching the Yellow Pages of telephone books, he found the phone numbers for scrap yards and military surplus stores in other big cities in Ohio. He then called the places and asked questions about aircraft items he was looking for.

Soon, we were spending an occasional Saturday on the road with the Suburban and trailer. One by one we searched scrap yards and military surplus stores in Akron, Columbus, Dayton, and Springfield, Ohio. Mostly, we just found old radial engines. Some were still configured with their aircraft cowlings and parts, like one we found for an F6F Hellcat. Even when we found something, it was usually in really bad shape. But no matter how ugly its condition, Dad still had to have whatever it was. About the only good news was that we seldom had to disassemble the item to haul it home.

Despite my growing doubts, I sometimes had to agree Dad knew what he was doing. One time he bought a fuselage and engine for a Navy N3N biplane. He paid $80 for it, and a year later sold it for $500. Once in a while he was able to buy an item and later trade it with another collector for a part he really wanted. More often, he'd buy parts for an airplane he didn't own, and within a few years would end up with a plane that needed those exact parts. When Dad got B-25 *Wild Cargo*, it was missing every escape hatch. Fortunately, he still had new hatches from the school busloads of B-25 parts. Another time he bought a set of outboard wings for a Navy AD Skyraider. A few years later, he bought a Skyraider, and it was missing its outboard wings.

One Saturday in the mid-1960s, we were doing our search of a scrap yard in southern Ohio. As usual, Dad and I split up to explore the yard quickly before it closed. I

More wings. A close up look at a pair of Republic F-84F Thunderstreak jet wings with a derelict Vultee BT-13 Valiant nearby. Many other stray wings not pictured ended up in the collection (courtesy Jason McKeon).

wandered a bit before getting to the other side of a mountain of scrap iron and then couldn't believe my eyes.

"Dad, Dad!" I yelled as I reversed course and ran about a hundred yards to get him.

"What is it?" he asked, annoyed that I was interrupting his search.

"There's a P-51 Mustang on the other side of that big scrap iron pile," I said excitedly, while pointing. Dad's face lit up. I never saw Dad run very much, but this made him hit his stride.

"Oh, my gosh. Look what they've done to her," he said sadly as we got to the plane. We paced near the P-51—or what was left of it. Strewn in a heap of scrap metal we found the forward fuselage, wings, and engine. Unlike the B-25, the scrapman beat us to this one. Scrap metal guys as Dad and I were, we recognized somebody had worked like a dog to remove every piece of steel from the P-51's aluminum airframe in order to get more money for it from the scrap dealer. Not only were the bolts and other hardware gone from the airframe, but most of the structural steel rivets were drilled out as well. "Can you believe the man-hours spent drilling those steel rivets?" Dad said as we both stood there in disbelief. Still, there was good news—the airframe had not been touched by a torch. Beat to hell as the P-51 was, Dad wanted it, and for once I agreed. Amazingly, the scrap dealer sold us the airframe for $60 and the engine for $200.

Besides airports and scrap yards, military bases were another source for Dad's collection. While the need to demilitarize airframes meant there was no hope of finding a complete airplane to salvage, he was able to get other things on his wish list. Many of

Property getting crowded in the 1970s: Left is the P-51 fuselage I found during a scrap yard hunt. We also got the P-51 wings and engine (not pictured). The Mustang was a photo recon version, so officially an F-6D or F-6K instead of a P-51 as we called it. Center is a derelict P-63 fuselage. Franklin B-25 is in background with Cutlass jet behind the B-25 upper left.

his aircraft were missing instruments, radios, and other electronics when he originally got them. Fortunately, military surplus items were often obsolete, yet still in excellent condition despite being sold as scrap. By successfully bidding on scrap aircraft and electronics, Dad could pluck the things he needed for his obsolete aircraft.

About half the items Dad equipped his planes with came from surplus bids at military bases in Ohio and Michigan. He typically limited his bids to scrap lots of 10,000 pounds. The Suburban and trailer could haul a load of that size in one or two trips. By bidding between $100 and $200, he was successful on a bid a few times a year. After picking out the items he wanted, he'd sell the rest to a scrap yard and get his money back several times over. Still, there were problems bidding on scrap sold by the military. The biggest problem was that his carpenter job conflicted with the Monday-through-Friday operation of the military disposal yards. It was hard enough to get Friday off to haul the stuff, but he considered it unrealistic to make a pre-bid trip to inspect what was for sale. As a result, Dad bid almost everything sight-unseen.

On one military scrap bid, we ended up with an F-101 Voodoo fighter plane. One of the century series jet fighters built in the 1950s, the Voodoo was fast, with a top speed over 1,000 miles per hour. There was just one problem with Dad's sight-unseen Voodoo. It had been recovered from what military jet jocks call a "smoking hole." With the exception of the tail section, disassembly wasn't a problem. We got the Voodoo the same time as the B-25. From the high point of hauling the B-25, the Voodoo took me to the basement of low. To load the wreck, Dad started loading the bigger pieces on the trailer

F-101 Voodoo wreckage: Around the same time we hauled B-25 *Wild Cargo*, **we also hauled the crashed Voodoo jet above. I'm up on the left tip of the plane's tail. As Walter's 11-year old son, I couldn't help but notice the extreme contrast of hauling this wreckage home compared to B-25** *Wild Cargo*.

as I got the small ones. Being only 11, I couldn't lift real heavy pieces, but not to worry: there was a huge abundance of small pieces.

The plane burned after the crash and had a terrible odor of burnt plastic, metal, rubber, and God knows what else. As I picked items, I'd find pieces of metal here, a chunk of a tire there, some smashed flight instruments and other cockpit items among piles of everything and anything.

There are different versions of this F-101 Voodoo story. In the version I know, Dad was told that two men died in the crash. I don't know who from the base disposal office told him that. We were regular customers buying bid-lots of scrap and salvage from Lockbourne Air Force Base near Columbus, Ohio, so we well knew the base disposal people who briefed Dad. As a young boy it was normal for me to consider what I heard from Dad to be gospel. That, of course, would change in a few years at the exact moment I became a teen. But for now, Dad's words were written in stone.

I vividly remember Dad assuring me that I was not going to find any human body parts in the jet's wreckage. Still, my eyes were on high alert. When I did eventually find what certainly was a busted piece of a flight crew helmet, I was stunned. After finding *that*, I grabbed things slowly and cautiously, afraid of my next surprise. "We haven't got all damn day," Dad barked. "We need to get this thing loaded before they close up for the weekend."

Despite my fears, I hurried up my pace understanding time was critical. The military disposal yards we bought from closed up tight at 4 p.m., with no exceptions. That meant we had to be loaded, weighed, government paperwork done, and headed out the gate. When you consider that we drove 200 miles and more sometimes just to get there, we put in some hectic days.

For over fifty years, that busted piece of flight crew helmet remained etched in my brain. Relentlessly searching the internet for tidbits of information about many of Dad's planes, I only recently found a very brief newspaper story dated September 10, 1962, telling about the Voodoo crash near Washington Court House, Ohio. That matches the crash site location we were told of by the disposal yard people. According to the published story, both men ejected safely from the Voodoo and had no serious injuries. After all these years of believing the worst, it was a thrill to read that they got out okay. Still, this mismatch of information is something I am unable to explain.

Other military scrap-bid road trips were a bit further than Lockbourne. For the longer trips to Selfridge Air Force Base, Michigan, and Wright-Patterson Air Force Base, Ohio, we left the house around 4 a.m. Getting up so early was very hard for me to do. Still, there was something special and mysterious about starting the day so early, especially on some winter trips to Selfridge. With the sunrise a few hours away, everything outside was so still, so quiet, like the whole planet was asleep. Snow crunching under my feet as I made my way to the Suburban was sometimes the first sound of morning.

By age 11, I was fully checked out for making winter starts of the Suburban and warming it up, manual choke and all. Like Chevy trucks of its day, the Suburban had a pedal for a starter button on the floor, just right of the gas pedal. The starter button took a lot of foot pressure to hold engaged, so I had to scoot my bottom to the front edge of the cold seat and hold the steering wheel tightly to work both the starter and gas petals. Since Dad didn't have a battery charger or spare battery, I had one shot at getting the ice-cold engine cranked. Luckily, Dad taught me enough about engines and carburetors by now that I could finesse the manual choke and gas pedal to get it going every time.

13. Treasure Hunting

As I got the Suburban warmed up, Mom and Dad did their final inventory check of lunches, clothes, money and paperwork. Likewise, as Dad directed, I did a check of all the tools, oil, tie-downs, jacks, and other equipment I had loaded the night before. As Mom waved from the doorway, we headed off into the frosty darkness. Luckily, as a kid, I was too young to drive legally and thus could sack out in the back seat as Dad drove. Typically, though, I stayed awake up front until we got on the interstate. I enjoyed the peacefulness of driving down the highway at that time of the morning. Back then, almost nothing was open 24 hours. It simply seemed like we owned the road.

As planned, we'd get to a military base about 8 a.m. when the disposal yard opened up. When hauling engines or electronic equipment, we could usually load up in a few hours and be on our way. However, if there was any dismantling or cutting to do on an airframe, we were hard pressed for time. With loads like the Voodoo or other aircraft, it would have been nice to take two days, but Dad's boss was mad enough that he was taking even one day off from work. Also, since Dad was an hourly employee at his carpenter job, no work meant no pay. To make things as manageable as possible, we always hauled on Friday. That way, Dad only missed one day of work, and we had the weekend to recover from each trip.

14

On the Outside Looking Up

I'll never forget the first time I heard that sound. A plane was taking off at an airshow, and it had a powerful racecar sound that was refined in a way that wowed my ears and made me an instant fan of whatever plane this was. The crowd was immense, with the spectator viewing fence packed so deep I couldn't see much. Suddenly, above the heads of the spectators, a yellow plane pulled up into a steep climb. The climb looked way too steep, and I immediately sensed great danger. Then, the yellow plane started a brisk roll and began to go upside down. All of this really startled me, as it just looked too soon after takeoff to be doing that. As the plane rolled upside down, you could see its landing gear retracting into the wings while the nose dropped into a shallower climb. With the saturating roar of the plane's engine filling the air, the plane continued its roll until upright again.

Bob Hoover had just completed his trademark takeoff in his yellow P-51 Mustang, and I knew right away that this was going to be my favorite airshow act. The Mustang is considered by many to be the best-looking propeller airplane ever made, and in any airshow it's a definite crowd pleaser. By itself, the powerful growl of the Mustang's Merlin engine is an intoxicating sound that airshow goers quickly become enchanted with. Even when a P-51 is far off in the distance, its distinct sound telling of brute power asserts strongly that the pilot has a real tiger by the tail. With tremendous grace and skill, Hoover put the Mustang through a series of intricate maneuvers that showed off the plane's swift speed and superb maneuverability, as well as his own unique precision flying. A World War II fighter pilot and postwar test pilot, Hoover was the man Jimmy Doolittle called "the greatest stick-and-rudder man who ever lived."

I was probably about nine or ten the first time I saw Bob Hoover perform, but actually I'd been going to airshows since I was a baby. Dad liked airshows and we were lucky he did. The only reason he'd take the family out of town was to go to one. And for many years, if you lived in the Cleveland area and wanted to see a big airshow, you had to go somewhere else. That was a bitter pill to swallow for Dad and other local aviation enthusiasts, since Cleveland had previously been home to the Cleveland National Air Races from 1929 through 1949.

In the golden years of the races, Cleveland had been the speed capital of the world. The event was so popular in those pre-television years that Cleveland's Thompson Trophy Race had a live radio audience nationwide. People were fascinated with the new speed records airplanes were setting, and some of the race pilots were the first humans

14. On the Outside Looking Up

to reach speeds approaching 300 miles per hour. To the embarrassment of the military, these civilian racers had pushed the frontier of speed significantly beyond what any frontline Army or Navy aircraft could do. Fortunately, some of these race plane innovations were later credited with helping the military develop more capable planes in time for World War II. The races were suspended during the war, but then returned from 1946 through 1949. Unfortunately, the races came to a disastrous end in 1949 when a highly modified P-51 Mustang crashed into a house killing the pilot along with a mother and her child in the home. With rapid growth of new residential areas around the Cleveland Municipal Airport (later renamed Cleveland Hopkins International Airport), the risk of another such tragedy was too much for the public to endure.

Years later, Dad found a few airshows to go to elsewhere in the state. With the entire family along, these trips were an adventure for my sisters and me. We saw a few airshows in the Akron and Youngstown area and quickly found that we liked the county fair atmosphere as much as the show itself. The popcorn, candy, ice cream, and soda pop were treats we didn't get much at home, so I was sold on airshows.

A few times we went to some huge airshows held at Lockbourne Air Force Base by Columbus and Wright-Patterson Air Force Base in Dayton. And when I say huge, I mean *huge*. In those days, military aviation differed greatly from that of today. In the '60s, America had an enormous Air Force. Back then, the Air Force was equipped with an amazing arsenal of fighters, bombers, transports, aerial tankers, electronic warfare planes, and helicopters. While the vast array of supersonic fighter jets captured the eye of many, there were also a lot of propeller-driven planes still around. When you added up all the Air Force jets, prop planes, and helicopters on display at one of the big airshows, it amounted to quite an armada. Then, when you included planes and helicopters from the Army, Navy, Marine Corps, and Coast Guard, it seemed like the rows of military aircraft on display were endless. Just to walk past it all took forever.

After touring all the display aircraft, I was totally captivated by the airshow that began early in the afternoon. One by one, civilian pilots like Bob Hoover did their airshow routines, which set the stage for bigger things to come when the military put everything in the air. Every type of fighter made a high-speed pass, bombers flew by in their air refueling position behind a tanker, and the transport planes dropped paratroopers. The big shows were an incredible show of force that perhaps reflected the Cold War politics of the time. It seemed America liked to flex her military muscles to make her citizens feel secure. America's military was high tech, large, powerful, and unafraid. When a little war started in an unheard-of tiny place called Vietnam, Dad was totally unconcerned: "The construction guys who are veterans say it will take just a few weeks for the Marines to mop up over there."

A few times, Dad planned his out-of-town scrap yard hunts to coincide with large airshows. After loading some of Dad's scrap yard treasures, we'd change into clean clothes, leave the trailer at a truck stop, and head to the show. Leaving the trailer behind, Dad would always worry that someone was going to steal his trailer load of stuff. I was confident he had *nothing* to worry about. While these airshows lifted my spirits, they again brought a sharp contrast into focus. In the morning, we'd be loading the trailer with aircraft engines or parts that were filthy dirty, beat up and corroded. Then in the afternoon we'd see all the airshow aircraft that were in immaculate condition. I'd end up so green with envy I could barely stand it.

Fifteen years after the Cleveland Air Races ended, airshows resumed there in 1964.

However, instead of taking place at Hopkins, they were moved to downtown Cleveland's Burke Lakefront Airport. Though that was very close to downtown Cleveland and the stadium then used by both the Cleveland Browns and Cleveland Indians, officials assured the public the aircraft would be mostly over the airport or Lake Erie, which would minimize any hazard to people on the ground.

Dad and other aviation enthusiasts were thrilled by the new airshows. I agreed, as the Cleveland Airshow quickly became my favorite. For one thing, I loved the setting. The shoreline location of this airport gave it an ambiance that was unlike any I'd seen. Since the airport was flat and clear of obstacles, you had a perfect view of the boating activity on Lake Erie. From small pleasure craft to large fishing boats, to huge cargo ships loaded with iron ore, the lake had a lot of traffic that was widely varied. As large flocks of birds soared freely about, a combination of nature, airplanes, ships and a huge crowd of people all nestled immediately next to the skyline of Cleveland's downtown presented an environment that was absolutely teeming with life.

Without exception, every Cleveland airshow was a big event. A large number of military and civilian planes were always on display, and the show soon drew the top airshow pilots in the nation. First, there was Bill Adams in his beautiful red and white Stearman biplane. Like other airshow Stearmans, Bill Adams's plane was highly modified from its original military configuration. Instead of the original 220-horsepower engine, Bill Adams's Stearman had a 450-horsepower radial engine. Additionally, the plane had 4 ailerons for quicker rolls, an airshow smoke system, a red and white starburst color scheme, and a brace on the top wing for wing walkers.

Bill Adams usually flew his Stearman three times in one show. He'd start by flying in the opening ceremony. As the National Anthem played, Bill Adams flew circles around a skydiver displaying a huge American flag. Later, Adams would fly the Stearman in an aerobatic routine that took the big biplane right to the limit. He'd do the usual loops, rolls, and hammerhead stalls, but also flew his daring triple snap rolls at very low altitude. Dad and I quickly became big fans of Bill Adams's performances, including his wing walker flight that announcer Bill Sweet joked could be Dad's or any man's mother-in-law for fifty bucks.

Even though I was always thrilled to watch Bill Adams fly his Stearman biplane, predictably, my favorite airshow act was watching and *listening* to a P-51 Mustang performance. Bob Hoover wasn't at some of the shows we went to, but instead a local area man named Dean Ortner did his own P-51 airshow routine partially similar to Hoover's. No matter who flew it, the P-51 Mustang was often the star of the show, and you'd commonly hear men say "This is what I came to see."

In those years, other than Bob Hoover and Dean Ortner performing in the Mustang, you just didn't see airshow acts in World War II planes or other warbirds, as they soon would all be called. A man named Bill Fornoff often flew a stunning performance in an F8F Bearcat. Fornoff's showmanship of flying vertical lines in the Bearcat left no doubt about its reputation for having great power and speed. Other than that, the warbird movement was in its infancy then. In the gap between the military retiring all of these planes and civilians emerging to fund, restore and fly warbirds, people like Bob Hoover, Dean Ortner, and Bill Fornoff were among the few who gave spectators a chance to see these planes fly at all.

Dad and I saw eye to eye with our excitement watching these three warbird pilots fly at airshows. We felt a small connection due to the F-82 Twin Mustang, Corsairs and other planes Dad owned. And while Bob Kucera didn't fly airshow performances in his F8F Bearcat, he had the plane on display at almost every airshow we went to. While I greatly enjoyed the airshows, they obviously tugged at me. It was neat that Dad had his planes, but I just wished we could take it one step further and get one of them in the air. Instead, we had to settle for being on the ground looking up. The high cost of flying that type of aircraft was obviously a big obstacle. Also, Dad himself had little flying experience.

Despite being the perfect age for the military in World War II, he never had a chance at becoming a military pilot or joining the service in any capacity due to his stuttering problem. During the Vietnam era, many men would have liked to be medically disqualified by the military. But during World War II, when it seemed everyone joined the service, having to sit out the big war put a monkey on Dad's back. Dad had built an armada of model airplanes as a young boy, so growing up and flying military planes would have been a dream come true for him, but it simply wasn't to be. Instead, he had to settle for a little bit of civilian flying. At Horn's Flying School in Chagrin Falls, Ohio, he did solo a Piper Cub during the years after the war. Before getting any further, he had a family, and his flying stopped.

About the closest Dad got to his dream of flying a warbird was all captured in a fake home movie. On movie film shot from behind Dad's race Corsair 74, he sits in the cockpit as the giant four-blade propeller turns slowly. From the movie it appears Dad will have the Corsair's huge R-4360 engine roaring to life at any moment. But not quite. Its propeller gearbox and engine were blown during its last flight in 1949 when Dick Becker was qualifying it for the Cleveland Air Races. A complication for Becker, besides the blown engine trailing heavy smoke, was that the Corsair had its flaps riveted up and sealed for less drag and more speed. Fortunately, Becker's incredible flying skill allowed him to dead-stick Corsair 74 safely onto the ground without a scratch. When it was later parked in our yard with its blown engine and gearbox, you could turn the Corsair propeller easily by hand. For Dad's fake movie supposedly starting Corsair 74's engine, that's exactly what powered the scene. Mom is moving the propeller blades by hand while cleverly hidden from the camera's view by the Corsair's big wing. We all laughed like crazy anytime Dad showed his fake would-be hero Corsair pilot movie.

As time for the Cleveland Airshow approached each summer, I looked forward to it with great anticipation. To me, it was the event of the summer. After the first few shows proved successful, the agenda was expanded to include air racing. However, there was a big limitation to the races. There was no unlimited class race for the Mustangs, Bearcats, and Corsairs to compete in. In 1967 there was a transcontinental race for the aging World War II fighters, but otherwise those types of aircraft were out. There were races for small homebuilt formula-one racers and that was all. Without the unlimited class race, I found the races kind of boring. For Dad, the races were a total letdown.

Quickly, Dad realized that compared to the legendary Cleveland races he grew up with, a lot of things were different now. The glory days of Roscoe Turner, Jimmy Doolittle, Jacqueline Cochran, Cook Cleland and others were long gone. While car racing still had the public's eye, air racing never caught on again with the general public. From 1964 to the present, air races at Reno proved successful with large crowds, but much of this audience consisted of people who were devoted aviation fans. Despite the fact that unlimited race planes at Reno were going more than twice as fast as Indy racecars, the general public hardly noticed.

Perhaps the main problem was far bigger than air racing. To the 1960s generation, an airplane was often viewed as just another machine. Probably the biggest reason for the lack of interest was the decline in the public's fascination with speed. In the distant glory days of air racing, daring pilots were pushing the frontier of speed in giant leaps and were the first humans to reach unbelievable speeds of 300 mph and up. But by the mid 1960s, anyone could board a new jet airliner and go a lot faster than any propeller-driven racing plane. And with astronauts launching into space, any airplane speed record seemed all but meaningless.

The other difference Dad noted about the modern races was the lack of press coverage. Newspapers once had frequent coverage of aviation events. Knowledgeable aviation reporters like Charles Tracy of the *Cleveland Plain Dealer* were busy reporting on the rapid advances occurring in aviation. But once the space race was on, the news media had little, if any, aviation interest.

There was one exception. Airplane crashes still made the news. And just when I was convinced that being an airshow pilot was the neatest thing there was, Bill Adams made his way into the news. He was flying at an airshow in Indiana when the propeller broke off his Stearman biplane during a maneuver. Instantly, the spinning propeller came around the side of the aircraft and destroyed the struts and structural wires that kept the wings in place. As the wings collapsed, the Stearman went straight in. Too low to parachute out, Bill Adams was killed.

I felt sick. Bill Adams had been at just about every airshow I'd seen. I just couldn't imagine that he was dead and I'd never see him fly again. The images played continually in my head. The sight of Adams flying around the skydiver with the American flag, the triple snap rolls, and the brave gal on top of the wing all came back to me over and over. As I recalled all those times I'd seen him fly, I began to wonder if I'd even want to go to any more airshows. A few years later, I found out bad news wasn't limited to accidents at airshows.

Just after school, Mom and I were in the kitchen on a Thursday afternoon in December of 1968. Outside the big picture window of our second-story perch, a gray sky with occasional light snow told of another dreary winter day. As I watched the swirling snow, a news report on the radio told of a light plane crash at Lost Nation Airport. They mentioned that the pilot and a passenger were injured and gave their names, which was still a common practice in those days of radio before privacy laws were enacted. The names didn't ring a bell at first. Then it hit me. "Mom, I think they mispronounced his name," I said, feeling a chill come over me.

"Who?" Mom asked.

"They said the pilot's name was Robert Ku-sarah. Could they have meant Bob Ku-chair-a?" I asked, hoping she'd disagree.

"Oh my," Mom paused. "I hope not, but you could be right," she said, looking worried.

"But they did say it was a light plane," I said. "So maybe it was somebody else, since the Bearcat is anything but a light plane," I added, trying to reassure myself.

Mom turned the conversation positive, reminding me the radio report told of people being injured, but not killed. I felt better. Often, on his way home from work, Dad would stop at Prott's Food Store and pick up some groceries. Today, he came home with more than groceries. Looking grim, he threw an afternoon newspaper on the kitchen table. Right on the front page was a picture that ruined my hope that it was all a mistake.

14. On the Outside Looking Up

The pieces of wreckage in the photo made it painfully clear that Bob Kucera had crashed in the Bearcat. It was obvious that the plane was heavily damaged, but it still appeared survivable.

"At least Bob's alive," Dad said grimly, pointing to the article about the crash. Mom and I looked at each other and then at Dad. A later news report on the radio provided an update on the crash. Mom and I knew the Suburban had no radio. "He survived, right?" Dad questioned as his looks grew anxious. Mom and I shook our heads. Though he initially survived, Bob Kucera died in surgery a few hours after the crash. It turned out the crash was caused by engine failure after takeoff. Kucera wasn't able to get the plane back to the runway. Fortunately, a mechanic riding in the rear fuselage did survive, though he suffered a broken back.

That night, a man called from Kucera's company to tell Dad about the crash and ask for a favor. Could we haul the wreckage away? As the man explained, employees and friends were obviously grieved by the crash. He thought it would be best to remove the wreckage as soon as investigators were finished examining it. Dad said he could do it and I got the creeps. I hadn't begun to accept the idea of Bob Kucera's death. Now the mental image of loading the smashed Bearcat onto the trailer just symbolized too blatantly what a terrible thing had happened.

On Saturday morning, Dad and I headed for Lost Nation Airport with the trailer in tow. The man who had called Dad greeted us there, and as we went in the office, I felt sadder than I ever knew. I had always been so happy the times we'd been there before, but now, it just seemed like a really bad dream. All I wanted was to wake up and find out that none of this was true. As bad as I felt, I was very relieved to find out we weren't going to be hauling the Bearcat wreckage.

On our previous visits, no matter what airplane discussions Dad and Bob Kucera started in the front office, they always migrated to the spot on the hangar floor where the Bearcat was parked. Now, with another man substituting for Kucera, we walked out into the hangar one last time. In the same location where the ever-polished Bearcat had previously stood like a proud trophy on its tall landing gear, its torn and crumpled mud-streaked wreckage was now scattered on the cement floor. From there, we went outside to where yet more wreckage was spread among some weeds off the edge of the parking ramp. Under the cold gray sky, a light snow fell. Callously indifferent to the sacred site of tragedy sprawled out along the ground, the snowflakes drifted carefree to settle upon the wreckage. As the snowflakes continued, their subtle message told a harsh truth. The world would go on without him.

With the shattered evidence of wings torn from the fuselage, bent propeller blades ripped from their hub, and other savage violence done to man and metal, the sobering reality continued to hit me. Bob Kucera was dead. The tall gentleman I'd known who walked with confidence, flew with confidence, yet never hesitated to be kind and warm to a ratty kid like me—just like that, he was gone. As we slowly and quietly made our way past the wreckage, I found myself fighting battle after battle to hold back the tears. But no matter how hard I fought each battle, a few times—I lost.

15

Chicago Clone

From a very early age, I realized that what Dad was doing was unique. A lot of people had airplanes, but nobody admired or acquired them in the manner he did. There were others who liked airplanes, but few with Dad's zeal for the clunkers, the outcasts. Those who were interested in the old birds usually saved their enthusiasm for airplanes that were in flyable condition. The more airplane people I met or read about, the more it appeared my father was in another world all by himself. Then I discovered he had company.

It was a typical Ohio winter day early in 1966. By my definition it wasn't bitter cold, yet there was a thick blanket of snow on the ground that had persisted for weeks. I was home after school when two men drove up in an old black Buick. I went out to meet them, and like most people who drove up, they had come to see the planes. Despite the weather, their visit was no surprise. Except during times of extreme blizzards with deep snowdrifts, people came all during the week and weekend to see the planes year around. As I greeted the two men, they told me they'd come all the way from Chicago to see Dad's planes. The man doing the talking introduced himself as Earl Reinert. The other man was his brother, Ray.

Earl was a tall and slightly heavy man who appeared to be in his early forties like Dad. His dark, sandy hairline was receding slightly in the middle, which added to the round look of a face that was slightly plump. Both he and his brother were dressed casually in dark pants, plain shirts and dark coats. Their clothes weren't ragged, but were fairly worn. The simple dark colors and baggy fit made the men appear as if they were from the World War II era. There was only one other man I knew who routinely dressed that way—my father.

Earl appeared excited about going out into the field to see the planes. As I led the men on a packed trail through the snow and started the tour, I quickly found the dialogue I usually used to describe Dad's airplanes wasn't going to work. Telling this man which plane was which was like telling a veterinarian how to distinguish a dog from a cat. This guy knew his stuff better than *anyone* who had visited before. Even people who knew a lot about airplanes often got tripped up at our place because Dad had such rare and unusual planes. Dad's Corsairs were Goodyear models instead of Chance Voughts. The F2G racing Corsair was unique in itself. The F-82 Twin Mustang and F7U Cutlass were never built in large numbers, and both were now almost extinct. Likewise, the Bobcat was rare, as its wood wing doomed most of them from any hope of longevity. But no matter how rare Dad's planes were, Earl Reinert knew them all.

"I've got a Bobcat myself," he nodded as we walked past ours. "But yours is in a lot

15. Chicago Clone

Corsair 74 in the snow just as Earl Reinert would have seen it upon his first visit that reunited him with the plane that took him back in time to the Cleveland Air Races to remember his fallen friend, Bill Odom (courtesy Jason McKeon).

better shape than mine," he added. Say what? I couldn't believe what he said. Dad had a plane in better shape than somebody else's? Now I knew I liked this guy. When he walked up to the F2G racing Corsair, something about his demeanor changed. Though he strode past the other planes, now he stopped and just stared.

As a light snow fell from the gray overcast, he seemed moved by the presence of the Corsair. "Cook Cleland's Thompson Trophy winner," he said, as if greeting an old acquaintance. "Have you ever heard of Bill Odom?" Reinert turned to me and asked.

"Yes, I have. His P-51 Mustang crashing into a house in 1949 ended the Cleveland Air Races," I answered. Reinert nodded softly. Then he surprised me.

"Bill Odom was a good friend of mine," he said sadly as he continued standing and staring at the Corsair. To me, Bill Odom had just been a name in the history book of air racing. Now I realized, to someone else, he meant a lot more. "I've got Bill Odom's P-47 Thunderbolt racer," Reinert added.

"I only heard of him racing the Mustang," I said, sounding confused.

"You're right, he was killed racing a Mustang, but he had a P-47 racer before that," Reinert explained. I felt sad that Reinert had ties to the Odom tragedy, but I was also intrigued. A Bill Odom P-47 air racer? Dad could talk for hours about the Cleveland Air Races, but never mentioned anyone racing a P-47. P-47 Thunderbolts were also very rare now. A big World War II single-engine fighter, the "T-Bolt" or "Jug" was as legendary to the Army Air Corps as the Corsair was to the Navy and the Marines. Over 15,000 P-47s were built, but only a dozen or so of the big brutes were believed to remain.

The P-47 didn't seem like a good choice for air racing. Big and heavy, the Thunderbolt was built like a brick outhouse. Arguably the sturdiest fighter plane, it served the Allies well, unleashing its tremendous firepower on the Nazis. On the receiving end, it

Me in 1966 with Reinert's rare P-47 air racer once flown by Bill Odom. Odom was killed when his P-51 Mustang crashed into a home during the 1949 Cleveland National Air Races, claiming the lives of a mother and her child, and bringing the air races there to an end.

was a tough and rugged fighter that could survive a lot of hits. Even when shot full of gaping holes, the P-47 was often able to limp its way back and get its pilot home safely. Perhaps a perfect match of man and machine, a P-47 named *Peggy* had years earlier served as the mount for Arizona Senator Barry Goldwater, who later ran for president in 1964. I was now anxious for Dad to get home. I'd escorted a lot of visitors around Dad's airplane collection, but this guy was proving to be something else. On the other hand, his brother hardly uttered a sound.

"How'd your father get these planes here?" Reinert asked.

"We towed some of them on that trailer, including the B-25," I answered as I pointed.

"You're kidding," Reinert smiled a somewhat shocked, yet amused look. "You hauled the B-25 on—*that*?" he pointed at the trailer while looking at me for confirmation. I'd seen many people react that way, but his intrigue seemed profound. He wanted more. It wasn't just about the trailer, he seemed particularly stunned that we even had a B-25 here among the other planes. Mystery solved, he told me he had a B-25 he was planning to scrap. He said he considered it impossible to haul a B-25 on the highway because the plane was so big.

I was wearing my boots, so I then escorted him off path through the deep snow to *Wild Cargo*. There I showed him all the seams where we unbolted the B-25 and explained how my father said it was like the plane was made to be towed down the highway. I also told of a second and much better B-25 Dad had bought that was still in Pennsylvania, and that I expected we would probably haul the same way. Reinert was beside himself with my show and tell. It was quite a personal moment. Here was this older man of tremendous aviation knowledge getting a surprise lecture by a 12-year-old boy on exactly how to haul a B-25, which he had considered impossible just a few moments earlier. Reinert was so thrilled by the news he seemed unaware that his socks and scruffy black dress shoes were now encased and packed with snow.

"I've got to meet your father!" he said emphatically.

"He'll be home soon," I assured him.

"Is he out at an airport?"

"No, he's a full-time carpenter. This is just a hobby," I answered. Like many visitors, I could tell it shocked Reinert that a man up to his ears in airplanes had that type of job. It just didn't make sense to most people. Of all the jobs for Dad to have, being a carpenter was about as far away from aviation as you could get.

As we continued touring the planes, Reinert established his own credibility by dropping the names of a few of his own aircraft. In addition to Bill Odom's P-47 Thunderbolt, he also had a number of Grumman-built fighters with the company's traditional cat names. Reinert's Grumman collection included an F4F Wildcat, F6F Hellcat, and an F8F Bearcat.

Before long, Dad got home from work, and I introduced Mr. Reinert, also mentioning the Wildcat, Hellcat, Bearcat, and Bill Odom's Thunderbolt. As expected, I could tell that got his adrenaline flowing. Reinert expressed his amazement at Dad's collection and his appreciation for the grand tour I'd given him. Dad wanted to give him the tour again, but Reinert wasn't interested. It was almost dark, and the temperature was dropping quickly. Like Reinert and his brother, I was ready to head inside. Dad still tried to persuade them to go for another look, but it was useless. He finally gave up and we went inside.

Dad handed Mom his empty thermos bottle and then scrambled for the airplane picture albums. Soon Reinert and Dad were sitting on the sofa looking at the pictures as they passed names and traded stories like two long-lost brothers. They knew a lot of the same people, and best of all, each owned a piece of legendary air race history. Reinert was awed by Dad's F2G Corsair, while Dad was amazed to learn Reinert had the late Bill Odom's P-47. Reinert's own rarest of the rare, it was a YP-47M.

"Would you men like to stay for dinner?" Mom asked pleasantly.

"Well, we ... uh ... we thought we'd find a motel and then get something there," Reinert answered, clearly not wanting to be any trouble.

Dad jumped in, "Oh, no, we've got plenty here, and there's no place to eat at nearby." Mom also told them the nearest motel was over ten miles away, after which Dad reported the roads getting slick and icy his last miles home, so they were best to stay put. Reinert tried to argue, but it was hopeless. Mom and Dad convinced him it was no trouble for him and his brother to stay.

Soon, Mom added two extra places at our small table and we were all eating supper. Dad and Reinert didn't miss a beat with their airplane chatter. Dad was more excited than I'd ever seen him, and soon it was like he was a hurricane of airplane talk, even with his stutter. Between bites of food, I'd bet he was talking over 100 words a minute, with occasional hurricane gusts to 300. But the true evidence of Dad's fascination with Reinert was his ability to listen. In general, Dad was in his own world and wasn't known to be a good listener. But when Reinert talked, Dad hung onto every word. And unlike Dad, Reinert didn't ramble. Instead, he spoke slowly, and even though Dad appeared impatient at times, Reinert kept on with his slightly deep voice maintaining its leisurely pace.

We soon learned that trading airplanes and parts was Reinert's livelihood. Unlike Dad, Reinert didn't have a job. While that was one way they differed, we found they had a lot of similarities. Neither had anything to do with small light planes or World War I planes. Instead, they both concentrated on World War II planes, which, while rare, were relatively cheap at that time. And while both had a lot of planes, neither had any that flew.

As he quickly gulped down his supper, Dad talked with Reinert about all the people and planes he knew. Who owned the planes, flew them, raced them, and worst of all, who scrapped them? It was Dad's personal crusade to lament about how many World War II planes were now almost extinct in spite of the more than 300,000 built. As the rest of us ate, Reinert nodded in agreement with everything Dad said.

"It's crazy," Dad complained. "Nobody thinks about the future. Not even the military. Sure, the Air Force saved a few planes for their museum, but not nearly enough. And the Navy didn't keep anything." Dad rambled on about how congressmen were writing him that it was his patriotic duty to donate his Corsair to the Navy museum being started at Pensacola. "The nerve of them!" Dad stood up and started pacing by his chair, gesturing with his hands. "Heck, they had over 12,000 Corsairs! They couldn't keep one, not one!" Then Dad told of the bum engine that kept Zero Zero from going to the boneyard. "Smart plane, she knew better," Dad repeated the story he had told so many times. "Unpatriotic!" Dad roared. "If it wasn't for people like us, there wouldn't be any World War II planes left at all."

After supper, Dad put on his coat, grabbed his flashlight, and pressed Reinert to head out for the official tour. Reinert was reluctant. Outside the corner of the sunroom, an outdoor light illuminated big snowflakes coming down in a heavy snow shower. Dad started asking Reinert questions about what I showed him and perhaps something I missed. It reminded me of when he had tried to interrogate Grandma Murray after the tour I gave her. Reinert was polite, but he didn't want to go outside. Dad could have asked Reinert if I showed him the original Wright Brothers plane and Reinert would have nodded "yes." Outside it was getting colder by the minute, and Reinert obviously wanted to stay in where it was warm. But Dad, as always, had trouble taking no for an answer. Like General Patton dragging a soldier from his cozy foxhole near the snowy German front, Dad kept pushing. With flashlight still firmly in hand, he finally got Reinert and his brother to go back outside for the official tour. For Dad, his chance to show off his planes was now or never. In the morning, he had to go back to work.

Initially, I tagged along while observing the deepening snow. As we went from one airplane to the next, Dad fired away with his rapid speech, getting in every detail. Soon, I decided I'd spent enough of my life freezing my fingers and toes off out there, so I slipped away to the house. After completing their tour, Dad still had a few more pictures to show and stories to tell. From newspaper articles to books and photographs, Dad had an immense and ever-growing assortment of aviation memorabilia. Reinert was a true airplane addict, and his interest and endurance for airplane trivia had outlasted everyone else's I'd ever seen.

Then he asked the question that made Dad's heart skip a beat. "How would you like to have a P-47?" he asked.

Dad's eyes grew wide. "You're not going to sell Bill Odom's Thunderbolt?" Dad asked, sounding confused.

"Of course not," Reinert smiled. "I have another P-47 fuselage I might be able to part with." Now he really had Dad's attention. Reinert told that the fuselage he had was the last available from a bunch of fuselages he got from the Republic plant after the war.

"What do you mean *bunch* of fuselages?" Dad asked.

"Oh, I had sixteen of them at one time," Reinert answered. "All of them brand-new from the factory."

"Who has the other fifteen now?" Dad asked uneasily.

"After I salvaged all the parts from them, I scrapped them," Reinert answered casually. There was dead silence. Dad didn't mumble a word. The look on his face said it all. Blasphemer! How could you scrap fifteen P-47 fuselages and show your face in my house? Dad held his tongue for now. He'd save his fit until after Reinert's departure.

Reinert sensed Dad's lust for a P-47, even if all he had was a fuselage. He had something Dad wanted very badly. In turn, Reinert wanted some of what we had, but not any of the planes. That was good. Dad routinely made it loud and clear to everyone that none of his planes were for sale. In a defining trend that would only grow stronger, once something was on Dad's property—it was there for keeps. But he didn't have to worry about Reinert's wanting to buy any airplanes. Reinert, like Dad, didn't have a lot of money. Since Reinert showed no interest in acquiring any of the planes, Dad had no reason to run him off.

What Reinert wanted were parts. Engine parts, in particular. It turned out that Reinert made his living by horse trading all types of airplane parts. At that time in the 1960s, there were still a lot of piston-driven transport aircraft that used World War II–type engines and propellers. Since parts for these planes were no longer being made, used parts were getting more and more scarce and expensive. Dad was all too familiar with why engine parts had gotten scarce—and it wasn't from being worn out. To Dad's chagrin, the countless thousands of engines he had helped melt down for fifty bucks' worth of metal would now be worth a fortune. As Reinert told us some of the prices that old engines were going for, Dad was beside himself. "Heck, we had new ones!" he told Reinert, almost in despair. "Thousands of brand-new engines with the cellophane wrappers still on them, and we cut them up with torches," Dad confessed.

Still, being almost as fascinated with engines as he was with airplanes, Dad now had a good collection of engines stored in his hangar. Depending on the type and model, some were worth a lot. Others were, as described by Reinert, "boat anchors." Then, like kids trading baseball cards, Dad and Reinert were soon talking about what airplane parts would make a fair trade. For Dad it was a difficult discussion. He prized his collection of engine and airplane parts to the point he didn't want to let anything go. Still, Reinert cleverly dangled the P-47. So back and forth, Dad reluctantly revealed the types of engines and propellers he had. Then the discussion would move to the P-47 and how Reinert could add a spare canopy or new engine cowlings to the deal. After about an hour of back and forth, they reached a deal. Dad would do all the hauling, taking the engines and props to Reinert's place in Chicago and then bringing the P-47 back.

The engines and parts Reinert wanted were, of course, in the back of Dad's shop. With Dad's passion for collecting, things in the hangar were packed tight. For me it was the biggest airplane parts aerobic workout I ever had. Gunsights, starters, magnetos, wheels, you name it, tons of stuff had to be moved out of the way. The premier of the popular TV show *American Pickers* would not air for another 44 years, so when it came to saving things, Dad was very far ahead of his time. Eventually we were able to back the boom tractor into the hangar and get the engines out that Reinert wanted.

Despite the parts-moving grind, there was no holding Dad back. Only his level of enthusiasm was subject to change. And just like when he had the B-25 in his sights, the thought of getting a P-47 put his enthusiasm in full afterburner. Following his well-established tradition, Dad studied everything in preparation for his next big adventure. Again, he found every book, every manual, and every picture of a P-47. I got to hear every detail several times over: how big it was, how much it weighed, how it disassembled. Heck, it was already apart! But never mind, Dad wanted to show that he'd done his homework and was well prepared—sort of.

It took us about a month to get everything together for the big trip. But finally, with the barter loaded on the trailer, Dad and I headed for the Windy City. Neither of us had been west of Ohio, let alone taken the 400-mile trip to Chicago. Until now, Dad had kept all hauling trips in the 100- to 250-mile range, except for hauling the Cutlass from Boston. Going to Chicago, Dad and the Suburban were quick to appreciate the flat terrain that characterized Indiana and Illinois. But it was a long grind. Dad lamented that I was too young to drive legally at age 12. He'd been letting me drive on county roads now and then.

"I wish you could take the wheel for just a few hours," he said. "But the cops would pull us over and throw the book at me. Even if you were big enough, I don't know if you could handle this thing," Dad said, suggesting it took superhuman skill to drive his junk Suburban. The Suburban was now nine years old and had been hauling heavy airplane loads for four years since its debut hauling the Cutlass wings.

"This thing is pretty tricky at times going high speed on these superhighways," Dad continued a familiar spiel as we cruised on the turnpike. "Gotta be careful and know what you're doing. You know the front end is worn out," he'd say as he'd briskly turn the steering wheel side to side without any effect, all to show how much "dead play" there was in the steering. "The clutch chatters and slips, half the tires are bald, and that heavy trailer has no brakes," he summed up the vehicle's condition. He forgot to mention broken taillights, rust holes, lots of dents, no radio, cracked windows, and the need for a two-gallon can of motor oil. Yet I thought Dad was exaggerating just a bit as he repeated saying, "You almost have to be an astronaut to drive this thing." Mom had the best reply once when she said, "No, I don't think so—the astronauts would be too afraid." But maybe Dad had a point. With its unbalanced bad tires and worn-out front end, plus blown shocks that we never changed, at freeway speeds the Suburban was prone to vibrate and shake. This powered the orchestra of tool boxes, jack handles, loose doors and other things that were vibrating as though we were in Chuck Yeager's rocket plane trying to break the sound barrier.

As we headed west on the turnpike toward Toledo, South Bend, and Chicago, I found the trip to be the most boring ever. I usually enjoyed the scenery on the other trips we took. The rolling hills and mountains in Pennsylvania made that state a very scenic one. But no such luck on this trip. As far as the eye could see—cornfields were about all we had to look at. Luckily, I took some books with me to pass the time. With good intentions, I took some of my schoolbooks and planned to do some homework. Soon, however, those books found their way to the floor and were stowed under the seat. Instead, I read books that had more appeal, like aviation or science fiction stories. My favorite book at the time was *Aerospace Pilot*, a book about becoming a jet pilot in the Air Force. While many aviation books were focused on the pioneers and heroes of the two World Wars, this book was all about the new and exciting jet age. I was mesmerized by reading about a new jet featured in the book and also on the cover, the T-38 Talon.

The T-38 was the hot new trainer the Air Force used to train all pilots. Besides having a sleek and cool appearance, the T-38 was obviously a real go-cart. With a top speed of nearly 1,000 miles per hour, it became the first jet trainer capable of going supersonic in level flight. It was a hot performer, even compared to fighter planes; aviation legend Jacqueline Cochran set eight world records in a T-38 in 1961. As I read more and more of the book, I couldn't get my mind off the T-38. Someday, somehow—I just had to fly.

Though still awaiting my first airplane ride, I had long dreamed of flying. From the Cessna light planes Dad scoffed at, to playing *Sky King* in the Bobcat, and Navy pilot in both Corsairs, I had played in and dreamed of flying everything on the property. A few times I was Jimmy Doolittle pushing hard on the B-25's throttles during my imaginary takeoff from the USS *Hornet*. As I continued reading about the supersonic T-38, the hot-rod jet took my yearnings to yet a higher level. But just when I thought Dad and I had an obvious topic to agree on, it wasn't so.

"A jet—that's not flying," Dad replied as I tried to tell him about the T-38.

"But it can go a thousand miles per hour!" I rebutted.

"So what? In a plane like that, you're up so high you can't see anything or even tell you're flying." He dismissed everything I said. Then, to pop my bubble more, he insisted I was born too late and had missed all the good flying. He repeated his spiel about the glory days of the "big recips" radial engine prop planes. "Now that's flying!" he asserted. With jets taking things over, he concluded the big recips would all be gone by the time I was old enough to fly. Keeping my thoughts to myself, I rejected his assertions. I knew he had never flown anything bigger than a 65-horsepower J-3 Piper Cub, yet he talked like he knew all about everything that flew. He, in fact, would live a very long life and never fly on an airliner or jet of any type. Still, I knew he wasn't totally alone in some of his thoughts.

A similar "born too late" refrain was something I often heard from visitors touring Dad's old planes. Mostly I heard it from the men who had been too young to fly in World War II. Yet, they were around to witness, to see, and to—*hear* the formations of B-29s, Corsairs, Hellcats, and other piston-engine planes. To them, it was *that sound* that captivated them as dozens, sometimes hundreds of cylinders and pistons laboring in fine-tuned harmony, galloped and thundered overhead while pounding out the thousands of horsepower it took to swirl the giant propellers on the big planes. The giant prop planes flew much lower and slower than the new jets streaking silent contrails so high above. This allowed young minds fascinated by airplanes to easily watch and hear the majesty of the big recip planes lumbering slowly overhead during a period of history now mostly gone.

By late afternoon we made our way through Chicago and found the Palwaukee Airport that Reinert directed us to on the city's north side. Soon we had Reinert's office in sight, and it was easy to spot. He'd told us to look for the small building with the F4F Wildcat next to it. Since the Wildcat was also a very rare airplane, we didn't have to worry about finding the wrong one. Reinert came out of his office next to the Wildcat and greeted us warmly. He then took a look at the engines and parts on the trailer. He was obviously content, and so it appeared the P-47 deal was a go. All we had to do now was unload the trailer and then pick up the fuselage—wherever it was.

Next, Reinert took us over to his Wildcat to show it off. He was clearly proud of the aircraft. I'd never seen a Wildcat before, except in photographs. Compared to the Corsair, it was a small fighter. Inferior to the Japanese Zero, it didn't last long as a mainstay Navy fighter. Still, the Wildcat gained fame in the early days of World War II, since it was the only fighter the Navy had a large number of at that time. Despite its being outclassed by the Zero, Navy pilots overcame the Wildcat's shortcomings and scored many aerial victories against the Japanese.

One of these Wildcat pilots was a Navy Lieutenant from Chicago named Edward H. "Butch" O'Hare. A Medal of Honor winner, O'Hare became the U.S. Navy's first fighter ace by downing five Japanese bombers in one mission. Unfortunately, O'Hare was shot down and killed later in the war. Like Chicago's international airport, Reinert's Wildcat bore the hometown hero's name. It was obvious that Reinert's Wildcat hadn't flown in a long time, but was still in good condition. Reinert glowed with pride as he explained how rare the plane was, and how it had been used in parades honoring O'Hare. With its wings folded back, the Wildcat was quite narrow, which made it well suited to be towed in parades. I was glad to see the Wildcat, but I wondered where the other planes he owned were located. The Wildcat was the only airplane here.

Reinert then led us to the small office building that he called "the den." As we headed in, he took a moment to point out a giant four-blade propeller from a C-119 Boxcar leaning against the building like a big X. The tips of two blades rested on the ground, while the other two reached above the edge of the roof. Reinert made note of the propeller by jokingly calling it his "sculpture." Since he paid only $25 for it, he figured it was a bargain compared to any official piece of art. The idea seemed a little

Dad with Earl Reinert's F4F Wildcat in Chicago in early 1966. American flag is taped to fly above the top propeller blade. Reinert proudly told of this Wildcat being used in a Chicago parade to honor Navy war hero Lieutenant Commander Edward "Butch" O'Hare.

strange at first, but by 1966, the new hippie movement and other cultural changes were pushing a lot of traditional boundaries, including in art. So if Reinert wanted to call his airplane propeller "sculpture"? Sure, you bet.

Inside Reinert's den, Dad and I were right at home. The airplane decor was wall to wall. Instrument panels, pictures, flying uniforms, empty practice bombs, you name it, Reinert had the place packed with aviation memorabilia, yet it was nicely arranged and neat. That alone made his collection very different from Dad's. As Reinert gave us a brief rundown about the items in his den, I could tell Dad had something else on his mind. He wanted to see his P-47. To his disappointment, he'd have to wait until the next day. As it started to get dark, Reinert invited us to have dinner at his sister's house. "You can spend the night there, too," he assured us.

I could tell Dad was uneasy, but with no time to argue, we hopped into the Suburban and followed Reinert's old Buick. The drive was about 25 miles, but seemed to take forever. It was not what Dad needed. He wasn't happy about getting back on the road after 400 miles of astronaut duty piloting the Suburban with a loaded trailer. I couldn't blame him.

Eventually, we arrived at Reinert's sister's house. It was a big two-story house in an old 1920s industrial-era neighborhood with nearly identical structures lined up side by side as far as the eye could see. Though the neighborhood was old, it appeared well kept. After climbing a few steps that led us onto a big front porch, we found Reinert and his sister waiting for us at the front door.

As we entered the house, Reinert's sister, Margaret, was quick to make us feel at home. Of medium height and build, and likely about the same age as my mother, she gave us a warm welcome and glowed with a powerful smile. A big apron covered her long casual dress, and from the billowing scent of freshly baked bread and other foods, it was obvious she'd been cooking up a storm. After taking a few moments to get acquainted, she escorted us to a spacious dining room and sat us down at the dinner table. By the sight and aroma of all the food, I'd have believed it was Thanksgiving!

The food was great and I was quick to let her know it. Dad nodded in agreement, but otherwise didn't say anything to thank or compliment her. His mum demeanor wasn't a surprise since he had previously explained his thoughts about compliments to me. I don't remember where or when, but I complimented someone with Dad present and he later admonished me for doing that. The way he explained his views, it suggested he was passing on something from the dog-eat-dog years of the Great Depression. He strongly believed that if you buttered people up with nice compliments, they would always assume you wanted something in return. Academically, he might have had a point. But right or wrong, I didn't like the sound of the advice he was giving me.

Margaret knocked herself out for our visit. She was so gracious, big-hearted and sweet. There was no act going on here to influence whatever deal may be going on with her brother Earl. So I complimented her every chance I got while giving her my best smiles. We talked for quite a while with her asking me the typical adult questions about how I like school, if I played sports, and stuff like that. Altogether she impressed me as a genuinely wonderful lady who left me with a sense that meeting her was worth the trip all by itself.

After dinner, Earl got his photo albums to show us his airplane collection. As we looked on, Dad's excitement grew. The rarity of Reinert's collection was quite impres sive. Once again, it was like they were long-lost brothers who were just reunited and had a lot of catching up to do. I could tell that Dad was just dying to see the actual airplane collection. Finally, we called it a night. I slept on the floor with some heavy blankets. Not to complain, though; as long as we weren't spending the night in the Suburban, I was happy.

The next morning, Reinert's sister treated us to a fine breakfast and off we went. Soon we were on what seemed like a wild goose chase. First, to one place to drop off the engines, then to another place to unload a propeller, followed by a few more stops. Finally, we headed to where the majority of Reinert's planes were, including our P-47. Reinert's "Victory Air Museum" was located on a country farm near Mundelein on the northwest outskirts of Chicago. There, he had his planes in two groups. Up front by the main highway were the best planes, which like Dad's were mostly complete. The second group we'd see later.

Sure enough, out front was Bill Odom's P-47 racer. It had a striking blue and white racing paint scheme that, like our planes, was faded from the weather. The P-47 was basically all there except, like most of his planes, the engine was missing. Unfortunately, the type engine used in the P-47 was still popular in a lot of other aircraft, and thus had been sold. Since Reinert didn't have a job, a certain amount of airplane cannibalism kept the bills paid.

Quickly, Dad and I surveyed the collection with Reinert now in the tour guide mode. Another man, Paul Polidori, who lived in a house at the airfield, soon came to

Earl Reinert with very rare cockpit and gun section of a German Henschel Hs 129 photographed during our 1966 visit. I really needed help identifying this. Thankfully, Aviation Historian Lt. Col. Jim Rice and his friends at the Warbird Information Exchange came to my rescue. Damaged PBY Catalina in background.

join us. The man appeared to be about the same age as Dad and of similar build. Though he seemed friendly, he didn't have much to say. On the tour, Reinert's collection included Odom's P-47, a PBY seaplane, an AT-6 Texan, a Lockheed Hudson, a Douglas RB-26, and some Army vehicles from the World War II era. We got a good tour, but I could tell Dad didn't want to spend all day looking. He was anxious to see his prize, the P-47 fuselage. But soon we realized—it wasn't there.

"Where's the P-47 fuselage?" Dad asked, careful to avoid sounding doubtful.

"It's back there," Reinert pointed to a line of trees far away at the other end of a long grass runway. Back behind the line of trees was the place where Reinert kept his second group of planes. From where we were standing, you wouldn't know anything was back there. Everything was hidden out of sight, and for a good reason.

As we walked along the wet squishy grass, it was obvious the ground was too soft to drive any kind of vehicle. Thus, we hiked the length of the long grass runway to get out to the site. Reinert continued to shoot the airplane bull, but it soon became a one-sided conversation. I could tell Dad was bothered and I sensed the same problem he did. "Is there another road back here?" Dad asked.

"No, this is it," Reinert replied. Now, Dad and I were mud masters of the caliber any pig farmer, dirt biker, or monster truck driver would be proud of. Usually we could drag, winch or roll anything a few hundred feet through soft dirt and mud. We'd used jacks, planks, pipes, cables and winches, you name it, to get a chunk of airplane onto solid ground. But this grass field seemed at least a half-mile long. Dad got even quieter. We finally got around the row of trees and could see the P-47 fuselage.

The "factory new, never been flown P-47 fuselage," was in rough shape. The cockpit was stripped badly and the fuselage had a lot of corrosion plus some "bullet holes." Some vandals wanted to make it look like an authentic warplane, so they used a pipe or tire iron to punch holes through the soft aluminum skin. Like everything else Reinert owned, the engine was missing. Reinert never claimed that it was in good shape, but still, I was a bit disappointed. It was, however, a very rare P-47. Like the gutted P-51 we had found the previous year, Dad wanted it.

It was obvious why this part of the collection was hidden behind the trees. As bad as the P-47 was, it wasn't the worst. When Reinert told me our Bobcat was in better shape than his, he wasn't kidding. His dilapidated Bobcat was totally rotted out and lying flat on the ground. All of the aircraft in this area were in truly sad shape. An F6F Hellcat and an F8F Bearcat were there, but except for being up on their landing gear, you couldn't say anything positive about them. Both were corroded and terribly stripped of parts. We understood that Mr. Reinert was a parts dealer, but were still shocked how these poor aircraft had been cannibalized to the bone. Repeatedly, people asked Dad to sell parts from his aircraft. Now I was glad he didn't.

Though Reinert's aircraft were not nearly as complete as ours, he did in fact have some rare birds. And though you'd never guess by looking at it, his skeleton of a Bearcat had a bright future. Years later, the aircraft was rebuilt and was destined to win the Reno Air Races under the name "Rare Bear."

After a brief tour of Reinert's collection, it was time to get back to business. Dad asked again, "Isn't there any other road somewhere nearby?" Reinert replied as before, that the long airstrip was the only way out.

"Don't worry, we'll get a wrecker truck back here to get it out," Reinert then said. Clearly, Reinert was blowing smoke. Nothing short of a large farm tractor had any chance of driving over the long stretch of wet and soft ground. Regardless, Mr. Polidori, who'd still been trailing us, suddenly spoke up.

"Absolutely not! You can't bring a wrecker or any other truck back here to get this thing. You'll rut up my whole airfield," Polidori said authoritatively. Another surprise we didn't need. Not only did Reinert live with his sister, but now we found the property his planes sat on wasn't his, either. Dad, I could tell, was totally dismayed. Reinert then spoke as if a flash of brilliance suddenly struck him. "If we have a hard freeze tonight, maybe we can do it in the morning." Unfortunately, this winter was beginning to give way to spring, and it was too late in the season for a hard freeze of that kind. No, this was the worst time of year for moving things out of a soggy field. Too cold for things to dry out, and too warm for the ground to freeze.

For Dad, there was no greater disaster than being on a trip and going home with an empty trailer. He would have been a great bomber pilot because with him there was just no excuse for an aborted mission. "I didn't haul those engines 400 miles to go home empty," Dad said calmly, expressing his disappointment. I could tell he wanted to choke Reinert. Then Reinert suggested Dad leave his trailer, and Reinert promised to haul the P-47 to Ohio after the field dried out in maybe a few weeks. I felt that was a good offer. It made Reinert look trustworthy despite today's disappointment. Dad wasn't for that idea at all.

It was a curious moment. What would I do in Dad's shoes? I kept my mouth shut, but I was for leaving the trailer behind as the best bet of getting the P-47 on our property sooner rather than later. There were risks Reinert wouldn't deliver, but I already liked and trusted the man. Then again, I was 12. But at 12, while I wasn't yet schooled on the

Getting ready to head home with Reinert's F-86 fuselage, which was a heartbreaking substitute for the P-47 we could not haul due its remote location in a soggy field.

issue of addiction, I knew my father well enough that the very idea that he would leave his trailer behind was out of the question. He now collected things with that trailer as certain as the sun would rise tomorrow. For that reason, Dad didn't just like his trailer, he was married to it.

Empty trailer mission abort avoided, we ended up buying and hauling an F-86 jet fighter fuselage that Reinert offered Dad for $100. As we followed Reinert's black Buick to yet another location to see the F-86, Dad unleashed a storm. "Can you believe this guy! I came all the way to Chicago, lost two days' pay from work, haul my engines here, and he knew all along there was no way to get that fuselage out of that muddy field!" Dad said heatedly. He expressed suspicion over Reinert having us unload all of our items before even seeing the P-47. Dad now suggested he was considering getting his engines and other items back on the trailer and heading home. "All the way here for nothing!" he fumed. Dad was upset, and was gesturing and waving so much, I was almost afraid he'd lose control of the Suburban. I kept my focus on the road while agreeing with my father that it looked like a bad deal.

While disappointed, Dad took solace in getting his first F-86 Sabre. More Sabres would follow, so we can thank Reinert for starting that trend. The Sabre was one of the most successful early jet fighters. The mainstay of the Air Force in the Korean War, the Sabre racked up an impressive dogfighting record against the communist MiGs. Like the World War II planes just a few years before it, the Sabre was now obsolete and out of the Air Force inventory. Using the usual array of jacks, planks, pipe rollers, and the bomb winch, we soon had the F-86 on the trailer. Though we weren't going home with the P-47 prize we expected, it gave Dad one more mission accomplished.

16

Plane Crazy

Dad's airplane collection really grew in 1966. His carpenter job kept going strong, enhanced by good pay raises achieved by the carpenters' union. We did an oddball series of road trips to haul stuff home that year, and two of those trips tested us to the absolute limit. The first of these was a scrap bid B-57 Canberra jet bomber from Selfridge Air Force Base, north of Detroit. The plane was another wreck. While not nearly as bad as the Voodoo jet, the B-57 had been in a serious accident. The belly of the jet was torn up badly, while a lot of fire damage was evident in the middle of the fuselage. The front and rear cockpits appeared to be in excellent condition, but sadly we were told that both crewmembers had died despite escaping from the aircraft.

While he didn't buy many wrecks, each one caused a serious rift between me and my father. I could handle the long hours we put in on airplanes like the B-25. I was proud he had a pair of Corsairs, Twin Mustangs and other historic planes. But wrecked planes that killed people? Count me out. The other problem was the wrecks revealed that Dad couldn't let go of his junkman roots. Yes, scrap metal helped pay the bills, but each time we worked a wrecked plane for scrap metal, it detracted greatly from what I believed we should be doing. We needed to focus on taking care of the good airplanes. And if there were more good ones to haul home—great. But to me, the wrecks did not belong.

Hauling the B-57 wreck became an exercise in pure misery. Dad got the plane in the middle of a brutally cold winter, and it required an extreme amount of effort for the two of us to cut it to size for the highway. The B-57 had giant wings front to back from the leading edge to the trailing edge. They were made of very thick aluminum compared to the B-25, and we had to chop, hacksaw, hammer and chisel our way wingtip to wingtip. The wingspan of this bomber was 64 feet and we had to cut the top and bottom of both wings. The work was slow and the conditions were terrible. There was a lot of snow on and around the plane, and the high temperature one day was eight degrees Fahrenheit.

After the despair of the B-57, things looked much better when summer came. After my years of pleading for an airplane ride, Mom and Dad took the whole family to a local fly-in at the Concord Airport near Painesville, Ohio. The small airport was bustling with activity as several hundred people turned out to view twenty or so small planes. Rides were being sold in several Cessna and Piper aircraft. The rides were priced at a "penny-a-pound," so for a total of about five bucks, Dad bought rides for his five children.

I got my ride in a four-seat Cessna 172, and my only disappointment was that I

Hauling wrecked airplanes drove a giant wedge between me and my father. It also generated the question in some members of the aviation community about whether Walter was an airplane collector who liked junk, or was a junkman who liked airplanes.

rode in the back seat behind the pilot. Still, it was a long-awaited thrill. The inside of the Cessna was so nice and clean it appeared new. We took off and flew leisurely above lush green dairy farms and fields of corn for about fifteen minutes with the vast waters of Lake Erie visible nearby. The view was spectacular. Having *finally* gotten an airplane ride, I spent the rest of the weekend jubilant as could be. Even on the dusty roads of our neighborhood, I rode my bike with a new zest and determination, as if more speed on my favorite downhill slope would make the old bike fly. Dad seemed indifferent to my getting my first airplane ride, likely because he was worried about something else.

As long as the P-47 fuselage remained in Chicago, Dad feared Reinert might get a better offer and pull out of the deal. Certain that Reinert knew we could not possibly get it from the muddy field on our first trip, Dad held suspicions that Reinert never intended for him to get the P-47 in the first place. Even though it was summer, Dad worried about rain spoiling our ability to drive the length of the grass strip to get the P-47. Like Eisenhower preparing for the D-Day Invasion, Dad kept an eye on the national weather listed in the newspaper for weeks leading up to our trip. He also called Reinert to insist he check the ground as the day of our arrival grew near.

As we headed back to Chicago, the old Suburban hummed along with an almost happy kind of vibration that triggered the familiar orchestra of rhythmic squeaks and rattles from all the items we carried, plus parts of the Suburban itself. Though the drive went well, I still had to listen to Dad fuss over and over about how ticked he was at Reinert for causing us to make a second trip. As for me, I had my own observations.

It was smack-dab in the middle of the summer, and it seemed all of America was

Top center: I walk behind a badly burned F-86 sitting on the trailer. It was burned so severely that Dad sold it for scrap—a rare thing for him to do. Other aircraft, left to right: T-28A nose resting on an empty 55-gallon drum; Navy UH-34 Sea Bat helicopter; C-82 Packet; B-25 *Wild Cargo.*

out on vacation to "see the USA in your Chevrolet," as a series of TV commercials from General Motors played who knows how many millions of times on American televisions in those years. Hour after hour we'd be in the right lane of the turnpike as countless streams of families would rocket by us driving in the left lane with nice new cars packed with kids inside. Rooftop luggage racks loaded with camping gear, canoes, and other vacation items told that these families were out for a good time. Quietly, I often found myself thinking, "I wonder what that's like."

If there was one thing that defined Dad best, it was that he was a working man. Vacations to go somewhere to relax and have fun were almost a version of heresy. And speaking of religion, there are various versions of how this happened, but one Sunday after Mass, our parents visited Father Mark to ask if Dad and his family's tending to his airplanes on Sunday was considered working on Sunday. It was not a question they would ever consider asking Father Moran, St. Helen pastor who was known to be very strict and stern. Today, people would barely understand why they would even ask this question. But back in the 1960s, almost nothing except churches was open on Sundays. So Dad popped the big question to Father Mark. As Dad explained it, the airplanes were his hobby, so working on them on Sunday was really an act of playing instead of working! When they came out of their meeting with Father Mark and told us how it went, I erupted laughing. Even Mom was fighting back the giggles. Father Mark did ask if Dad was making money from the planes. When Dad answered no to that question, Father Mark gave him the green light to work on Sunday.

Upon our arrival in Chicago, we met Reinert and with little delay drove the long grass airstrip to the P-47 site. Soon the trailer was in position to winch the P-47 fuselage aboard. Initially, Dad was a little cold toward Reinert. But as we got the fighter plane's fuselage further and further onto the trailer, Dad warmed up proportionally. Reinert made good on his promise to give us a new canopy, complete flight control tail section, engine cowlings, exhaust system and other P-47 parts, which quickly patched the rift between them. By the time we left, they acted like best buddies, often laughing over each other's stories. With Reinert proving Dad's worries about a bad deal to be false, forgiveness came quickly. Despite a few differences, they had uniquely common traits that formed a strong bond between them. From then on, they would remain good friends for the next 26 years until Reinert's death in 1992.

After the trade Dad worked with Reinert, word of the deal must have spread. Dad wouldn't sell airplane parts to anyone, but now, he had made a trade. No sooner did we have the P-47 home than another man named Bill Strube showed up who

P-47 fuselage arrives home in the summer of 1966 after being hauled from Earl Reinert's Victory Air Museum at a small grass strip near Mundelein, Illinois.

Third fuselage from left is the P-47 parked next to the C-82 fuselage. Silver vertical tail of P-47 with dark rudder behind it is visible in right section of photo (courtesy Jason McKeon).

wanted to make a trade. Unlike Reinert, who liked to talk, Strube was quieter and more reserved. Probably in his early forties, he had short dark hair and was a bit less than six feet tall with an average build. Though he was quiet, he presented an air of strong self-confidence and exactness. With him was a younger man with black hair of about the same build. The second man had a technical kind of presence that easily could cast him as one of the gadget wizards on TV's *Mission: Impossible*.

Dad was home when they arrived, and he wanted to give them the full-blown tour of his 13 airplanes. But unlike Reinert, they weren't very interested. The tour was over quickly, and Strube got right to the point. He had some trading he wanted to do. Also unlike Reinert, who was interested in engines, Strube was interested in instruments and electronics. He explained that he ran a big military surplus operation near Harrisburg, Pennsylvania, and had some aircraft he might want to trade.

That was the good news. The bad news was that none of his aircraft were of World War II vintage. He did have a pair of P-80 jets and some T-28 parts, but that was about all he had to offer. Noting that the T-28 we owned had a broken front canopy, he proposed right away to get Dad a new canopy if they could do some trading. Dad set the rules right away. He explained that he wouldn't trade or sell anything that belonged to any of his aircraft. But the extra things he had in storage were available for trade. Strube had no problem with that. He was only interested in the modern things we had, which eliminated most of the old equipment mounted in Dad's planes anyway. Dad showed Strube where he stored his extra instruments and electronics. Quickly, Strube and the man he came with were talking model numbers, part numbers, and nomenclature that was a foreign language to us. Soon they had about a dozen instruments picked out.

Strube offered $100 for the items, which Dad quickly agreed to. Having bought them by the pound, Dad figured he had paid a dollar at the most.

Strube wrote down a wish list of what he wanted to trade for one of the P-80 jets. Dad was quick to accept the idea of adding a Lockheed P-80 to his collection, especially if it just involved trading parts. He looked at the list Strube gave him and told that he probably had most items on the list. To know for sure, he'd have to do some digging and phone the answer to Strube. I knew exactly what that meant. I was in for another aerobics workout lifting airplane parts.

The P-80 Shooting Star had a very significant role in aviation history. Though another plane, the Bell P-59, was America's first jet, it was the P-80 that first became operational in large numbers and best signified the end of the propeller-driven fighters. Although the P-80 was subsonic, its performance greatly outclassed everything before it. The P-80 flew extensively in the Korean War, and afterward a two-seat derivative known as the T-33 "T-Bird" served Air Force student pilots as an advanced jet trainer until the 1960s. Even when replaced by the supersonic T-38 Talon, the Air Force continued to fly T-33s as targets for intercept training until the mid-'80s. Thus, with many T-33s still in service in 1966, Dad was happy to have basically the same airplane.

As we headed off to Harrisburg, it was my first time traveling back to Pennsylvania since hauling the Bobcat five years earlier. But unlike the Bobcat trips, this would be a much longer drive. What made it seem especially long were the mountains. On our way to Harrisburg, we encountered mountains so big the Pennsylvania Turnpike tunneled through them. I'd never been in any kind of highway tunnel before and learned right away I didn't like them. The idea that zillions of pounds of rock were just above my head gave me the creeps. Fortunately, the Suburban had no trouble going up the mountains. But on the way there, the trailer was empty.

When we found Strube's place, it was obvious he ran a major business selling parts and equipment. His business was set up on a large industrial lot with several giant warehouses. Though the facilities were old, the place was impressive. He even had rail access to his lot with some railroad cars parked on the tracks. In addition, he had a lot of equipment stored outdoors.

We found the P-80 jets disassembled and stored among the outdoor stuff. Both jets were in fair condition. There weren't any holes or dents like we found on Reinert's P-47. One was in Air Force markings and the other was a Navy jet. As we'd learned to expect, the Air Force jet had a lot of corrosion. Navy planes built for sea duty had better corrosion protection, we observed. Both jets were missing a lot of parts. The pilot seats, instruments and controls were gone. Neither jet had an engine, but not to worry, Dad had a P-80 engine in the shop. It didn't take him long to make up his mind. He agreed to trade with Strube for one of the P-80s and picked the Navy jet.

Before we closed the deal and loaded up, Strube took us on a tour of the site. His warehouses and railroad trailers were packed full of parts and equipment. Most items were electronic in nature, but he also had a lot of wings, canopies, and engine cowlings from T-28 trainers. Besides the P-80s, however, he had no other aircraft. Dad was excited about all the T-28 parts, as Strube had exactly what we needed to put ours in top condition. As promised, Strube had a new front canopy for our T-28. Dad and Strube agreed to do some further trading to get the rest of the T-28 parts at a future time. Despite the huge stockpile of parts, Dad anxiously scanned it all, looking for something that simply wasn't there. "Do you have anything from World War II?" Dad asked Strube.

"That stuff's not worth anything anymore," Strube answered. He then told of junking railroad carloads of World War II airplane parts just a few years before. Dad was alarmed. If a huge parts dealer like Strube had no World War II parts left, did anybody?

Soon, we moved on to the task of hauling the P-80. Hauling the forward fuselage was relatively easy. First, the jet was already disassembled. Also, Strube had a big forklift for loading. After all the planes we had jacked, blocked, and winched onto the trailer, I greatly appreciated the forklift. Using the forklift, one of his men had the forward fuselage loaded in no time. It fit nicely on the trailer and wasn't too heavy. Soon, we were heading home.

The Suburban and trailer handled the load well. Except for climbing the mountains, we were able to maintain normal speed on the turnpike. The trip home was uneventful, but we had one observation that concerned us. The long climb up each mountain caused the Suburban's engine to get hot. With each climb, Dad had to shift into second gear, and as the Suburban labored up the long hills, the engine temperature climbed as well. Although the engine never boiled over, it came close enough that it made us worry about the next trip.

The P-80 had a straight wing with a span of nearly 40 feet. The jet was so old that the concept of sweeping back the wings of jets wasn't done to the P-80. For us, the straight wing was perfect for hauling down the road. The bad news was that it was one piece from tip to tip. Nowhere could you disassemble the wing by unbolting any segments. At first Dad planned to cut the wing in half with a torch to make it easy to haul. But the more he thought about it, the more he didn't want to cut it. The fact that this jet was not demilitarized was rare in itself. Now that the military was destroying its surplus aircraft, Dad didn't want to do the dirty deed to one that had escaped. Also, though the likelihood was remote, the jet did have the potential to fly again. As a result, Dad quickly rejected the idea of cutting the wing. I had my doubts we'd be able to haul the whole thing on the trailer. Even though we had succeeded at hauling the B-25 center wing section, the P-80 wing just looked way too long for our trailer.

With little delay after our arrival, Strube had one of his men on the scene with the big forklift. Carefully he drove the forklift tongues under middle of the wing and began to lift it. Even though the forklift looked big and powerful, it struggled hard as it lifted the entire wing. That made me worry. The wing seemed heavier than expected. With Dad and me spotting, the driver carefully set the wing on the trailer. Dad had the forklift driver place one wingtip just behind the rear doors of the Suburban. It was immediately obvious this wasn't going to work.

Loaded this way, the other end of the wing hung far beyond the end of the trailer. To make matters worse, the center of the heavy wing rested on the very back of the trailer. Not only was this going to make the trailer extremely tail-heavy, but the rear of the trailer wasn't strong enough to support all the weight. The steel truck frame from which Dad made the trailer only extended a short distance behind the axle. The rest of the trailer bed behind that was supported by hardwood beams. Hardwood or not, it looked like the rear part of the trailer was about to snap and break off. "I think you're gonna need a real truck here or you're going to have to cut the wing," Strube said to Dad.

"No, I really don't want to cut her. I've got to get her home in one piece," he answered. We all stood around for a few moments, and then Dad began pacing the length of the Suburban and trailer. He apparently had a new idea. "Lift it up again and put part of the wing over the roof of the Suburban," Dad instructed the forklift driver.

16. Plane Crazy

"You don't want to crush the roof of your wagon do you, Walter?" Strube asked.

"No, I'll shore this end of the wing up so it hangs over the roof," Dad answered while pointing to the area between the wing and the front of the trailer bed. He asked if he could borrow a stack of wood pallets to put there. Strube approved, and we soon had four pallets stacked on the front of the trailer. Strube and his forklift driver exchanged some doubting looks. With the pallets in place, the forks were slowly lowered until the wing rested on the trailer. We all stepped back to look. The tip of the wing now sloped up over the roof of the Suburban, but wasn't clearing it by much. Also, the trailer looked ridiculously short to be hauling such a long wing. The good news was that the center of the wing was over the steel frame of the trailer and near the axle. Still, from the looks of the trailer tires and springs, I could tell the wing was very heavy. We worried that perhaps the rubber fuel bladders in the wing had filled with rain water. We discussed ways to reduce weight by checking for water and removing both main landing gear that were retracted inside the wing. But loaded as we were, Dad was not a man to ever consider retreat. Thanks to Dad's stuttering problem disqualifying him from the military, General Patton's Army legacy was safe from Walter's competition.

Absurd as our overloaded trailer already looked, may as well add some more. As Dad directed, the forklift operator soon had the rear fuselage resting on the wing. By hand, we loaded the horizontal stabilizer on top of the wing. Now we definitely had a load that worried me about weight. Dad tied the load down while I did my familiar task of connecting taillights and wires to the wingtip. As we worked, he assessed the drive home. "We'll never be able to go down the turnpike with this thing," Dad lamented.

Lockheed P-80 Shooting Star wing is yet again too much airplane on too little trailer. Wood pallets near front of trailer elevate the wing to fit over the roof of the Suburban. The World War II bomb winch we used for so many hauling trips can be seen (looks like a guitar in this photograph) atop the front of the trailer frame.

He studied our road map to find an alternate route home. As he decided his route, he pointed out which highway numbers I needed to help him watch for. On the treacherous long trip home, I was navigator, and I knew there was no room to mess up. We said our farewells to Strube and crew and departed.

The way the Suburban handled the long P-80 wing was reminiscent of the final B-25 trip hauling the bomber's center wing section. The long wing, plus the location where we loaded the rear fuselage, combined to make the trailer tail-heavy, and it swayed on the highway as expected. As a result, our max speed was about 50 mph. With some of the wing hanging over the back of the Suburban, the roof got pounded every time we hit a dip in the road or crossed railroad tracks. Each time it happened, it sounded like we were inside a big drum. If the road dipped pulling into a gas station, the drum announced our arrival to the gawkers awaiting us.

When Dad decided not to drive on the turnpike, I didn't see the loss of the turnpike as a big deal. So what if we can't drive on the turnpike? A few more traffic lights, a few more towns, and a two-lane road. No big deal. But I soon found out there were *big* reasons to wish we were on the turnpike. The reasons were steep mountainous roads. I quickly realized that among other features, turnpikes can be far less hilly than two-lane mountain roads.

As Dad approached the first mountain, I got a real pit in my stomach. The so-called hill we used to worry about near home on Route 306 was just an ant mound compared to this one. As he learned from hauling the B-25, Dad got in first gear early while the road was still flat. The Suburban pulled the load fine, but we soon had another problem. "She's rising steady," Dad said as he pointed at the engine's temperature gauge. We both started comparing our progress up the hill with the rate the temperature gauge was climbing. As we slowly made our way up the long hill, cars started stacking up behind us. On level roads, Dad pulled off every four or five miles. But while climbing the mountain there was no way to pull over because Dad was afraid that if he stopped on a steep hill, he'd never get the Suburban going again.

Up the first big hill, we barely made it to the top when the temperature gauge hit full hot and steam began blowing up over the hood. Dad pulled off the road at the first place he could. We got out, popped the hood, and looked at the steaming engine. "I can't wait all day for this thing to cool down," Dad said, sounding anxious. I knew well that when hauling a plane home, Dad hated to stop. His stops for gas were like pit stops at the Indy 500. If I wanted to go to the bathroom, speed was of essence. His main reason for being in a rush was the police. By now, our many trips with oversize loads on an undersized trailer taught us to be nervous at the sight of a police car. And Dad figured the best way to avoid the police was to spend minimum time on the road home. Donut shops were definitely off limits.

Luckily, Dad was prepared for the overheated engine. Back then, it was still common for service stations to sell motor oil in two-gallon cans. The way the Suburban used oil, we had lots of empty cans. In addition to traveling with spare parts, tools, tires, and everything else, we carried two cans full of water. No matter what disaster was awaiting us, we were prepared. We learned early into our hauling trips that if something hadn't gone wrong yet, it was about to. Like a lot of the preparations we made, having four gallons of water paid off.

As we looked at the sizzling-hot engine, small oily bubbles oozed from the rocker cover and head gasket seams, somewhat like Mom cooking buttered toast in a frying

Overheated Suburban takes a break near the top of a Pennsylvania mountain towing the heavy trailer loaded with the entire P-80 wing, rear fuselage and tail.

pan. Dad warned me of the extreme danger of removing a hot radiator cap as he directed me to get far away. He then put an old rag around the radiator cap, extended his arm as far as he could reach, twisted the cap off and ran. More steam escaped, but fortunately our radiator cap was so worn it didn't hold much pressure. "Get me a water can and start the engine," Dad said. I did as instructed, but was uneasy as the temperature gauge was still showing full-hot. Holding the brakes as I ran the engine, I peeked through a gap below the open hood to watch. Very slowly he poured water into the radiator. We both knew if he poured too fast he'd crack the hot engine. Eventually the radiator was full and the temperature came down to normal.

Soon, we were heading down the other side of the mountain and the engine cooled down even more. But now we encountered a different problem. Dad had to ride the brakes so long that they overheated. Before long, an acrid, burning smell filled the Suburban. Dad kept the transmission in low gear so the drag of the engine would help keep the speed down. But even then, the burning brakes smelled awful. I opened every window I could. I hated the smell of the brakes, but whenever he tried to ease up on them, the tail-heavy trailer started to sway again. With steep drop-offs along the side of the road, I was glad Dad was able to keep the swaying problem under control. I became worried about the brakes failing. Our chances were probably very slim if that happened.

Unlike the turnpike, our new route home took us through a lot of small Pennsylvania towns. We hit many of them during Saturday afternoon, so the sidewalks were full of people. Like the gas station spectators on the B-25 trips, the people gawked as we made our way through each of the towns. To add to the spectacle, some dips in the road added the sound effect of the wing bashing the Suburban's roof. Before long, I found myself sliding way down in my seat while passing through the towns.

When not in a town, it seemed like we were always going up and down mountains. The engine overheated almost every time, and soon we had the water can routine down pat. Periodically, we did a quick pit stop to fill up the water cans, but otherwise just kept on truckin'. It was beginning to look like nothing could stop us. Then, we approached the mother of all hills. This time when we climbed the hill, the Suburban boiled over before we got to the top. As Dad pulled over, hit the brakes, and abandoned the climb, I felt sick. Would we ever get going again?

Dad was afraid to let go of the brakes, and asked if I could handle the radiator routine. I reluctantly said I could and did things exactly the way he had. I was still nervous about getting burned. The engine cooled down, but I was still worried that the Suburban would be unable to climb the hill from a dead stop. Anyone who's driven a stick-shift knows that getting started on a steep hill takes some quick foot work to handle the clutch, brake, and gas pedals all at the same time. In most cases you can let the vehicle roll backward slightly as you move your right foot from the brake to the gas. In our situation, we couldn't let the Suburban roll back an inch.

"Scoot over and put your foot on the gas," Dad instructed. I put my foot on the gas petal and revved the engine to a high speed with Dad coaching me on how high to go. As I worked the gas, Dad used his left foot to hold the clutch, and his right foot to hold the brake. "When I count to three, get your foot off the pedal—fast!" he prepped me. On his command, I slid my foot off the gas as he released the brake and quickly mashed the gas himself. Still, when Dad tried to let the clutch out, the Suburban's engine wanted to die immediately. Clearly, the engine was no match for the load. As a result, he had to quickly cycle the clutch in and out to slip it enough for the engine to stay alive while trying to get us rolling. As he did that, the whole Suburban started shaking violently.

The P-80's nearly 40-foot wing rests on the trailer as we unload the rear fuselage and horizontal stabilizer. Left to right: B-25 *Wild Cargo*; F2G Corsair 74; T-28A Trojan; Corsair Zero Zero.

Within moments, a burning smell followed by wispy fingers of gray smoke curling up from the floorboard told me things were bad—real bad. Just like the terrible brake smell that sickened us while going downhill, now the burning clutch was doing the same thing trying to go uphill. For a few moments I thought we were doomed, but then slowly, very slowly, we were starting to move. Dad continued slipping the clutch until we got a little more speed. Finally, he was able to let the clutch out all the way. The shaking stopped, and though crawling slow, we were rolling.

Fortunately, we never had to stop on a hill again. The Suburban did boil over a few more times, but at least it could hang in there until we got to the top. What also helped was a new idea Dad had. Even though it was the middle of summer, he turned the Suburban's heater on. While going up the hills, the air coming from the heater felt red hot. Even though it made us miserably sweaty, using the heater slowed the rate at which the engine heated up on each climb.

Regardless of what we did to keep the engine cool, nothing could cool off some of the motorists who were stuck behind us. We got used to them roaring past us each time Dad pulled off the road. We understood hearing car horns, glaring looks, and a variety of nasty gestures. But along the way, there was one guy riding as a passenger who really took the cake. This passenger was a large man who appeared to be in his forties. As his car passed us, he stuck the top half of his stout body out the passenger window, faced backwards and angrily shook a fist at us while screaming obscenities. Dad and I were upset about it for a few moments, but then laughed our butts off. We were years ahead of our time learning about *road rage*. We of course were stopped by the police now and then. Dad's airplane-saving sob story got us off the hook each time. And compared to the big man that screamed at us passing by, the cops were all very nice.

The P-80 hibernates for the winter surrounded by two B-25s and the Cutlass jet (courtesy Jason McKeon).

17

Delusions of Flight

After hauling the B-57, P-47, P-80 and an F-86 all in 1966, we still weren't finished. We hauled his second B-25. With one look, it was easy to see why he wanted it. Compared to *Wild Cargo* and its damage from the gear-up landing, the next B-25 was in excellent condition. Following a lead from a visitor, he found this B-25 in Franklin, Pennsylvania. After being surplused as an Air Force multi-engine trainer in 1959, it was flown to Franklin and had remained there ever since. While he hadn't kept it in perfect flying condition, owner Curtis McKinney ran the engines periodically and taxied the bomber around the airport.

Dad actually purchased the bomber in 1965, but after he bought it, he did something very unusual. He left it at the airport rather than bring it home. This B-25 was in such great shape Dad wasn't sure he wanted to take it apart and haul it. McKinney had his pilot type rating in the B-25 and explained he piloted five other B-25s to their new owners. Ours was the last of a batch of six he had purchased surplus from the Air Force, so he offered to do the same for us. He likewise offered to work the ferry flight permit with the FAA as he'd done with the previous five. Dad sounded receptive to the idea: "It would sure be nice if you could fly it home for us." Do what? Fly it? One of our airplanes? I couldn't believe my ears. Yet, as I examined the B-25, its condition left little doubt that with some work, it was flyable. The flight control surfaces needed new fabric, a couple of instruments were missing, but otherwise everything looked to be in order.

With the prospect of flying the Franklin B-25, as we called it thereafter, I was more excited than ever. For the first few months Dad owned it, he seemed to be in favor of flying it home. Unfortunately, as time went on, he started to change his tune. Even if McKinney flew it to Ohio, Dad had no runway on his land. Since we did everything on a shoestring budget, the expense of keeping the plane at a nearby airport really concerned him. And then there was Mom. She wasn't excited about the idea of flying the old bomber at all. Dad's biggest pitch for flying it was that he could avoid damaging the aircraft while hauling it. Due to our severe equipment limitations, minor dings and dents usually occurred while hauling airplanes home. But when Dad tried to sell this idea, Mom had her own view. "Wait until you crash it," Mom said sternly. "Then if you're still alive, you'll see what real damage looks like!"

Every couple of months, we made the 80-mile trip to check on the Franklin B-25. Each time, Curtis McKinney offered to start the engines and taxi it around for us. That sounded real exciting to me. The Bobcat was the only plane whose engines we had run up until this time, so I was more than ready for the excitement of cranking the B-25 engines. Dad worried about running airplane engines at home and the noise bothering our neighbors. With the B-25 still parked at the Franklin Airport, there was no worry about that. But to my complete dismay, Dad wasn't even willing to put electrical power on the B-25 and turn a prop. Shoot, even Mom approved of running the B-25 engines! But every time it seemed like we were maybe going to do something really fun and exciting like this, Dad would bail out. It really made me wonder. On the flip side, when the junkman in him decided to haul a wreck like the crashed B-57, there was absolutely no stopping him.

Still, I kept my flying hopes up. Each month that the B-25 remained in Franklin gave me more hope. Eventually we made the trip that ended my dream. Behind the Suburban, we had the trailer in tow. The fall weather in Franklin was cold and dreary. While I was happy to see Dad get a gem of a B-25, I was sad to know what we were going to do to it. I wanted to see it fly! In little time, however, the extreme to which my dream was an illusion would hit me—cold.

On one of the early trips, Mom went with us. We were heading home on a Sunday night with me riding in the back seat. The right-side window by my seat was broken with about half of the glass missing. Because of that, I froze from the cold air blowing in as we drove down the highway. Finally, I made the situation better by stuffing a bundle of rags in the opening while being careful not to cut myself on the jagged edge of broken glass.

Before getting home, we had another problem. One of the Suburban's tires starting thumping loudly. A tire change on the Suburban was a routine occurrence, so I expected we'd be underway shortly. I was wrong. Due to a combination of having a badly worn tire iron and likewise worn wheel lugs, Dad could not get the bad tire off. One wheel lug wouldn't budge, and after several attempts to loosen it, the lug became chewed to the point the tire-iron could no longer grip it.

As Dad kneeled in the mud and gravel while using a hammer and chisel to tap away and eventually split the stubborn wheel lug, I couldn't help but sum up the situation quietly in my mind. With Mom looking on as I held the flashlight for Dad, the word "junk" flooded my brain. Barely a teen, I was faced with a vivid reality check. What on Earth had I been thinking? Stuck in the cold next to a junk Suburban with busted windows and worn-out tires, one of which we can't even remove—I'd been thinking and dreaming of *us … flying* a World War II B-25 bomber? Talk about being delusional! In the future, I told myself I'd have to keep my expectations much more realistic.

18

Plane Folks

By the summer of 1967, Dad's airplane collection was indeed impressive. Not only did he have a wide variety of vintage aircraft, but having some exceptionally rare and historic ones like his F-82 Twin Mustang, the partial XP-82 prototype, and rare F2G National Air Race champ Corsair was beginning to put him on the map. His many complete aircraft included a gaggle of trainers, fighters, and two bombers. For trainers he had two Vultee Valiants, one a BT-13 and the other a BT-15, a T-50 Bobcat and a T-28A Trojan. Fighters included the two complete Corsairs, the F-82 Twin Mustang, the F7U Cutlass, and the P-80 Shooting Star. For bombers he had two B-25s. Additionally, though not complete, he had the P-51 Mustang, P-47 Thunderbolt fuselage, C-82 Packet fuselage, XP-82 Twin Mustang left fuselage, another Corsair fuselage that had also raced in Cleveland, and an odd assortment of other fuselages, wings, cockpits, and engines. Even a number of his aircraft engines were exceptionally rare. The most stunning and sobering aspect of his collection was the fact that if he had not saved these treasures, it was all but certain that most if not all of them would have been cut up for scrap metal. He alone, on the shoestring budget of a carpenter raising five children, had taken on this Herculean endeavor in a way that no one before or after him could ever hope to duplicate.

As Dad gathered this collection, word spread about its existence. Though we always had people dropping by to see the planes, the number of visitors continued to grow each year. By the late sixties, it wasn't uncommon to have groups of a dozen or more visitors on the property at the same time during the weekends. After newspaper articles were written about Dad's collection once a year or so, we saw our visitor turnout grow. Local gas station attendants were also telling us they were getting many requests for directions. With our location very remote and hard to find, we sometimes wondered how many would-be visitors gave up trying to find us.

Dad was quick to greet every visitor. Immediately, he'd ask if any of the visitors were aviators. Those who were not got a polite go-ahead to look around while also being asked not to smoke or climb on the aircraft. On the other hand, if a visitor turned out to be a crewmember or mechanic, and especially one who served in World War II, Dad latched on. Bubbling with enthusiasm, his voice would rev up like an airplane propeller at full throttle. He would point out everything about each plane to include what type it was, how many were left, and how he got it home. If we had the type of plane that one of these aviators flew or worked on, Dad offered a trip to the cockpit. Frequently, they showed a lot of excitement upon being reunited with a B-25, Corsair or other airplane they hadn't touched in the twenty years since the big war. Of all the reasons Dad continued his airplane-saving endeavors, it was this experience that gave him the greatest satisfaction.

Some interesting moments developed sometimes when Dad latched onto a visitor. These visits began with men parking their car in our driveway. They often had a lady in the car, who most likely was their wife. Our driveway was almost always woefully short of gravel and frequently muddy. As the man got out of the car, it was very common for the lady to stay seated. Many of these men had nice dress shoes on. God only knows how many hundreds of pairs of men's dress shoes, perhaps thousands, were ruined during tours of Dad's collection over the years. Undeterred, the men would spend thirty minutes or longer touring the planes while walking the squishy and muddy soil throughout the property.

When people showed their enthusiasm about the collection, it spurred Dad to a heightened level of show and tell. He would open the huge doors to his hangar and point out some of his rare engines. Of these, his favorite was an inverted V-12 German engine, possibly from a Focke-Wulf Fw 190. Each time he showed it off, Dad made sure to point out where a cannon had once been bolted to the back of the engine to shoot its deadly ammo through the propeller shaft. People were really wowed by that.

Dad had quite a collection of rare aircraft engines, almost all of which were purchased from his contacts in the scrap metal business. How did so many rare engines end up in Ohio scrap yards? They probably came from Wright Field near Dayton, where so much experimental flight testing was done. It is well known that captured German aircraft were flight tested at Wright Field. So our best guess was the German engine likely

Visitors: Names unknown, a typical small group of people tour the Soplata collection in early 1970s. Hoops of steel water pipe over F2G Corsair engine and BT-15 in background are sometimes used to support corrugated sheets of salvage-yard metal to partially shelter the planes. Distant far left is front of Cessna T-50 Bobcat.

Top: Engines: Dad liked to show visitors his rare aviation engines. On trailer is this X-24 cylinder dirigible engine. Its dataplate states it was the first engine built by the Allison Engine Company in 1916. Hood on Suburban slightly open indicates the one good 12-volt car battery the family owns is on loan to the 6-volt boom tractor towing the trailer. *Bottom:* Firewall forward (R-2600 engine) from a rare Curtiss SB2C Helldiver Dad found at a scrap yard in Oklahoma after my college graduation from Oklahoma State. I never counted how many engines he collected, but my best guess is around fifty.

came from there. Dad later got a batch of about ten very rare engines from a scrap man, and every engine stand had a metallic sticker with the words "U.S. Air Force Museum." Among these was the very first engine manufactured by the Allison Engine Company.

Always excited by having an experienced aviator visiting, Dad would send me to get his photo albums. He'd set the albums on the splintered and beat-up hardwood trailer bed. Then he'd thumb through his favorite airplane-hauling pictures and tell his tales of the road. Initially, people enjoyed seeing the pictures of the jet in the school bus, followed by photos of too much B-25 on too little trailer. But, no matter how much enthusiasm a visitor had, about ten pages into the photo album, it was usually clear his clock was ticking. About then, he started getting signals from the lady in the car.

The first toot of the car horn was usually very brief, almost as if the lady in the car accidentally bumped the horn. The man would politely stick his hand up and gesture that he'd be on the way shortly. This almost never got Dad to stop talking. It only made him go faster. "Can you believe the Navy is begging for my Zero Zero Corsair because they don't have one for their museum in Pensacola?" He'd then ridicule the Navy and other services for not saving enough airplanes for museums, while also complaining of congressmen writing him to donate his Corsair to the Navy as part of his patriotic duty.

The next toot on the car horn was longer than the first, and it was usually effective. You could see the anxiety set in on the guy. He'd reach in his pocket and pull out his car keys. Yet, despite the anxious sound of the man thumbing through his keys, Dad wouldn't even slow down. He'd next tell the story of the Marine Corps also begging for

The loudest visitor to come by the Soplata collection was a Fairchild C-119 Boxcar that flew over our place and orbited for a few minutes. I shot this photograph of a C-119 at the 1969 Cleveland Airshow, where I drew a map to our home for the Air Force flight crew a few weeks before the flyover happened.

the Corsair because they likewise had none for their new air museum. Dad just couldn't stop. Car horns or not, he couldn't let an aviator type get away without getting his digs in on how dumb the military had been in scrapping their aircraft to near extinction.

Though we enjoyed meeting and talking to airplane buffs, not everyone who liked airplanes got a warm reception. The airplane homebuilder visitors were people who built their own *Popular Mechanics*–type airplanes in their basement or garage. As a group they were great, and if they came just to look, they were warmly welcomed. But if they came to shop, they were at the wrong place. One day during the week, a man showed up in the afternoon and pulled a toolbox from his car. Then he headed out toward the planes. Dad was away at his carpenter job.

"Can I help you?" Mom asked the man as she looked out the sunroom window.

"Yes, ma'am, I'm building a homebuilt plane and am looking for some control cables and pulleys to salvage for my plane," the man answered matter-of-factly.

"I can't let you do that. We don't sell any airplane parts," Mom said firmly.

"These airplanes aren't going to fly again, are they?" the man asked indignantly. "I mean, this is an airplane *junkyard*, isn't it?"

Navy test pilot Dick Becker visited us frequently to check on F2G Corsair 74, which owner Cook Cleland flew to victory in the 1947 Thompson Trophy Race. Cleland then assigned Becker to race Corsair 74 in 1948 and 1949, which explains Becker's name forever painted on the side. In yet another F2G Corsair 94, Cleland won the 1949 race, becoming only the second pilot to ever win the Thompson Trophy Race twice (courtesy Jason McKeon).

"Airplane junkyard!" Dad growled when Mom told of the rude visitor. But as time went by, Dad began to encounter critics. To some, there was no excuse for his aircraft being out in the weather. If Dad wasn't home, I often experienced the criticism myself. Like my father, I was quick to remind people that if not for us, every aircraft in the collection would have been scrapped. For most, that reality quickly made them change their tune.

Despite the occasional critic, Dad continued to welcome everyone who came, always free of charge. Overall, he got a lot of satisfaction from the sincere gratitude most people expressed at the end of their visit. What people liked most was how they could see the planes up close. And with the least little hint, countless kids and adults found themselves in the cockpit of a B-25, Corsair, or F-82. "You can't do this anywhere else!" one woman said. As she smiled with amazement, her kids were busy playing in one of the B-25s making loud engine, propeller, and machine gun sounds. She told of being at the Air Force Museum, where the planes were roped off so you couldn't get near them. She complimented Dad that she'd rather see them like this where people could touch the planes, climb inside to feel and to even smell what the old planes were like.

It meant a lot to hear compliments like that. Anything bringing reassurance about our unique collection, home, and lifestyle was encouraging. While I never dwelled on it much, I felt some doubt and insecurity as a result of living such an unusual life. A typical apple-pie American family was clearly something we were not. The visiting

Dick Becker in Dad's F-82E Twin Mustang in 1965. Dad had his work cut out getting Navy test pilot Becker to grudgingly pose for this photo in "a dang Air Force fighter plane." Becker visited so often I almost thought of him as my airplane uncle. There was always a relaxed yet thoroughly competent air about Becker that inspired me enormously and fueled my inspiration to become a pilot.

No stream of visitors would be complete without Earl Reinert paying another visit in the mid-1970s with this vintage military ambulance. The house staircase seen on far right leads up to our second-story living area with a left turn at top of the stairs. Three sets of second-story sunroom windows make that room one of our favorite places to hang out.

public's acceptance of what we were doing was therapeutic. It helped reassure me that while none of this was normal, it was still okay.

Though almost all visitors arrived by car, others paid us a different kind of visit. If the weekend weather was good, we could count on some light planes circling around the area throughout the day. Eventually, Dad became worried about the light planes buzzing for several reasons. First, he was afraid someone would get carried away and have an accident. Also, he was afraid the neighbors would be annoyed by the noise of the frequent flyers. Fortunately, most pilots stayed high, circled around gently, and used good judgment. But not all the planes that made a flyby were light planes.

One day we were out in the yard and heard an airplane approaching. The distinctive sound told me some powerful radial engines were turning giant props. With tall trees all around our property, there were times you couldn't see an approaching airplane until it was right overhead. Suddenly, an Air Force C-119 Boxcar thundered loudly overhead. The giant plane began circling, and as it did, I thought of a Boxcar crew I had met at the Cleveland Airshow a few weeks earlier. I had no way of knowing which Air Force base the plane was from, let alone if it was the same crew. But I had my suspicions, especially considering the map I drew for them after spilling the beans about Dad's airplane collection. Soon, family members and neighbors were outside in yards and driveways looking up. Dad, again, was away at work.

"What's that?" someone asked.

Dad and I play the visitor role, returning to Earl Reinert's Victory Air Museum in 1975 when I was on summer break from college. Here Dad sits in the cockpit of Bill Odom's former air race YP-47M. Reinert got the Thunderbolt repainted from its air race colors to a D-Day paint scheme in honor of the 30th anniversary of D-Day.

"It's a Boxcar!" I yelled. "Maybe they're the ones I talked to at the airshow," I added. We all started waving and the plane continued to circle. From across the yard, I heard a familiar voice holler, "I know *exactly* what *that* is!" I looked over and saw our next-door neighbor, Mr. Naymick, smiling as he walked over to join us. I had no doubt he knew what he was seeing. During a tour in the Army as a paratrooper, Mr. Naymick jumped out of Boxcars.

After flying several circles, the Boxcar rolled out of its turn and flew away. We all just stood there for a while. I was mesmerized. Somebody in the Air Force actually stopped by, so to speak. Not everybody gets that kind of attention.

19

Along for the Ride

As visitors continued coming to see Dad's planes, the question they kept asking was what did he plan to do with all of them? The collection was big now, and so was the unanswered question people were asking. I'd been wondering the same thing. Where is my father heading with all this? And as his airplane son, do I fit somewhere in his future plans? When I pondered these questions, a more frightening question arose. Does he have a plan? Any plan?

What I did know was what he wasn't going to do. Long before the Gulf Wars gave us the term "no-fly zones," my father was no-fly zone Walter. For Dad, the Bearcat crash that killed Bob Kucera was the most personal to date of the fatal warbird crashes that continued to occur around the country during that time. Besides the loss of life, Dad was outspoken about the historic aircraft being lost. Just a few months before Kucera's crash, a historic P-39 race plane named "Cobra II" was destroyed in a fatal crash. This same P-39 won the 1946 Thompson Trophy Race in Cleveland with test pilot legend Alvin M. "Tex" Johnston at the throttle. The loss of this and other rare historic planes convinced Dad these aircraft belonged on the ground.

The vision Dad began to talk about was to start an air museum in which all aircraft would be on static display and none would fly. And though we had some differences of opinion about his collection, I wished in every way for him to achieve and realize his dream of having an air museum. Trying to envision the museum he talked of and dreamed of, I frequently picked my young and inexperienced mind to try to figure some way by which he could reach this goal while also wondering where I might find myself in that journey. In his collection of airplane books, magazines, and museum newsletters, I examined what other air museums were doing and tried to imagine how their blueprint might apply to us.

The more I looked at the challenges he would face attempting to start such a museum, the more it occurred to me that there were a number of barriers he would have to overcome for this vision to become a reality. First was the barrier of trust. Dad had a serious fear of trusting others. I wasn't sure where that fear came from, but it was strong. He often spoke of observing people's looks as "throwing daggers at me." I was slow to understand that at first. But the more he said it, the more I realized he was ever reading people with a trained eye, seemingly on alert for any negative looks. Feeding his fears of trusting people, he made occasional mention of business stories he'd read in which the founder of a company was ousted by others who arrived on the scene after all the difficult start-up work was done. By repeating this observation as often as he did, it appeared to me that he predestined himself to conclude such would be his fate.

More precariously, Dad was afraid of the potential consequences if someone else invested money into starting a museum with his aircraft. He worried that if any investors later decided to sell or back out, they'd take his aircraft to recoup their investment. This fear boxed Dad into a dilemma. He needed outside financial help to upgrade his airplane collection and acquire the proper facilities for a museum, but he could end up losing everything if the deal went bad. So while the movement to collect and restore World War II aircraft was getting stronger, Dad seemed hopelessly stuck on the outside from having the air museum he envisioned.

While he would routinely identify money as the single main barrier keeping him from having an air museum, I observed other barriers that stood in his way. First was the unconventional way he did many things. That could often be a strength for him, but also a liability when he insisted others do things his unconventional way. As one example, the top fabric on the Bobcat wings rotted through. Dad decided to fix that by using some rusty scrap sheets of steel. He insisted I help him use roofing tar to stick the sheet steel to the top of the wing. We made a giant gooey mess with the black tar, and the steel was too stiff to bend and follow the curve of the wing. To try to force the steel to bend as needed, we then used long pieces of scrap electrical wire to wrap around the wing and pull the steel down where its edge was sticking up above the wing. That helped a little, but not nearly enough. The end result looked terrible when we finished, yet the Bobcat wing would endure this ugly duckling fix for many years. Over and over I tried to talk Dad out of doing this to the Bobcat. And I had to be very careful doing that.

Over a period of many years, I discovered my father to be the most thin-skinned person I would ever know. If someone said anything that included criticism, he would get terribly angry and have what one of my uncles would later describe as volcanic "Walter eruptions." Even worse, you could say something totally innocent, and he would sometimes twist the words into an imagined criticism and get almost as upset. So there were issues like that with my father. But there was also something else, and it puzzled me to try to understand what it was. Hollywood to the rescue: a new airplane movie came out and its theme hinted at some possible answers.

As Dad and I sat together in the old Geauga Theater watching the 1970 film *Catch-22*, the movie's theme of being trapped by contradiction got my attention. I couldn't articulate exactly how it applied to my father, but the general sense that he was caught in a trap like Yossarian and other characters in the movie made me wonder. I wouldn't go so far as calling my father crazy for hauling a jet in a school bus. Really? Am I his crazy son now? But occasionally eccentric, he was that for sure. Yet, and I mean this as a compliment, it took a gifted eccentric to haul the Cutlass with a school bus and two B-25s with a Suburban. Had he not been ever willing to tackle these and other challenges by savagely slaying orthodoxy with near reckless abandon, his mission of saving historic airplanes would not have been possible.

Unfortunately, the trap was that the same eccentric talents enabling him to collect his airplanes by being freed from conventional thinking, ironically imprisoned him from being seen as credible to others he would need to establish an air museum. As we watched *Catch-22* together, we were both thrilled as we exchanged giant smiles watching the B-25 flying scenes. We especially enjoyed the wild and crazy B-25 mass formation takeoff, which is still an epic scene to airplane enthusiasts to this day. As father and son airplane fanatics, we were clearly on the same page enjoying the movie together. Yet

I don't know if it ever occurred to him that the paradoxical personal dilemmas defining the movie's theme might apply to his own situation. For me, I didn't realize it at the time, but I was getting a double dose. I had *Catch-22* on the movie screen before me, and I had *Catch-22* sitting beside me.

Despite my many concerns about my father, I deeply respected that he almost single-handedly rescued many historic aircraft and artifacts. I also recognized that his stubbornness, intense obsession, workaholic lifestyle, and total self-reliance were among the attributes that made his many proud accomplishments possible. But it seemed every time I held some hope that these many strengths would overcome his handicaps, he'd do something that would dash my hopes. More exactly, it was what he soon refused to do that crushed my hopes for him.

Having worked for the same construction company for five years or so, he'd been offered a promotion to foreman. A good pay raise was part of the offer. Hearing the news, I felt so proud of Dad. Despite my growing doubts about him, perhaps I was wrong. Trust me here, I wanted to be wrong! I wanted the best for my father, and therefore wished and hoped for someone to prove my worries about him were false. With the foreman job offered to him, it was obvious the people at work thought highly of him, and I was thrilled to hear the great news. And knowing how intensely Dad clung to every dime, I figured he'd jump at the chance to make more money. But no way. As my spirits plunged, he told me how he had quickly declined the promotion. He was adamant he wanted "absolutely nothing to do" with supervising other carpenters. He continued talking, but I quit listening as I sat there devastated. The interesting irony was that the same man who had no problem being very controlling at home didn't want to supervise anyone at his carpenter job.

Unknown visitors tour Dad's carpenter reconstruction of a junked and destroyed B-36 Peacemaker. Didn't matter what shape an airplane was in, if it was a down-and-out airplane orphan nobody wanted, Dad would rescue it and give it a home.

19. Along for the Ride

No matter the pay raise, Dad's haunted expression told me he was afraid to take the foreman job. When hauling an airplane with an overloaded trailer, he could tackle any mountain despite the risk of being killed plunging down it. But lead a group of men? I could tell he deeply feared the thought. That caused me to wonder. If he was afraid to lead other men in his carpenter job, would he ever be able to lead the group of adults it would take to start and run an air museum? So again arose the question, where was he going with all this? I was soon starting to see a trend with the visitors that I was afraid was beginning to answer that question.

"You hauled the B-25s with *that!*" visitors would say as Dad pointed to the Suburban and homemade trailer. After the story about the Cutlass jet in the school bus, it was hard to imagine them being shocked about anything. But shocked again they were. That two B-25s like Doolittle's Raiders had bombed Tokyo with were hauled down the highway with a Suburban and homemade trailer instead of a large truck—people visiting us were beside themselves in disbelief. Learning to enjoy this notoriety immensely, Dad embraced it to the point he eventually all but proclaimed the highway as his personal stage.

His legacy as the man who saved and hauled big airplanes despite being totally ill-equipped soon appeared to become his newfound calling. To a man whose aircraft criteria were sometimes defined by size, in the early 1970s he reached the pinnacle of "size matters" by acquiring a giant B-36. Never mind it was smashed to pieces when the Air Force sold it for scrap. That didn't matter. It was rare, it was huge, and down the highway it went as he towed it behind a later model 1966 Chevy Suburban. As his

Mom poses with the reconstructed B-36 fuselage stitched back together with wood 2×4s and salvage-yard sheets of aluminum. In some ways it looked like a giant aluminum quilt sewed together in a hurry.

stage for doing the impossible on the highway grew, he'd use his rusted, worn-out and beat-up Suburbans as a visual aid for visitors touring the property. "I use the Suburban for everything," he would say with a sincere and meek humble pride. Heck, he should have been doing advertising for General Motors, telling how the do-all Suburbans took him to his carpenter job, hauled his airplanes, took the family to church and brought home the groceries. "You drive your *family* in—*this*!" a lady asked with a look of dismay as he showcased the '57 Suburban one day in the late sixties.

"It's all I've got," Dad answered, explaining how it took every penny to save the airplanes, and that's why his family couldn't have a nice car. "And the family don't mind—right, Wally?" he asked as he looked toward me. With everyone in the habit of slowly walking around each plane on the tour, the Suburban now became the focus of attention. As the visitors circled around, Dad proudly pointed out which airplane caused each of the numerous dents in the Suburban's body. And beyond the dents, there was so much more to see.

By the late 1960s, his first Suburban had rust galore despite the things we did to try to stop it. The front fenders had rusted so badly, we literally had to patch them with sheets of aluminum and iron bars to keep the headlights from falling out. Inside, the floorboard rusted through in a few areas near the front seat. But just like the derelict planes it hauled, Dad was endeared to his derelict Suburban. "She's been my faithful airplane hauler," he'd tell the group while gently patting a jagged aluminum patch on one of the fenders. "Can't let her rust away any more, though. I spray her with oil—just like the planes she's saved."

For years Dad had me use a garden pump sprayer to coat the aluminum insides of the planes with a mixture of oil thinned with kerosene to help fight corrosion. Then he

The giant ten-engine Cold War Convair B-36 Peacemaker (National Museum of the United States Air Force).

got the idea to do the same to his Suburban. I wasn't having any part of that, so Dad gave his beloved Suburban a periodic oil bath. It drove me up the wall. Aware by now that millions of men spend half their Saturday cleaning every speck of oil and tar off their car, I've got a father who smiles as he makes a mess splattering oil all over his. This was unconventional—on steroids!

In addition to all that, virtually every side window in the Suburban was cracked or broken. As we hauled the assorted loads of stuff home, objects inside the Suburban such as landing gear doors, engine cowlings, and other items would slide around and occasionally bang into a window. We drove for months with the chunk of window gone that nearly froze me while hauling the Franklin B-25. He eventually fixed that with a piece of B-25 Plexiglas that fit poorly. As Dad persisted showcasing his pitiful Suburban to groups of visitors, I soon tired of it and would leave. Despite my objections, he'd explain to me his belief that people were impressed by this intense self-sacrifice, given for the cause of saving historic airplanes. He'd tell me he was making this pitch hoping somebody would show up with a lot of money to help. I saw things differently as I strained to grasp what the future held for our father-and-son relationship.

It was always abundantly clear the airplane collection would remain totally under his direction and rigid control. My experience thus far was that he took almost no inputs from me, if I dared even suggest. I wasn't surprised for things to be this way. Looking at how he dismissed suggestions from adults such as Grandma Murray, I had to expect that, as a kid, I would get the same response. More importantly, beyond Dad's dismissing advice from other adults in our family, it was the way he did so that caught my ear. Dad strongly rebutted them by saying that ignoring his critics was the smartest

When the Marines offered to make an even trade of this airworthy F4U-7 Corsair for Dad's Corsair Zero Zero, he totally refused to consider the offer.

Mom with Corsair Zero Zero in 1965.

thing he'd ever done. "Glad I didn't listen to all the people who thought I was nuts—I wouldn't have the planes I've got now." He had a good point.

Dad now had many historic aircraft that others wanted. And as the years went by, they wanted his aircraft even more. He was getting a lot of phone calls from people begging him to sell this plane or that one. Flatly, he told every caller he wasn't selling anything. I began to wish he would. I figured in someone else's hands, the aircraft would be restored to pristine condition and sheltered from the weather in a proper hangar. Unless destroyed in a crash, their future would be secure. With their value escalating rapidly, the threat of a scrapman's torch was long past.

But to Dad, they were more than a collection of rare and historic aircraft. Their very existence made them symbols of his personal crusade. Dad felt he alone had put forth the toil, the financial sacrifice, and creative-hauling methods that accounted for the existence of this rare fleet of aircraft. Not unlike the stray dogs he fondly adopted, his planes were orphans he had given a home. And so it was in the safety of his sanctuary the planes would remain. Only from this perspective could I later understand a decision he made that was incomprehensible to me at the time.

A man from the Marine Corps came to visit us one day. Fitting what you might expect from a Marine, he had a stocky build and a razor-sharp crew cut, and he wore a crisp, decorated Marine Corps uniform. As his no-nonsense appearance suggested, he got right to the point. The Marine Corps wanted Dad's Zero Zero Corsair for a new aviation museum they were building. Quickly, the man informed us that they had a Corsair in tip-top flying condition, but since it was a later model Corsair built during the Korean War, it wasn't what they wanted for their museum. Instead, they needed a World War II Corsair like Zero Zero. Thus, they were willing to trade Corsairs. "Wow, a flyable Corsair!" I thought to myself. I was more excited than ever. But to my dismay, Dad had no interest in the offer.

20

High Hopes

Late one summer evening in 1968, I returned home from cross-country practice at Newbury High School, where my sophomore year was about to begin. A white 1964 Chevy Impala was in our driveway, and Dad was beside the car talking to a man of medium height and build, slightly bald, who appeared to be about forty. Dad's smiling face was beaming like the sun. A woman whom I assumed was the man's wife was happily talking with Mom. Seeing a definite liveliness going on with this visiting couple suggested something very special was going on. In addition, I observed something unusual about the man. Under his thin white shirt, I could see a big cast covering much of his torso. As I walked up, Dad introduced me. "I'd like you to meet my son, Wally. He's a runner," Dad said while pointing out my sweaty running attire. The man smiled nicely and I could tell he was in some discomfort.

"Hi, I'm Dean Ortner," the man said nicely as he shook my hand. He then introduced his wife, who seemed very sweet as my ears went deaf. *Dean Ortner!* Like an Elvis groupie meeting "The King" for the first time, I was stunned and speechless. Year after year, I had watched Dean Ortner perform his P-51 routine in Cleveland, as well as at other airshows. While all airshow pilots were special to me, nothing captivated me like watching someone roar across the field in a Mustang. After years of being one of my top hero pilots, now Dean Ortner was standing in my driveway! I was completely spellbound that he was at our house, but through the excitement I couldn't help wonder why my hero was wearing the big cast.

"Broke his back in a Piper Cub crash at an airshow in Pennsylvania," Dad said. While his comment fulfilled my curiosity, I felt uneasy that he told me with the man present. Fortunately, Ortner seemed relaxed about it. He just smiled and acknowledged by shrugging his shoulders. By the time I arrived home, they had completed the airplane tour and Ortner was ready to leave.

"My doctor doesn't want me up like this too long, so I need to head home," Ortner said as he opened the right rear door of the Chevy and gently eased into the back seat.

"Just let me show you a few pictures from my scrapbooks," Dad said, all revved up. "It'll just take a minute."

"I really need to get going," Ortner said politely.

I almost wanted to scream, "Daaaaad! My hero pilot has a *broken back!* Let him go!"

Luckily, Mom came to the rescue with a sweet sendoff. "Mr. Ortner, I hope your back heals up real soon, and God bless you!"

"Give me a call when you want to come see the plane," Ortner said through the car's open window.

"We'll be over soon," Dad replied happily. We all waved as they left, and Dad quickly told me he was thinking about buying Dean Ortner's T-6.

"Wow!" I thought. I saw that T-6 at the 1967 Cleveland Airshow. It was one of the best ones at the show. It was painted with a very appealing red and white sunburst paint scheme. "You're gonna buy Dean Ortner's T-6 we saw at the Cleveland Airshow?" I asked, totally excited.

"No, not that one," he answered. The nice red and white T-6 wasn't for sale, but Ortner had another T-6 he was planning on restoring. Due to the accident in the Cub, he decided to sell it. The price was $1,700 and I could tell Dad was thinking hard about buying it. He said that since Ortner was planning to get the plane flyable, maybe we could. I wanted to believe he was serious, but I knew better than to get my hopes up. He then spoke of Dean Ortner and told how he had spent about an hour at our place. Dad was really impressed. "He's a real nice guy, not at all like the big-shot airshow pilot I expected."

"What did he think about the planes?" I asked.

Beaming with pride, Dad replied, "He was really excited about the Twin Mustang and the Corsairs, especially Cook Cleland's racer."

"Wow!" I almost couldn't believe it. Dean Ortner was excited about Dad's planes, and we would get to visit my hero at his family airport!

The next weekend we packed the Suburban and hooked up the trailer for our first trip to Ortner's place. It was located out west of Cleveland in Wakeman, Ohio, and I couldn't wait to get there. From what was written in airshow programs and told by airshow announcers, plus what we'd heard from some of our visitors, I knew that Dean Ortner and his brother Andy ran a big and highly respected air freight company. They were well-known aviation legends, building Ortner Air Service from the ground up on their father's farm.

As we arrived at the Ortner airport, I felt overwhelmed. Like any airport, airplanes were everywhere. What was different was the flock of big propeller-driven cargo planes and ex-military aircraft scattered all around. And unlike ours, these flew!

Dad and I hopped out of the Suburban and went inside the Ortner Air Service office building. Neither of the Ortner brothers were there, but a tall man named Lou Boone greeted us and offered to take us out to see the T-6. He got in the Suburban with us and we headed across the airport. It was a good distance out to where the T-6 was parked, so on the way we had a little time to admire the scene.

Right away I could tell this airport had the kind of planes Dad really liked. Instead of just having those lawnmower-sounding light planes Dad scoffed at, this airport had a lot of the manly-type airplanes. About a half dozen planes were large C-46 transports, accompanied by a few DC-3 transports and some smaller Beech-18s. I was drawn to the C-46s since we still had the cockpit of one in the shop. I quickly spotted the stylish red and white T-6, which I originally hoped we were buying. The fantasy of getting *that* airplane was a tremendous thrill, though short-lived. Among the other airplanes, we quickly spotted a P-51 Mustang, though not the one we were used to seeing Ortner fly at airshows. We were always excited to see a Mustang, but what really caught our eye was a Corsair. From a distance this one appeared to be the same model as Dad's Zero Zero Corsair.

As we drove up to the T-6, which was actually a Navy SNJ version of the T-6, I could tell Dad was excited. While the plane wasn't in flying condition, it looked like a solid airplane. The outboard wings had been removed, but otherwise, it was all together. As we got out and examined it, Dad made up his mind quickly—he wanted it. Before long, Dean Ortner drove up. As he got out of his car, I noticed his cast was off as he walked up with a big smile.

"Looks like your back is healing up well," said Dad as he and Ortner met.

"Yes, thank you, I'm doing a lot better now," Ortner said happily while telling us how great it was to be done wearing the big cast. "What do you think about the SNJ?" he asked.

Dad stuck out his hand with a bank check. "Sold!" Dad laughed lightly.

"You sure?" Ortner asked.

"I'm sure. I've always wanted a T-6 or SNJ," Dad smiled with a new-owner pride.

Ortner seemed startled by Dad's quick decision. He took the check, smiled and said, "I wish everything in this business was that easy. Would you like to take a look around?"

"Sure would. I'm in airplane heaven here!" Dad replied. First on the tour, we checked out a C-46. From playing in Dad's C-46 cockpit, I thought I was familiar with the plane. But until seeing one up close, I never realized what a giant the C-46 is compared to a DC-3. Soon an airborne C-46 appeared on final approach, and Ortner then focused on monitoring the approach and landing. Dad and I were impressed by the nice landing as Ortner nodded his approval toward the hired hands flying the plane to home base.

Used extensively in World War II, the C-46 was best known for airlifting supplies to China in the war against Japan. The supply routes flown took the C-46s over

Curtiss C-46 Commando transport plane. Many C-46s and their crews were lost airlifting supplies to China by flying over the treacherous Himalaya Mountains during World War II. They later became popular civilian cargo planes with companies like Ortner Air Service in the 1950s and '60s (courtesy Robert Garrard at AirHistory.net).

the treacherous Himalayan Mountains in what became known as "Flying the Hump." These missions, flown with C-46, C-47 and other freighters, represented perhaps the most dangerous transport flying in history. Twin engine propeller transports like the C-46 didn't have an abundance of power to fly above high terrain, so any engine trouble over the Himalayas often spelled disaster. And unlike the reliable jet engines used on transports today, the big radial engines of the World War II era C-46 had their share of problems. In addition to the high terrain, the air routes over the Himalayas were known for frequent bad weather, with aircraft icing being a particularly dangerous threat. By the end of the war, an estimated 415 aircraft and 1,360 crewmembers were lost flying the Hump.

Fortunately for the Ortners, the Himalayas weren't in Cleveland. While we were there, one C-46 was getting an engine change after the engine seized on the flight in. Another C-46 was getting an engine cylinder changed. Looking around the field, I noticed many C-46 engines lying around in different places. Since these were early versions of the Pratt & Whitney R-2800 that also powered the Corsair, I began to think it was good that our Corsair didn't fly. Still, Ortner told that the C-46s were holding up well, despite an occasional engine problem. They didn't haul people, just cargo. Mostly they hauled car parts for the auto industry still going strong in Detroit.

Next, we headed over to the Corsair parked outside a big hangar. As I walked up to this Corsair, it suddenly occurred to me the only Corsairs I'd ever seen belonged to Dad. Compared to the Mustang, of which over a hundred were said to still be flying, the Corsair population was rumored to be a dozen or so with maybe two or three flying. "Don't let me get my trailer near this thing!" Dad kidded Ortner.

"Hey, you've already got two, you can't have all of them!" Ortner laughed. "I haven't had it long and it needs a lot of work."

"This Corsair needs work?" I asked. Sure, the paint was a bit faded and a missing engine cowling told some engine work was underway, but still, it looked great.

"Oh, definitely, I've got a lot of fixing up to do to get it in shape," he answered. He told of a carburetor problem with the engine and how the hydraulics needed a complete overhaul, plus a new paint job was planned. He told of ferrying the plane home with the landing gear down. He was afraid that if he retracted the gear, he might not get it back down because the hydraulic system was in bad shape.

"Had you ever flown a Corsair before?" Dad asked.

"No, just the one flight here," Ortner answered.

"How'd you know how to fly one?" I asked.

"Just like the World War II guys did, I read the flight manual, climbed in, and flew it," he answered casually.

"It's amazing they never had a two-seat training version of the Corsair or other fighters," Dad remarked.

"That's exactly right," Ortner replied. He told of his great admiration for the young World War II pilots who earned their wings flying the 600-horsepower T-6, and then had to climb into these single-seat 2,000-horsepower fighters and solo on their first flight. "Yes, I soloed this Corsair on my first flight, but I've got a lot more experience than those young guys had. It's truly amazing what they did." Dad and I nodded in agreement.

"You know, I didn't realize it till now, but it's these World War II model Corsairs that are suddenly in demand," Dad said.

"What do you mean?" Ortner asked. Dad explained how the Navy came begging for his Zero Zero Corsair, and now the Marine Corps Museum at Quantico wanted it so bad they offered to trade a late model and flyable F4U-7 Corsair to get the one he owned.

"Really?" Ortner's face lit up with intrigue.

"Yeah, they say the Corsair they want to trade has a freshly overhauled engine and they've rebuilt everything else. They'll even fly it to the airport of my choice if I'm willing to trade," Dad continued.

"Why are they so eager to trade?" Ortner asked, clearly puzzled.

"Because they want a World War II model Corsair for their museum," Dad answered. He explained to Ortner that the Marines said their F4U-7 Corsair was built in the 1950s, and they didn't consider it historic because it was built after the war. "Heck, I told them to just put it in the museum since most people don't know one Corsair from another," Dad said to Ortner. Shrugging, Dad explained the Marines wouldn't listen to him and they insisted they had to have a World War II Corsair like his or Ortner's that we were looking at now.

With the tour finished, Ortner showed us the spot in an open-air hangar where the SNJ outboard wings were stored. He then rounded up a group of men and we quickly had the wings loaded on the trailer. The men got some old car tires and used them for padding the two wings riding on top of each other. "Walter, you sure know how to haul airplanes," Ortner said. "I hope you don't mind these guys loading your trailer this way, but I think you'll be happy."

"Men helping me load my trailer!" Dad laughed. "Usually it's just me and my boy working like dogs to get loaded," he smiled.

My hero pilot Dean Ortner in 1968 with the early model Corsair he later traded to the Marines for the same F4U-7 Corsair my father turned down.

20. High Hopes

"Dean has not stopped talking about seeing your airplane collection," one of the men said as the others smiled in agreement. "Can we come look sometime?"

"Come anytime, we're always open, and it's free of charge," Dad said cheerfully.

After the men loaded the trailer, we drove across the airport back to where the SNJ was parked in the grass. Dad wanted to study the SNJ more to help decide how he was going to get it home. One option was to hook the tailwheel to the trailer bed and tow the plane backward behind the trailer. That idea didn't last long. The Suburban, trailer, and SNJ would make a train of three wheeled objects that might go out of control. We quickly agreed not to try that. Another option was to use a pickup truck Ortner offered to loan us. That was how his men towed the SNJ from Hopkins airport. But Dad was hung up on the idea of borrowing the truck. Self-sufficient as a rule, he didn't like to borrow anything. Another option was to separate the center wing from the fuselage and trailer the two sections home. While much easier than dismantling the B-25, it still would be a lot of work to take it apart and then reassemble it. So towing the SNJ on its landing gear was our first choice, but we didn't have the correct vehicle to do that with.

I was exploring around the SNJ cockpit as Dad headed to the Suburban parked in the thick grass. In a few moments I looked and saw something very strange. Dad was on his back under the rear of the Suburban with just his feet and work boots sticking out in the grass behind the rear bumper. It reminded me of the scene in *The Wizard of Oz* after the house fell on the sister of the Wicked Witch. "Just what we need," I thought. We had to fix the overworked Suburban a lot, so I figured Dad had spotted a bad problem under the vehicle. "Is something broke or leaking?" I asked as I got down in the grass and looked under the Suburban.

"No, nothing's wrong," he answered. He wiggled out from under the Suburban and had a serious investigative look I was well familiar with. Next, he opened the rear doors and studied the door hinges. Then he smiled to himself, and clued me in. "I've got it," his face was all lit up. "We'll take the rear doors off, hook the tailwheel to the floor in there, and tow the sucker home tail-first on its landing gear," Dad explained while showing how the rear fuselage of the SNJ would fit inside the rear of the Suburban.

He then told me that he had crawled underneath the Suburban to confirm the passenger and cargo areas of the floor were made of thick marine-quality plywood. He was certain he could nail wood blocks to that floor to capture and secure the tailwheel axle of the SNJ and use that as our hitch to tow the plane. I was good with that, but asked how he would turn corners without the fuselage getting dented by the Suburban's door frame. Dad answered he would just have to turn really shallow while also depending on me to be his spotter.

We soon went home, towing the outboard wings on the trailer. A total non-event getting home, and we then revisited our plans during the week as we planned our next trip to tow the SNJ the way Dad envisioned. Early the next Sunday morning, we were back at Ortner's, making our final efforts to secure the SNJ tailwheel axle to the Suburban's rear floor. We were alone that sunny Sunday morning when Dean Ortner drove up. "Walter, you and your son absolutely amaze me!" Ortner said. He had a huge smile on his face and shook his head as he leaned in the Suburban examining wood 2 × 6s and other short pieces of lumber Dad had nailed into the Suburban's plywood floor to attach the SNJ tailwheel axle. It was very crude, but effective. Dad's carpenter skills made his rough and tough use of wood blocks look secure. "We even crawled under and bent the nails under the floor to be sure they won't pull out on the drive," Dad reported proudly.

Ortner laughed, "If you guys can haul two B-25s with this Chevy, I guess a little old SNJ should be a piece of cake." It felt good seeing Dean Ortner appear both amused and supportive. We were undoubtedly a little strange in our approach to doing things, but people like him seemed able to look past that. It was the end result that counted. But just when I felt like maybe we had impressed my longtime airshow hero, Dad did it.

"Can't afford a real truck. Spend all my money on my planes," he sighed, sounding like the poor destitute airplane collector charity case again. "I use my Suburban for everything," he continued as he listed how his derelict Suburban took him to his carpenter job, towed his planes, took his family to church and met all his needs.

"You mean *this* is your family car?" Ortner asked.

"Yep, it's all we've got," Dad answered. It was bad enough that Dad repeatedly said these things to strangers who came to see his collection. But at least they were strangers. Dean Ortner was my hero! After years of watching him perform in airshows, I finally got to meet this man. To my delight, his friendly manner, self-confidence, poise, and other traits all met or exceeded my high expectations. He was the perfect role model for a kid pilot-wannabe like me, and I was tickled pink just to be standing next to him. Then Dad had to do this. *Never* was I more embarrassed.

It was mid-morning when we headed home, and we mostly had the road to ourselves. Other than some families heading home from church, traffic was light. We took two-lane roads the whole way home since it didn't make sense to try the turnpike. From west to east, we had to travel the entire Cleveland metropolitan area. Fortunately, Dad was an expert navigating the big city and knew which roads to avoid. He actually drove the route he envisioned on the way to Ortner's to be sure of no surprises.

I spent a lot of time facing backwards spotting the landing gear that was riding near the shoulder of the road. As cars approached from the opposite direction, Dad moved to the right as far as he could, based on my reports of where the landing gear was tracking. Of course, with the rear doors missing, seeing the landing gear was not a problem. Much of the road was wide enough that staying clear of other traffic was no sweat. But there were some narrow stretches of highway that made things tight. "How much have I got?" Dad would call anxiously. I would shout back in inches until the SNJ tire was on the edge of the pavement.

"You're on the edge now, can't go over any more!" I'd tell him. After quite a number of these events, it was like I was Scotty on *Star Trek*. "That's all she'll go, Captain, can't give you any more!"

On the edge, Dad would hold position, slow down, and then look for a reaction from the driver going the opposite direction. Most spotted the tight clearance and eased toward the shoulder of their lane. But a few drivers didn't budge. When Dad couldn't delay any longer, he'd swerve right and put the landing gear off into the grass. Luckily, we only hit a few big bumps during the times the SNJ tire went off-road. Still, the big bumps made the SNJ bounce up and down wildly. To my surprise, Dad wasn't bothered at all. "Remember, this plane was designed as a military pilot trainer," he laughed after I reported a giant bounce.

"So?" I didn't see his point.

"Hell, when Navy student pilots flew this plane, I'm sure the landing gear got pounded a lot harder than that!" he laughed harder.

Between zigging right to miss cars and zagging left for mailboxes, Dad was on his toes all the time. On top of that, we also had to make a few hard turns here and there. Again, I faced backwards and reported exactly how much room he had in each turn as the fuselage got close to the Suburban's doorframe. A few times Dad had to let the Suburban go wide and drive through the grass across the highway. In the end, it all worked out. After ninety miles of flying backwards, the SNJ was safely in our driveway.

The SNJ-7 Dad purchased from Dean Ortner in 1968. Ortner enjoyed seeing our Jed Clampett method of attaching the SNJ tailwheel to the floor of the Suburban. Top center of photograph shows salvage-yard corrugated steel pitching a tin roof over the folded wings of Corsair Zero Zero.

Author Note Concerning Aircraft Manufacturers:
This is a good place to mention North American Aviation (NAA). NAA was a leading aircraft manufacturer for many years, and designed and built many of the aircraft in this story. These include both the XP-82 and F-82E Twin Mustangs, the P-51 Mustang, a T-28, both B-25s, the SNJ-7 in the above photograph, and all versions of the F-86 Sabre.

Other aircraft manufacturer information can be referenced in the Aircraft Make and Model Index.

21

Carrying a Load
Not Measured in Pounds

By the late 1960s, many things were changing at home, including two of my older sisters growing up and moving away. I felt a powerful sense of emptiness when they left, and Dad's shadow loomed larger with them gone. Their departure and others that would follow led to some growing questions about the direction life at home would take as our parents inched closer to becoming empty nesters. If Dad's past history suggested anything about what the future would *look* like, his passion for collecting would play a big role. And if there was ever any doubt about Dad's obsession with airplanes, an experience at church one evening helped confirm his obsession was total.

The same priest, Father James Moran, whom Dad had earlier feared asking the question about working on Sunday, remained our pastor during all of our school years. While no doubt a good priest, he could be very harsh like an Army drill sergeant. In fact, he'd been awarded the Silver Star for bravery in combat during World War II in the Pacific as a *chaplain*. Certainly an unusual military award for a priest. Dad was terrified of Father Moran. As young kids, we were often more afraid of Father Moran than the Wizard of Oz.

We were late for Mass one evening on a holy day during the week. For large crowds, the church had an extra room behind the altar, which doubled as a classroom for the school. As a family we often sat on metal folding chairs in this room, but it was already packed. Mom and my sisters got seats, but Dad and I stood at the open doorway with other men and boys. From the doorway, a long flight of iron stairs went down to the parking lot.

Father Mark was saying Mass when a plane flew overhead. Dad leaned out the doorway, and like an air defense radar antenna, he kept his eyes locked on the plane as it slowly tracked across the sky. "Twin Beech," he said softly. Suddenly, I saw Father Moran heading up the stairs. Dad was so fixated on the plane, he was oblivious to Father Moran hurrying up the stairs toward us. I wanted to alert Dad, but Father Moran already had eyes of rage locked on Dad. I should be awarded an Oscar for then acting my attentive altar boy look.

Dad jumped as he felt his arm being grabbed tight by the priest, who was also said to have been a collegiate championship boxer before he was ordained. I turned to watch just in time to see Dad's eyes erupt with terror as he realized who had grabbed him. Father Moran kept a death grip on Dad's arm and yanked him down the iron stairs with their feet thumping and scuffling on the iron. I didn't know what to do. Father Moran then looked up and motioned for me to come. I mowed grass and did other fix-it guy chores at the church and school, so I'd been on mostly good terms with the priest. Still, I was anxious. Finally, at the bottom of the stairs, Father Moran tore into Dad and gave him a flaming butt chewing I'm sure he never forgot.

Dad was then angry at me for not alerting him that Father Moran was approaching. I let the criticism roll off me. It was simply hilarious to see Dad's obsession with airplanes be so complete that he could not make it through Mass without being distracted by an airplane and getting nailed for it by Father Moran. Even Mom, his ever loyal and devoted wife, could not stop snickering for days.

As I became old enough to drive, I became obsessed with the independence of getting some wheels. I took driver's ed in the summer of '69 and was paired with—Mom. We had an absolutely wonderful time learning to drive together, and both passed our driving tests on the first go. Needing a car, Mom and I found a fifty-dollar '62 Ford Falcon. The car body and interior were in great shape, but its engine was missing a number of parts at the car dealership where it was stranded. The dealer wanted it off the lot, so if I could get it running, it was ours for the low price. We had a rusted-out '61 Falcon on the property that had all the parts I needed to get the '62 Falcon running. With my years of experience fixing Dad's Suburban, boom tractor, and other engines, I had our Falcon running in a few hours with the parts I salvaged.

As I began to travel a road of my own, I figured the end was near for my airplane-hauling trips with Dad. Interest in the old planes was continuing to grow, as were prices. Throughout the country the last of the relics were being snapped up. Many were restored for flight, while others were placed in museums. But just when I thought Dad would finally give up the hunt, he'd find another plane. Still, the condition of each plane suggested we were scraping the bottom of the barrel.

In the spring of 1969, we hauled home a Douglas A-26 Invader that Dad bought on a lead from Earl Reinert. The plane was flying just a few months before Dad got it, so the good news was that it wasn't all weathered and corroded. The bad news was that it slid off the end of the runway at Chicago's Meigs Field and plunged into Lake Michigan. By the time Dad bought the plane, it was in bad shape. In the accident, the plane suffered significant damage. The nose of the bomber was smashed, as was a section of the tail and one wingtip. Like a lot of Douglas A-26s, this old bomber had undergone an On Mark conversion to be used as a corporate plane to fly executives around. Until the Learjet ignited the corporate jet boom, many On Mark A-26s earned their keep as VIP planes. As a result, the parts on the A-26 were of high value, and by the time Dad got the plane, it was a shell that was missing its engines, landing gear, instruments, and just about everything of value.

A few months after getting the gutted A-26 home, we towed home two more aircraft that were stripped even worse. Both, however, were quite rare. From an aviation mechanic school in Columbus, we got a Fleetwing BT-12 trainer and a Curtiss O-52 Owl observation plane. Of all the planes I'd seen by now, the BT-12 had to be the strangest. Its shape resembled that of our BT-13 and BT-15 trainers, but the way it was built was totally different. Unique in its construction, it was made from strips of stainless steel that were spot-welded together. The nice thing about it was that there was no corrosion despite years of being in the weather. However, inside the cockpit, numerous sharp edges from the stainless steel structure looked ready to cut and injure the pilot

Very rare stainless steel Fleetwings BT-12 we got from an aviation mechanic school in Columbus, Ohio, in 1969 (courtesy Jason McKeon).

Fuselage of rare Curtiss O-52 Owl we purchased from the same aviation mechanic school that sold us the BT-12. Lower right is front of '61 Ford Falcon from which I salvaged parts to get a '62 Falcon running so Mom and I could have a car (courtesy Jason McKeon).

if any kind of accident happened. Dad and I speculated this may have been the reason very few were built.

The O-52 Owl was built with a conventional aluminum structure and had a high wing held in place by wing struts. Even in good condition, I couldn't see this as an appealing airplane to anyone. There just wasn't anything exciting about it. Its only value now was limited to the fact that it was rare. Like the BT-12, the Owl was very outdated. For that reason, the FAA asked the aviation mechanic school to get rid of the two aircraft, since they weren't good examples for students to work on. For a few hundred dollars, Dad got both aircraft.

Continuing his airplane hunt, in 1970 Dad found a very rare experimental XBD-2D Dauntless II. The plane was for sale at a scrap yard in the Philadelphia suburb of Fairless Hills. As a propeller-driven surface attack plane, it was large and bulky compared to fighters like the Corsair. Still, it was a very versatile plane with missions that varied from search and rescue, to hunting submarines, to carrying huge loads of bombs, rockets and other weapons in support of troops on the ground. Built after World War II, the Dauntless II was later renamed the AD Skyraider, and saw action in Korea and Vietnam, serving with the Navy, Air Force, and Marines.

It was about 400 miles to Fairless Hills, which meant there was almost no way to make a hauling trip involving aircraft disassembly within a normal weekend. By now, Dad knew better than to ask me to cut school to haul a plane home. In his own way, he accommodated me. We hauled the Skyraider during spring break of my junior year. There was a Sadie Hawkins dance at school that coincided with our trip. I had hoped at least one of the few girls I knew well would ask me to go, but no luck there. As Dad and I went on our first trip to get the Skyraider, I was struck by how much had changed from our early days on the road. Physically, I was about finished growing and could do virtually any task he could do. On the road he even put me behind the wheel for astronaut duty driving the old Suburban for a hundred miles or so. Clearly, I wasn't his little boy anymore.

We took the time to catch up on what was happening, share our outlook on life, and more importantly, discuss the future. With a little more than a year to go until graduation, I wasn't sure what I was going to do after high school. And it gave me a chill to realize Dad had very little advice to offer, except what not to be. "Whatever you do, don't be a carpenter," Dad laughed. "You freeze to death in the winter, half the companies go broke, and it's hard, hard work."

Not a problem on the carpenter thing, I assured him. I sort of knew what I wanted to do, but it seemed so far out of reach that it was a crazy pipe dream. I wanted to be a military pilot or an airline pilot. The latter was kind of academic as I saw no way to get enough flying time for the airlines without flying for the military first. And to be a military pilot, you had to be an officer, which required you to have a bachelor's degree. Dad, however, scoffed at the idea that military pilots had to be college graduates. "What do pilots need to go to college for?" he expressed contempt at the idea.

"I didn't make the rules, that's just how it is," I answered.

"Well, it's stupid. Everybody's got to go to college now," he growled. With the Vietnam War protests and hippie movement, Dad viewed college campuses as unpatriotic hotbeds of dope-smoking brainwashed commies. "And they spend their parents' hard-earned money going to college and doing all that crap," Dad said, indignant. Even though the college campus antiwar movement was aimed at the war in Vietnam, the movement at times seemed broader than that. While many men of Dad's age were extremely proud of their contribution to the victorious outcome of World War II, many youths displayed a "so what" attitude about it. As a result, Dad saw the anti-war movement as a slap in the face to his generation that had fought World War II. "I suppose they would have wanted us to let Hitler take over the world," Dad continued to vent. "These college kids don't appreciate all the people who died for their freedom!"

Coincidental with the growing antiwar movement, the term "warbirds" continued to gain popularity in the aviation community as a collective reference to the surviving World War II airplanes. That made Dad worry. He wished aviation people would avoid using that term until the Vietnam War was over. "Next thing you know, I'll have hippies protesting in the driveway and splattering blood on my airplanes," he said, truly worried.

I had my doubts that anything like that could really happen, but then again, times were hot. Only thirty miles from our home, the deadly shooting at a Kent State war protest was barely a month into the future. The first time some hippies came by to look at the planes, we got a little edgy. Dad wasn't sure what to do for a few moments, but then he fell into his routine and showed them around just like he did everyone else. Other than comments like "cool" and "far out," nothing was much different. Like everybody else, they and the other hippies who followed seemed to enjoy the tour. Later, one hippie even complimented Dad, saying something about him "expanding the definition of individual freedom." That we could agree on.

The Vietnam War had our country deeply divided then, somewhat similar to what we are seeing in current times. In contrast to the hippies touring our collection, the World War II veterans visiting us seemed mostly to be flag-waving conservatives. Despite the wide gap between the views of these two groups, I sensed their take-away view of my father was surprisingly similar.

It was as if they recognized there was an only-in-America symbolism to the efforts Walter A. Soplata unwittingly put his stamp on. He fully embraced the patriotic ideal that America stood for freedom and believed his efforts to save historic warbirds represented his personal commitment to honoring that. Deeply as that became etched in his DNA, I doubt he ever realized how the highly unusual manner of his efforts reflected his push to expand the envelope of individual freedom. And not unlike aviation pioneers discovering there were dangers in pushing the flight envelope of speed, expanding the envelope of individual freedom did not come without risks. Having the freedom to do whatever the heck you want can be a double-edged sword.

As for the hippies visiting us, if there was any link between the Vietnam antiwar movement and our airplane symbols of World War II, we never saw it. With some exposure, we all mellowed about the hippie crowd. Some of them even offered us a *joint*. "No, thank you, we don't smoke," was the standard response. Still, hippies or not, the war protesters made Dad's blood boil. Like probably all Americans, he was also sick and tired of the war by now. But he didn't see protests as the answer. He believed they were actually encouraging the North Vietnamese to keep fighting, which was making the war last longer. As applied to my future, Dad said it simply: "If that's what they're teaching at college, I'll be damned if I'm going to pay one dime for any of you to go to college!" To me it seemed like the ultimate irony. I was thinking of going to college exactly because I wanted to be a military pilot. But due to Dad's opinion about war protesters on campus, there was no way he'd even consider helping me financially.

After Dad's soliloquy solving all the world's problems, we finally got to Fairless

Hills, Pennsylvania. We arrived at yet another scrap yard, where the heaps of rusty steel, dilapidated trucks roaming the yard, and a cluttered, run-down office were all familiar backdrops. The scrap yard manager was expecting us since Dad had prearranged his purchase by phone and through the mail. A friendly man, he soon had us out of the office and on our way to check the plane out.

The Skyraider was in fair condition. The cockpit was badly stripped, and the plane was missing many parts, including its canopy, some lower engine cowlings and its outboard wings. Since Dad's collection of miscellaneous airplane wings still included a set of AD-5 Skyraider outboard wings, this is the plane those extra wings ended up on. The Skyraider's airframe had a lot of corrosion, but all things considered, this plane was a good find. The price was $400.

We hauled a wrecked AD-5 Skyraider home years earlier. It was a massive single-engine plane, and we worked like dogs cutting its heavy and muscular wing spars with hacksaws in order to fit the plane down the highway. Dad and I were determined not to cut the wing on this Skyraider. Instead, we wanted to dismantle and separate the wing from the fuselage. But the more we examined the plane, the more we realized this would be a nightmare project requiring far more man-hours than we had available. Wherever you looked, the wing and fuselage were fastened together with endless rows of rivets holding many pieces of structure together. We also realized there was a lot of internal structure we could not even see.

The only other option was to separate the rear fuselage somewhere near the back of the wing. We looked closely at the fuselage trying to find a seam, with no success. It appeared we were going to have to cut this airplane instead of unbolting it. Still, Dad had a hunch. After removing some access panels, he crawled into the tail section and was delighted by what he found. Structurally, the fuselage had four big longerons that formed a large frame within the aluminum skin body, much like the B-25. All four longerons were bolted together just aft of the single-seat cockpit. "Great, all we have to do is cut the skin and unbolt the longerons. Putting it back together will be a snap," Dad explained, feeling very relieved.

With that, we got busy. Dad's overall plan was to take the airplane completely apart and haul the thing home in three trips. By getting it all apart now, he wouldn't need me for the last two trips. As we got going with the disassembly, I got concerned. I thought I'd seen corrosion before, but this plane took it to a new level. Screws and bolts that normally should be easy to remove were near impossible due to the rust. Of course, the plane was chock full of those nasty Phillips screws I'd come to hate so much. Some of them were so bad that Dad and I learned to work as a team. We'd start by applying a lot of oil to the screws. Then, to keep the screws from chewing out, Dad would push the screwdriver in as hard as he could. With a pair of pliers gripping the screwdriver handle, I would do the turning. It was slow and tedious as ever, but as the day wore on, we made progress.

The salvage yard manager let us stay until about 5 o'clock, and then we had to go. Dad and I figured we had about a half day's work left, so we were pretty satisfied with our progress. We checked into a motel, and after getting cleaned up, we went to dinner. Not interested in any more driving, we found a nearby place to eat that turned out to be more of a beer joint than a restaurant. Dad had his doubts for a few moments, but after seeing they had some meat and potatoes on the menu, he decided to stay.

It was our first time together sitting at a beer joint on barstools. I looked the dim, smoky place over. About fifteen people were there, and most of the patrons were men who appeared to be about the same age as my father. Likewise, they appeared to be blue-collar folks, except they were a rougher steel-worker crowd that would feel right at home lighting a cigarette with a cutting torch. A few were playing pool, some were watching TV, and others were just there perched on their barstool. "Well, you're big enough now I don't think I'll get in trouble bringing you here," Dad said as we sat on our barstools after ordering our food.

"Does that mean I can try a beer?" I asked Dad as I grinned.

"A beer? Forget that. Your mother would kill me," Dad laughed lightly. Then his expression changed slowly and he looked troubled. Badly troubled. I didn't get it. I had no idea what was happening, but I should have known. The bar was talking to him.

"My real father, my stepfather Charlie, and your mother's father—this is where they lived. Every one of them—a goddamn drunk. The only time I've been in a place like this was dragging Charlie out at 3 a.m.," he said in a low sad voice. "Time after time, my mother sent me to the beer joint to drag Charlie home. So drunk he couldn't walk. You kids think I haven't spent time with you? How'd you like me to spend all my time at a place like this, and then come home as a raging drunk? That's what I had for a family." He didn't really say anything I hadn't heard before, but the way he said it was different. His tone was inviting, and he wasn't talking down to me like I was a kid. It was like I was an adult who was now his confidant.

Then he continued, "The last time I saw my own father, I was eight years old. He was drunk and got in a big fight with my mother. I was in front of the house when he came storming out. On his way to the car, he picked me up in the air and then threw me. I hit the cement sidewalk so hard I thought my bones were broken. Then the mean bastard left and never came back. You think I miss that goddamn son of a bitch—hell, no!"

We sat quietly on our barstools, and as I looked over at Dad, I again saw that wounded expression in his deep, shadowy eyes. Over the years I had never quite figured out just what was the haunting knock on the door that hid behind those eyes. Now, I felt like I knew. As he rubbed his callused workingman hands over his weathered and leathery face, the man who never shed a tear looked like he was moments from a giant flood.

I felt really bad. I thought back to all the times Dad went on a tirade about how tough he had it as a kid, and how I had dismissed it all. His past was something I hadn't cared about. But his future, or more honestly and selfishly, *my future*, was the only thing I'd been concerned with. I realized now that I should have been more sympathetic about the hardships in his past. At the same time, the way Dad presented those stories, it was difficult to do that.

On most occasions when he talked about his childhood, it was usually a sharp, bitter recollection about how hard he had it "back when I was your age." Word for word, the rant was repeated over and over. I grew tired of it fast, especially the part where Dad expressed resentment because "you kids have it so good." Considering how hard he worked me during my childhood, he didn't get a lot of sympathy from me.

Now, perched on my barstool next to him, I sensed a different issue was the real problem. It wasn't the child labor he did, or the money and possessions he didn't have, or the playing he missed out on, that really mattered. Even though those were the things he usually talked about, it wasn't entirely about those things. Instead, I sensed it was the decades-old pain of a young boy being rejected, abused and abandoned by his own

21. Carrying a Load Not Measured in Pounds

father. Among the things that haunted him and made him bitter, I came to believe that was tops.

I thought back to when I was eight. That was when he brought the Cutlass home in the bus. He'd been gone for that week, and it was the only time in my life that he wasn't home at night. The loneliness the six of us felt that week was something I never wanted repeated. And now, when I tried to imagine his father leaving for keeps at the same age, I couldn't begin to imagine the lingering and terrible pain that experience left him with.

Early the next day we were back at work. I made sure not to whine or complain about anything. I now had a renewed sense that maybe I was lucky to be where I was. We worked hard throughout the morning, and by noon were done removing the engine, the rear fuselage, and tail surfaces from the plane. What I appreciated at this point was that the salvage yard had a crane they sent an operator with to load us. Having winched so many loads onto the trailer, I *loved* cranes. With a trailer load that included the engine, propeller, flaps, and tail surfaces, we headed home.

X-Prototype Dauntless II (XBT2D-1), later renamed AD Skyraider, that Dad and I hauled from a Fairless Hills, Pennsylvania, scrapyard (courtesy Jason McKeon).

Fortunately, the load handled well, and the Suburban could manage the hills on the Pennsylvania Turnpike. Still, Dad did all the driving home. Even though I was now legal to drive the Suburban, plus had years of underage experience, none of that counted for Dad's astronaut requirement to tow an airplane load of stuff on the highway. In bringing the plane home, all three trips went fine without a problem. Despite the shape it was in, Dad was now the proud owner of an X-prototype Skyraider.

22

A Hollywood Part

The studio 20th Century–Fox had recently finished filming the movie *Tora! Tora! Tora!*, about the Japanese attack on Pearl Harbor. For publicity, four of the planes were sent on a nationwide tour, including a stop at the Cleveland Airshow. Since there were no flyable Japanese aircraft to film *Tora! Tora! Tora!* with, the studio commissioned a California aircraft shop to modify thirty-one American-built AT-6s and BT-13s to look like Japanese aircraft. One of these planes had a landing gear problem while landing at Cleveland, so there was a call on the PA system asking if anyone knew where they could find BT-13 landing gear parts. I had been separated from Dad for about an hour when I went to the announcer's stand to tell them I knew where parts could be found.

I was barely 17 when the BT-13 pilot who came to escort me to the stricken plane gave me some very doubting looks. I quickly went on a verbal burst of details about Dad's airplane collection. I clearly startled the man, but I had his attention. In a huddle around the disabled landing gear with him and several other men, I confirmed my father had the parts they needed. Realizing what I had just done, I knew Dad would rightly take my head off for volunteering *his* airplane parts. But that could wait—I had a backstage pass. I told the men I would find my father, but in the meantime, I wanted to see the nearby Corsair on the airshow line. I convinced them I knew the owner, and they allowed me about ten minutes to go see the Corsair.

As I closed in on the Corsair, I was torn. Dad didn't trust the Marines Corps' story about wanting to trade Corsairs. He figured they would suddenly come up with some red tape regulation to trick him out of Zero Zero. Instead, it was Dean Ortner who traded Corsairs with the Marines, and the flying F4U-7 Corsair the Marines had once offered to my father was now right before me. I was alone for a few minutes walking in the grass around the Corsair that could have been ours. The original military paint on the Corsair was a bit rough and worn, but otherwise the Corsair looked to be in perfect condition.

I was mesmerized. My eyes glistened at the sight of its perfectly clear canopy and windshield contrasting with our Corsair's chalky white, hazy and cracked canopy. Likewise, this Corsair's clean cockpit and inviting instrument panel were electrifying as viewed from the tail. Even seeing the right kind of dirt excited me, as it told of a recent flight. At home all I had was my imagination. But here, I wasn't imagining a thing. Fresh thin streaks of oil left a swirling path under the engine that flowed magically along the contours under the wings and fuselage. The oil streaks meant cleanup rags to some people, but to me they were the fine-lined artistry painted by the roaring wind of Corsair flight. Likewise, there was fresh exhaust soot just above the wing on both sides of the

I'm holding Dad's thermos as I stand near one of the *Tora! Tora! Tora!* planes at the 1970 Cleveland Airshow. I later got myself in big trouble volunteering an airplane part of Dad's to fix one of their other planes.

fuselage. I felt lost in my wide-eyed wonder, but so be it. I was standing next to one of the few remaining Corsairs then that could, that did, *that dared* to reach the sky! "How do you like it, Wally?" a familiar voice startled me. I turned around and there was Dean Ortner.

"Hi, Mr. Ortner, you sure have a nice Corsair," I answered. "You don't mind if I look, do you?"

"Look all you want, but you can't haul this one home!" he laughed. "Unless maybe your father would like to work a deal on that racing Corsair?" He was happy and sweet, telling me briefly about the trade with the Marines and pointing out a few details about the Corsair while telling of the new paint job he was going to get done soon. He asked if Dad had made any progress restoring the SNJ for flight. I wanted to say anything but the truth. We had used paintbrushes to give the SNJ a blue, red and yellow civilian paint scheme with cans of hardware store paint. Beyond that, the painful truth was the SNJ would sit in the same area of our yard for the next fifty years. Cleaning oil streaks or exhaust soot off it wasn't anything we'd have to worry about. Dad did run the engine a few times, so I answered Ortner's question with that. "Well, if your father ever does get it ready to fly, tell him to let me know. I'll be glad to check him out to fly it."

"Thanks, Mr. Ortner, I'll tell him. You know, much as I've been around our Corsairs, I've never watched one fly. So I'm really looking forward to seeing you fly it today!"

"Well, great. I'll make sure I put on a good show for you and your father," he smiled. Ortner and I shook hands and parted, and then I returned to where the Tora-Tora pilot was. Soon the pilot escorted me toward a security guard controlling an opening in the fence. As we made our way we agreed on a location to meet at when the airshow was finished. As we neared the security guard, I spotted Dad with the airshow crowd. He looked puzzled and disturbed, wondering what the heck his son was doing with an airshow pilot on the flight line side of the fence. In a moment my clandestine backstage visit was over.

I could see the fire erupt in Dad's eyes as he found out what I'd been up to. "I can't believe you went to these guys and told them I have airplane parts!" he screamed, furious as ever. "You know I don't sell parts and you had no business telling anybody we had BT parts and now they'll never leave me alone!" he continued, enraged. I explained hearing the PA announcement asking for help finding BT parts, thinking he'd missed it.

"I heard the announcement, too," Dad acknowledged. "But it's not my problem that they flew these old planes all the way here from California. If they want to fly them all over the country like that, and something breaks, it's their problem, not mine!" he said, still red hot. Going into orbit was a recent space-race addition to the American vernacular when describing someone with a hot temper. But a good trait Dad had was he would often come back down to Earth and calm down almost as quickly as he went up. In this case his rage was totally justified by my teenage lack of judgment. We walked around silently for about ten minutes, then he asked me, "Did you get a good look at Dean Ortner's Corsair?"

"Better than that, I got to see him and he was really friendly," I answered with a big smile.

"To think we could have had a beauty of a Corsair like that—I guess I blew it," Dad said. We stood quietly for a while. It seemed Dad was pondering how the Corsair had slipped between his fingers. "I'd never be qualified to fly it anyway. So if it wasn't mine to have, I'm glad to see Dean be the one to get it," Dad said with a nice smile. The F4U-7 was a fork in the road for Dad. He realized that now, and so did I.

About 30 minutes before his scheduled performance, we watched Dean Ortner come out and preflight the Corsair. Now I just couldn't wait. Before long, he put on a parachute and climbed in the cockpit.

"Don't tell me he'd jump out of that thing!" Dad said, laughing lightly.

"If he has to bail out, he has to," I replied, matching Dad's laugh.

"Well, if he does parachute out, there will be *no question* that both of my Corsairs will be in better shape than his!" Dad laughed hard.

Finally, the four long and slender blades of the Corsair's propeller slowly began to turn. The scene reminded me of Dad's fake home movie, but nothing fake here. After several turns of the giant prop, a few cylinders fired and big wicked fingers of light blue smoke curled their way behind the engine and around the cockpit. The prop kept turning, and after a series of pops and burps, Ortner brought the powerful engine to life. As the swift air from the propeller quickly cleared the smoke, the scene gave me chills. Every time I played in Dad's lifeless Corsairs, I wondered what it would be like to do what was happening before me. Now, I stood behind a Corsair full of vigor. Even with the throttle back as Ortner waited for the oil temperature to rise, the engine made a galloping thunder. As the huge four-blade prop spun around, it seemed ten times bigger than when it was still. As a sign of its power, the thick green grass behind the Corsair flailed wildly, like a hurricane had come to shore.

Knowing Dean Ortner was at the controls really gave me a good feeling. I had not seen him fly since he recovered from his broken back. Now seeing him back in the saddle was a comforting reassurance. Before long, he was roaring down the runway and pulling the gear up. Spellbound, I kept my focus on the Corsair for the entire performance. I thought the plane looked cool on the ground, but that didn't compare to seeing it in flight. As expected, the Corsair was powerful, noisy, and fast. More than ever, I was impressed. And as I watched each pass and maneuver, I couldn't help wondering what could have been.

The last part of the airshow was a small-scale reenactment of the attack on Pearl Harbor with the *Tora! Tora! Tora!* planes. The plane with the bad landing gear was unable to fly, but the group still had the other three movie planes to fly. They took off in formation and soon were flying low just above Lake Erie to make their pretend Pearl Harbor attack. Though they didn't drop any bombs, a series of explosives prearranged on the ground went off, making loud booms and giant clouds of thick black smoke. While the explosions weren't exactly enough to make John Wayne dive behind sandbags, it was still an impressive show.

Dad enjoyed the show so much we ended up meeting with the *Tora! Tora! Tora!* pilots after the show to discuss the part they needed. While in Cleveland, the pilots had heard about Dad's airplane collection from some locals. A group of them got together and decided it was something they had to see. Dad smiled while telling them, "We're always open," but explained our location was very hard to find. One of the men then suggested I ride with them.

"You don't mind riding with a bunch of Hollywood pilots who shot the movie, do you?" Dad asked jokingly with an approving smile. I quickly agreed, and before long I was riding home with a carload of strangers. I don't remember what type of car we were in, but it was big and nice—very nice! Typical of the big luxury cars Detroit made

After the 1970 Cleveland Airshow, a sparse crowd gets their chance to see Dean Ortner's F4U-7 Corsair up close.

in 1970, a car like that almost qualified to be a yacht, and I enjoyed the splendor. As we headed home, the men talked about some golf a few managed to get in. That amused me. Dad didn't like sports in general, and men playing golf in particular. Their pilot golf secret was safe with me.

Before long, the men started asking me questions about the collection. After I mentioned the two Corsairs, F-82 Twin Mustang, two B-25s, the F7U Cutlass and other planes, I started getting questions about Dad, as well as our property. They rightly expected Dad was a commercial pilot or airplane mechanic, so my carpenter answer raised some eyebrows. When they asked what airport we were at, my answer left everyone puzzled. "We aren't at or near an airport. Dad keeps the planes in the yard by our house," I answered.

"In your yard?" a man riding up front turned to look at me. I was getting a little uncomfortable. I may as well have started singing "Old Soplata had a farm, E-I-E-I-O, with a Corsair here, and a BT there, here a jet, there a prop, everywhere a prop prop, old Soplata had a farm, E-I-E-I-O." Luckily we soon got on the topic of Corsair 74 and its giant R-4360 engine. I got questions about that and responded with a flurry of details, explaining the very different motor mount, engine, and supercharger configurations of our two Corsairs that made the F2G Corsair the perfect airframe to hang the big engine on. There was an eerie silence for a few moments. Then the man up front who'd been turned my way gave me a smile. "How old are you?" he asked with a kindly smile.

"I just turned 17," I answered.

"Well, there's not a teenager anywhere who could make all that up! I can't wait to see this place!" He erupted laughing, as did the other pilots. The nearly hour-long drive eventually turned into the adult version of "are we there yet?" Finally, a familiar cloud of dust formed around the car as we joined the gravel road that zigzagged the last half-mile. The men exchanged looks as tall overhanging brush occasionally encroached upon the road, suggesting we were maybe heading for a scene in *Deliverance* yet to be filmed instead of an airplane collection.

As we reached the top of the hill, suddenly we could see the SNJ and an F-86 in the yard. Soon, partial silhouettes of many more airplanes appeared through the scattered trees. The reaction was instant. Everyone was perched up in their seats and full of smiles. We pulled into the driveway and everybody scrambled out. Almost like kids arriving at an amusement park, these middle-aged men were ready to run and check the place out. Dad was still gone, no doubt staying at the airshow grounds being among the last to leave. With the pilots in tow, I started to head out to the field when Mom came out of the house with several of my sisters. A few of the men looked surprised as my family came out. "Amazing, your family lives right here in the middle of this," one man said.

"Home, sweet home," I smiled. Despite the initial enthusiasm of the pilots, I had my doubts they'd be very impressed when they saw up close that these were a bunch of old planes that had seen better days. I was relieved to see they were incredibly fascinated by the planes despite their condition. What they appreciated most was how rare some of Dad's aircraft were. Even as much as they had been around, some hadn't ever seen aircraft like the Twin Mustang, F2G Corsair, or F7U Cutlass. Of course, I explained how if not for our efforts, they all would have been scrapped.

About a half hour after our arrival, I saw Dad pull into the driveway. One by one the pilots shook his hand, thanking him repeatedly for single-handedly saving so many rare

TWENTIETH CENTURY-FOX FILM CORPORATION
P. O. BOX 900, BEVERLY HILLS, CALIFORNIA 90213
PHONE: (213) 277-2211 CABLE ADDRESS: CENTFOX, LOS ANGELES · TELEX: 6-74875

September 15, 1970

Mr. Walter Soplata
P. O. Box 65
Newbury, Ohio 44065

Dear Mr. Soplata:

On behalf of Twentieth Century-Fox Film Corporation and the pilots of the "Tora, Tora, Tora" aircraft, we wish to thank you for your assistance and the donation of such a vital part to the damaged "Tora, Tora, Tora" aircraft at the Cleveland Air Show on September 6. It would have been impossible for our aircraft to continue its exhibition without your help. Once again, many many thanks for your cooperation.

I am enclosing a photograph of our aircraft over Honolulu.

Very truly yours,

FRANK E. BROWN
Head, Property Department

FEB/mlh
Enclosure

Thank-you letter Dad got from 20th Century–Fox for donating a part to keep one of the *Tora! Tora! Tora!* planes flying.

planes. They were very gracious and kind toward Dad, and simply seemed overwhelmed by what he had accomplished with the collection. Then Dad asked if they had any leads on locating a new part for the BT landing gear. They shook their heads. Dad grabbed his tool box and led the group to his BT-15. He unbolted the part from his plane and simply gave it to them. "We don't want to take the shirt off your back," one of the pilots said. Everyone was deeply moved. Dad explained that this was the fastest way to get the group back on their way.

"This gal isn't flying anywhere. We have lots of time to dig out a spare part to put

A year later, Dad took this shot of Dean Ortner's F4U-7 Corsair long after the crowd left the 1971 Cleveland Airshow. I wonder what he was then thinking about this Corsair that he refused to trade for with the Marines.

back on her," Dad smiled. About a week later, we got a large envelope in the mail from 20th Century–Fox. A warm thank-you letter was enclosed along with some large photographs of *Tora! Tora! Tora!* movie scenes. We were delighted by the letter and the pictures. Dad was totally thrilled by the movie, and knowing a small airplane part of his got one of the birds flying gave him some sweet satisfaction.

23

As Is, Where Is—
The Fate of the Hunted

(With sincere apologies to Ernest K. Gann)

By the fall of 1970, there was no doubt in my mind that Dad was destined to remain on his go-it-alone path. For me, the same unanswered questions lingered. Did he have a plan, and what role would I play, if any? And if I had a role, would I simply be there to do physical labor, or would I have some say in the direction things went? My instincts at the time suggested he'd continue to call all the shots. As I began my senior year of high school, the clock was ticking for me to decide about my future. And beyond Dad's control, things were changing in the warbird community that signaled he would have to change course regardless of his wishes.

It was now so hard to find affordable warbird aircraft to haul home, I figured the time had come to park the trailer and start some restoration work on the planes he had. So many visitors kept asking about his future plans that I figured this would be a good place to start. "Since we're about done hauling, why don't we fix up the Corsairs, B-25s and some other planes?" I asked.

"What do you mean fix up?" Dad replied coldly. "Are you saying something's wrong with my airplanes?" He gave his stern look. I explained about finishing the wiring in the Franklin B-25, putting systems back together, and other projects he had mentioned himself. What I really wanted to discuss was painting, sheet metal work, repairing broken canopies, windows and other items in need of repair. He didn't want to hear it. "Nothing's wrong with my planes, and besides, I'm not done hauling yet."

"Hauling what? You keep saying the good planes are all gone now, or else they cost too much," I turned his own words on him.

"I don't know," he replied sharply. "There are still a few good planes out there somewhere, but I just have to look a lot harder. I did find the Skyraider, and who asked you anyway?"

"The Skyraider was okay, but what else?" I kept on.

"The A-26 is nice," he answered.

"Nice?" I rebutted. "Sure, it's not all corroded, but look how damaged it is and how much it's missing. It hasn't even got a landing gear to stand on," I countered as I visualized the wood pallets we used to support the poor naked plane. Unknown to Dad, this back-and-forth was about more than airplanes. This was about me trying to answer the questions about my future with him. I was also hinting that I was done hauling if planes like the gaunt shell of the A-26 were all that was left. And some new info recently convinced me it was time to change course. Dad missed a few purchases of derelict airplanes because the Confederate Air Force beat him there by a few weeks. So I made my pitch. "The little bit of stuff that's out there—it won't get scrapped. The Confederate Air Force will get the little that remains. Let them have it," I finished.

"And let them *crash* what they find!" Dad fired back. "Look at the planes they've lost in crashes! It's sickening." He had a point, I had to admit. He then conceded that he could never restore his planes all "spit and polish like those guys," but since none of his would ever be lost in a crash, that fully justified his way of doing things. "Nope, I don't plan to give in to those guys at all. If they find something, that's fine. But if it's in my neck of the woods and I find it first, it's mine!" he asserted.

He had me beat, up to this point, but I figured I had one last silver bullet. "Okay, but why collect more engines, electronics, and other stuff?" I asked next. I then complained how we had nowhere to put things and there were so many engines under airplane wings that people couldn't get a clear photo of the planes anymore. He argued back that many of his engines were rare and if that's what it took to shelter them from the weather, then that's what he'd do. His voice was irritated, yet he seemed curious with my nonstop interrogation. I could tell he was holding back his temper despite my continued nagging. That in itself was quite a moment.

"Okay, but then you have another problem," I said.

"What's that?" he asked sharply.

"You get so upset if someone calls this place a junkyard, but it's stuff like the BT-12 skeleton and all the engines lying around that makes them say that."

"So what?" Dad replied. "If some people call it junk, that means they don't appreciate what they're looking at." He elaborated that people who know airplanes don't mind what shape something like the rare BT-12 or the engines were in. They'd appreciate what they're seeing, he reasoned. I was dumbfounded and couldn't believe my ears. After all the growling Dad did when anyone dared say the forbidden J-word, now it was okay. I admit I was trying to push his button with the word junkyard. Still trying to pin him down, I was grasping now, trying to find another button to push.

"What about the neighbors?" I asked next.

"What about them?" he snapped.

"Well, you've always been worried about them complaining if the planes and the yard don't look good."

"Look, I was here before they even had a zoning board. People can say what they want, but nobody has the right to bother me about my stuff!" Dad's anger was at the tipping point. With that, I decided to quit before he exploded. I was actually surprised I got to question him this long and in this amount of detail. I hated to grill him like that, but I had waited long enough to ask questions I wanted answers to. I was double sad. He was heading down a path I knew I couldn't follow as I neared the threshold of my adult years. And I was sad because I saw that the end of our father-and-son team was near. I think he saw it too.

Looking back, our father-and-son relationship was a mixed bag of extremes. In his darkest moments, Dad could easily go on a tantrum, turning into a terse, profanity-screaming tyrant who used cutting and vulgar insults to put me and others down in order to elevate himself. And just when I didn't need any fuel on that fire, Father Moran preached a number of sermons in which he insisted fathers be tough on their sons in order that they be raised to become strong men. Maybe that guy in disguise at church one day was Johnny Cash taking notes for the tough dad song "A Boy Named Sue," which became one of his biggest hits.

But in addition to the role of tough-as-nails father he often played while raising me, he conversely beamed with tremendous pride at times such as turning me loose to drive the boom tractor at age 11. He soon started sneaking me on country roads driving the Suburban at age 12, and had me backing the Suburban and trailer on Air Force property at the same age. Despite his short temper and the occasional ability it taught me to know when I was walking on eggshells, there were countless good times when he took me gently under his wing on incredible adventures that other boys can't begin to imagine.

Following his example of adventure, I sometimes did things incredibly risky. One risky and stupid thing I once did should have gotten me in a lot of trouble. For some reason, we had to park extremely far away from the Burke Lakefront Airport to attend one of the Cleveland airshows. I was either 13 or 14, and the show took place on a hot sunny day. Mom was with us at this airshow, and I got the bright idea I was going to do something special. Dad always liked to hang around after each airshow was over and watch all the military planes like C-119 Boxcars, P2V Neptunes, S-2 Trackers and others start their smoke-belching radial engines and fly away. By the time we would leave, most people were usually gone. About 30 minutes before they were ready to go, I told my parents I was going to walk to the Suburban. They gave me the okay.

Quickly, I hoofed it for the Suburban, which was parked about a mile away. For an odd reason, we long had a backup hotwire rigged for the Suburban's ignition. Also, since some of its door locks didn't work, I had this great idea I would get in and drive to the airport to pick them up and save them the long walk in the heat. This idea quickly turned into fear as I almost went the wrong way down a one-way Cleveland street. I was almost to the airport when they spotted me driving as they walked down the sidewalk. As I stopped in the middle of the street, the shock on both of their faces was like nothing I'd ever seen.

They quickly jumped in as I surrendered the driver's seat to Dad. Then I got what was decidedly the sweetest butt chewing of my life. Mom and Dad laughed like crazy almost to the point of tears, but then realized parental discipline was needed. They each took turns telling me nicely that I did a really dumb and bad thing, only then for both of them to erupt in laughter and giggles, again consumed by the amusement of what their son had just done. Of course, they each made me promise to never do this again, to which I easily agreed before all three of us resumed laughing. We didn't always stop for ice cream on the way home, but I'm pretty sure we did that time.

One crazy adventure Dad and I went on should have long told me he never would be the kind of man to get the right equipment needed to restore his airplanes. My earlier interrogation of him about fixing up the airplanes had been a waste of his time and mine. Among our many lack-of-equipment woes, we didn't have an air compressor. Between all the planes and vehicles, we had a lot of tires. Also, tires on airplanes like the B-25 were very large. We needed an air compressor badly. Instead of buying one, we did something else. In his parts collection, Dad found an aircrew oxygen bottle and rigged it to pump up his airplane tires. Soon we had the oxygen bottle in the Suburban and were pulling up to the air hose at the nearby Texaco gas station.

"See how high you can crank the pressure up," Dad instructed me as he pulled the gas station's air hose into the rear of the Suburban where the oxygen bottle was. I started turning the crank on the air pump control and was surprised it went as high as about 110 pounds. That made me a little nervous as no car or truck tire the pump was meant for would use nearly that much pressure. Anytime you used the air hose, a loud bell inside the service station went "ding, ding, ding," as the air flowed out the hose. The greater the air flow, the faster the dings. I'd heard that bell go fast filling up an empty car tire, but no tire made it go crazy like Dad's air bottle did with the meter set on 110 pounds. That bell was going "ding, ding, ding," so fast it sounded like it was going to ring itself off the cement-block wall. With the bell ringing like crazy, some curious men approached the Suburban. One of the men pointed at the meter setting of 110. That raised their eyebrows. Soon the men were peering in the Suburban windows, watching Dad as he leaned over the yellow oxygen bottle holding the air hose to it.

"Not gonna blow up, is it?" one of them asked.

"I hope not. I've never filled it up before," Dad answered. The men took off in a

Race Corsair 74's fabric rudder looking sketchy. I'm not sure who the guilty person was for this workmanship, but I was once asked what kind of mop I'd used to apply a paint job. Most of the hardware store navy blue paint we brushed on the Corsair looked good, but there was never a chance we'd start a warbird restoration shop (courtesy Jason McKeon).

Salvage-yard corrugated sheet metal gives Corsair 74 some shelter from the weather in the 1980s and beyond.

hurry. Unaware they'd split, he continued saying, "It's supposed to be rated at 450 pounds, so I think…"

"They're gone!" I interrupted.

Dad laughed hard. "Well, it does kind of look like a bomb," he said while holding the air hose to the bottle's fill fitting. Then he got serious, suggesting maybe the oxygen bottle got junked because a crack had been found. Now Dad had me feeling nervous. Finally, the bottle had all the air the pump could give it. We then raced home with Dad driving like crazy. Since he didn't put any sealant on the threaded pipe fittings he rigged the bottle with, it was hissing and there was no time to waste. At home we hurriedly pumped up a tire or two until the bottle was spent. Then we raced back to the Texaco station four or five times to get more air. Silly story though this is, our trips to mooch off the local Texaco gas station air compressor clearly told that we were not destined to build an airplane restoration shop.

Given all the dangerous things we did with ratty equipment that we often modified or slapped together with what Dad could scavenge, my uncle Chuck in recent years remarked it was a miracle none of us got badly injured or killed. On many family visits in earlier years, he saw through his eyes as a structural engineer the often unconventional methods we used to haul and reassemble the planes. As his perspective suggests, we had some close calls. The worst of these happened in 1966 while the boom tractor was holding up the right engine and prop on the Franklin B-25. Dad crawled completely under the engine to move something. He got clear of the engine and took just a few steps when a steel rod broke on the end of the boom tractor cable. The thud of the 3,000-pound engine and prop hitting the soft soil shook the ground. Dad stood frozen as he looked

23. As Is, Where Is—The Fate of the Hunted

The SNJ we got from Dean Ortner likewise got a brushed-on paint job using hardware store paint. Not painted on this snowy day, of course, but a blue top, red middle and yellow bottom were nice colors picked by Dad. The plane needs a wash here, but mostly looked good. Its outboard wings were put in storage and never installed (courtesy Jason McKeon).

back at the scene. A man who would live to age 87 came within a few seconds of dying that day.

Another close call also involving this same B-25 happened when towing its left engine home. The right trailer tire let go as we were climbing a steep mountain road in Pennsylvania at night. The extra weight of the giant propeller riding on that side of the trailer not only finished off the old tire, but made jacking the trailer more difficult. As Dad held the Suburban's brakes on the steep hill, he also figured he'd need to be the one changing the tire. Now comes the crazy part. The Suburban's driver door was bolted shut.

The previous winter, Dad was backing the Suburban with the driver door open when the door snagged a heavy snowbank. The door got sprung so bad it couldn't be shut without using a lot of force. Rather than fix the badly sprung door, he eventually bolted it shut. Now, to get me on the brake pedal to free Dad for the tire change, he had to slide to the middle of the front seat as I waited in the rear seat to then climb into the front seat to get myself behind the wheel. Dad then slid his foot halfway off the brake pedal as I got my foot on the pedal so he could leave.

With a sister holding the flashlight while helping him dig in his packrat tool boxes for the one socket that fit the trailer lugs, I began to wonder how long my legs would last. Our Suburban, like many vehicles built in the '50s, lacked power brakes, and used drum instead of disc brakes. It took a lot of leg and foot pressure to hold it on the hill, and soon my legs were shaking. I tried to lighten up just a little, but the brakes creaked the moment I reduced my foot pressure.

"Don't let up or you'll kill us back here," Dad called out. "We're working as fast as we can." His tone was firm yet understanding. He knew I was wearing out. I began to worry—what if the brakes fail? The Suburban was nine years old, had over 200,000 miles on it and was worn out from doing the work of a big truck on ceaseless hauling trips. I thought about all the heavy-scale rust I'd seen on the hydraulic brake lines. I remembered once how a line burst when I barely moved it to get at some bolts while changing the differential. I looked down the steep drop-off by the side of the road. If the brakes failed, I'd sail off the side of the mountain into the darkness. With the driver's door bolted shut, my chance for escape would be slim. Also, if the brakes let go, the trailer would spill off its jack and likely injure both my father and sister before it and/or the Suburban would run backward over both of them.

We made it home fine despite all those worries, but got in so late there was no way to get to school on Monday morning. Mom and Dad decided to take us to school at lunchtime, figuring half a day was better than none. We got in the Suburban and were set to leave when it happened. Dad touched, I mean just *touched* the brake pedal—and it went to the floor! We got out and looked to see what was wrong. Underneath, we found that a rusted brake line had failed and squirted a puddle of brake fluid on the ground. Back then, cars and trucks didn't have independent front and rear brakes like they do today. If the brakes sprang a leak anywhere, you lost all the brakes.

I was stunned. Just last night I was standing on that pedal with both feet! I realized now that my fears were more than just imagined. Some would say it was sheer luck that

Me rope-tugging the TBM Avenger's left landing gear to retract the gear as the center wing is lowered to remove it from the fuselage in 1970. Dad and I would haul a few vagabond planes in 1971–72, but this TBM would be the last complete warbird we would haul together.

23. As Is, Where Is—The Fate of the Hunted

allowed us to make it to our driveway before the brakes failed. But you'll never convince me. Instead, I'll always be thankful and I'll always believe—God sent an angel to save us that night in 1966.

Despite the many risks we took hauling airplanes, and my growing doubts in 1969 that there were still affordable warbirds available, Dad proved me wrong and found a TBM Avenger torpedo plane. The model was originally designed and built by Grumman as a TBF Avenger, but as one of many examples in which automobile plants shifted to making airplanes for the war, it was General Motors who built the TBM Avenger.

The TBM Dad found was at a small grass airstrip in Rising Sun, Maryland, which is about halfway between Baltimore and Philadelphia. The plane was reported to be in fair condition, and except for missing its engine and propeller, the rest of the plane was complete. The price was $1,400. The TBM was the Navy's mainstay carrier-based torpedo plane in World War II. In many ways its single-engine profile made it resemble a fighter plane, but in reality it was too big and underpowered for that role. As a torpedo plane, though, it was quite effective. Of the many Navy pilots who flew TBMs in the war, one of them was future president George H.W. Bush.

With winter approaching, Dad planned to get the outboard wings and tail section

We put an unusual amount of effort into fixing up the TBM Avenger. It was originally missing its engine and prop, so Dad borrowed an engine from B-25 *Wild Cargo*, and had an FG-1A Corsair prop we installed. Our typical brush paint job using navy blue hardware store paint got the TBM looking pretty good. Its folding wings saved space on Navy aircraft carriers, and also helped on the Soplata property where space was getting crowded.

during the fall. He figured it was difficult enough pulling airplane loads over the Pennsylvania mountains during the summer, but he feared the ice and snow of winter. The owner agreed he could leave what remained of the TBM until after winter was over. Dad planned his first trip for the TBM to occur on a weekend in September and expected me to go. However, I had a cross-country meet to run that weekend known as the Kirtland Invitational. In a major test of wills, I told Dad I couldn't go due to the race. His reaction was exactly as I expected—he was furious.

Between school, my job, my car, and cross-country, he grew increasingly frustrated that I had other priorities besides his airplane collection. He insisted that missing one race wouldn't hurt anything, but I knew it was one of the most important ones of the season. Our cross-country team would in fact go undefeated this season, so this invitational race mattered a lot. I looked at Mom and could tell she had an idea. "I'll go," Mom said.

"Do what?" Dad replied, sounding surprised and caught totally off guard.

"You heard me. I'll go," Mom restated. She then suggested getting her mother to stay with me and my younger sister during the days they'd be gone. "I've handled a few wrenches, and I've got small hands—just right for getting at bolts in some of those tight spots," Mom grinned confidently. I was very curious how things would go with Mom taking my place on this and the other TBM trips that followed. I had my hunches. As I kind of expected, things boiled over a few times between them. Dad got frustrated and

F-86E Sabre Dad salvaged in 1969 after it had been partially burned for firefighting practice. This plane again told of Dad's orphaned airplane obsession. We crawled and kneeled in this gooey and oily mud-pie pond for many hours as we removed fifty or so wing bolts under the wing, plus more of the same bolts on top. The bolts were Allen heads recessed in aluminum channels that took many hours to remove. We were well prepared for a FEMA oil tanker disaster after all the time we worked in that oily pit.

23. As Is, Where Is—The Fate of the Hunted   175

Top: By our standards, this was a very nice F-86L Dad found in the late 1960s. It was missing its engine but otherwise was totally complete. It even came with a retractable rocket pod located immediately behind the nose landing gear. Dad and I joked about hoping there was some sort of safety to prevent pilots from shooting off their nose gear! *Bottom:* Sitting on high ground, the F-82E Twin Mustang looks down on the winter hibernation of Dad's two B-25s, F7U Cutlass, P-80 Shooting Star and other items in his collection (courtesy Jason McKeon).

angry that Mom didn't know tools and when he'd holler for her to go get a tool, she almost always came back with the wrong one. Privately, she told me about the fights, including when she told Dad *exactly where he could stick* his giant TBM! She and I really cracked up laughing over that.

To get Grandma Murray, I drove into Cleveland by myself. When I arrived all alone, she was shocked for a moment, but then happy and excited. "Driving in the city all by yourself! You kids have grown up so fast I just can't believe it—got my grandson as my personal chauffeur now!" Grandma Murray beamed proudly. Quickly, we were packed up and heading home. At that time in my life I enjoyed her company more than ever. We could talk openly about almost anything, which led her to give me some kindly advice now and then. My favorite among her pearls of wisdom was one that was quite funny. Seeing me now as a young man, she jokingly told me to beware that "slow horses and fast women were often the downfall of many men." We shared a good laugh over that piece of advice. I am forever thankful for those times. I was glad I fought my father, and in doing so got to spend some great weekends with my dear grandmother.

Over the winter months, Dad showed me photos of the remaining TBM fuselage and its massive center wing. Because it was a torpedo plane, the wing ran through the upper part of the fuselage instead of being attached at the bottom like most warbird planes. This was done by Grumman to make room for the giant torpedo to hang in the bay below the wing and cockpit. As Dad explained, he was perplexed on how to remove the wing with it so completely embedded in the fuselage structure. He did his best to

Walter A. Soplata, the mastermind and one-man band who pulled it all together, poses with his F2G race Corsair 74 early in 1971. The white top of the A-26 Invader fuselage can be seen between the Corsair and the Franklin B-25 at far left.

study the problem by buying TBM manuals from an aircraft book seller he often did trades with. The TBM manuals he got still weren't much help.

Within a week or so after I'd finished my junior year of high school, we went to the Rising Sun Airport to get the center wing and fuselage of the TBM. Parked off in the corner of the grass strip, it looked really decrepit. It was normally navy blue, but someone had painted it yellow. We had sometimes joked that my early painting efforts were done with a mop, but the yellow paint was almost certainly applied that way. The only role left in life for this torpedo bomber was to serve as an airport marker. With its bright yellow paint, pilots could spot the small field from many miles away. As some pilots stopped by to visit, they lamented that we were taking away their big yellow navigation aid.

As with all airplanes we hauled, the first thing I had to do upon seeing this one was to explore it thoroughly. Except for looking at some photographs in books and magazines, I'd never seen a TBM before. In those pictures, it looked to me like a big fighter plane with a bomber-styled gun turret added behind the cockpit. But upon seeing the real thing, I found it to be vastly different from any fighter I'd seen. The folding torpedo bay doors were open, so after I ducked under the front of the plane, I was able to stand up inside the bay. I was stunned to find the bay of this single-engine plane was longer than the bomb bay of our twin-engine B-25s. From front to back, I'd say it was the length of a midsize car. Most eye catching in the bay was the circular rack that had once held the TBM's torpedo. Though the rack was empty, its presence seemed menacing. Overall, the TBM was so big in size, I now considered Dad's Corsairs to be small.

No matter how we initially looked at where the TBM disassembled, it appeared impossible to get this giant plane down the highway. Unlike the big Skyraider of an equivalent size, there was absolutely no way to haul the TBM with its cockpit and center wing connected together on our trailer. Even with the engine and tail removed, the center part of the fuselage was far too big to go sideways down the highway while attached to the wing like we did with the Skyraider. To haul the plane home, we had no choice but to separate the wing and the fuselage.

As we examined the plane more closely, we noticed small panels forward of the wing attached to the plane with screws. Below the panels, we found vertical seams going down the walls of the torpedo bay. Quickly we realized this was how we'd disconnect the front of the wing from the fuselage. Behind the main wing spar was a big section of inboard wing we would have to remove to separate the rear of the center wing. Based on all that, we figured we could drop the center wing and torpedo bay as one unit and separate the fuselage and wing that way. But even though we had found a solution, the work we faced was difficult, tedious, and long in man-hours.

Like the Skyraider, the TBM had a lot of corrosion. That made many rusty screws and bolts almost impossible to get out. And if all the screws weren't enough, we also had hundreds of rivets to remove. As Dad and I worked hour after hour taking the TBM apart, we got along great and seemed to be more of a team than ever. On a day-to-day basis we just didn't spend much time together anymore, but hauling an airplane once again had us joined together like glue. The end of our teamwork was much closer than I realized, so I now look back on this TBM as our strong finish.

24

"Your Place"

During the fall of 1970, Dad became very frustrated with me. Attending my last year of high school, running cross-county, and working my part time job conflicted with almost everything he wanted me to do. My next distraction made his airplanes nonexistent. A brewing romance with a very smart and pretty girl in my senior class took off like a P-51. By the end of the month, the two of us were inseparable.

At or near the top of our class in every subject, this young lady was viewed as one of the "brains" by the guys. But if being a brainy gal discouraged guys from dating her, it was fine with me. Though I'd known her casually since first grade, it wasn't until we both got jobs at the Punderson Manor House that I got to know her well. Witty and fun as heck to be around, she also would have passed Dad's test for being a very hard worker. As it grew obvious we were head over heels with each other, her mother established a rule that all visiting be done at their house. Most guys wouldn't think of that as a good deal, but for me the timing was perfect.

At this exact same time, Dad entered a new phase in his hobby of collecting. The opening event was a big "white elephant sale" in Cleveland. Since my Manor House job occupied most weekends, I missed the sale. Upon seeing the results, I was glad I did. The way the Suburban was packed upon his return, an elephant could have been hiding in that stuff somewhere. "Where are you going to put all this?" I asked, as I peered in the windows of the stuffed Suburban and looked at the stacks of books, magazines, electronics, and airplane memorabilia.

"I'll make room—I always do," Dad snarled. Seeing this type of stuff come home greatly increased my despair. The house was already crammed to the gills. Dad's library room was so packed, the door only opened partway and you had to squeeze through the remaining gap to get in. Also, the sunroom where my sisters and I played as kids now had its walls fully lined with shelves that Dad's carpenter skills had enabled him to put up quickly. The shelves were already stuffed full. Throughout the house there were stacks of boxes, combined with piles of things here and there that Dad was "waiting for a rainy day to sort." So now he brings home a huge load of more stuff. With a sense of gloom, I helped Dad carry his loot into the house where we added it to several existing piles while also starting some new ones.

As we carried the stuff in, Mom made a futile attempt to hold back the flood. "You can't leave this stuff lying around the house," she said. "When is this going to stop?"

"Not you too. Wally's already giving me a bad time," Dad responded. "I'll get it all put away, don't worry."

"Put away where? There's no more space," she said as she pointed at several of his piles.

"Well, I'm not sure right now, but soon I can start using the kids' bedrooms."

"Do what?" Mom expressed her alarm.

"Once the kids are gone, they don't need a room." Dad said flatly, as though clearing us out were the same as getting rid of an old washing machine. Mom tried to argue that this was our home and it would be wrong to convert the bedrooms into storage rooms. But like trying to overturn a long-decided court ruling, she had long lost her meek fight for our place to be a normal home. Other evidence of precedence against her: she looked the other way for years as Grandma Murray complained about Dad's growing stacks of boxes. Still, despite the obvious upcoming verdict of the supreme ruler, I was glad to see Mom try to make a stand now. What was different was that instead of boxes trickling in a few at a time over weeks and months, this Suburban load from the white elephant sale was a sudden tsunami. Altogether I feared the future as my gut instinct told me this was one of those pivotal moments under Dad's authoritarian rule that was going to change the future in a way none of us would like.

As I expected, Mom's effort to push back was a lost cause. She'd caved into Dad so many times now, he just steamrolled her. He insisted the stuff would be priceless someday and therefore he had no choice but to get all he could. Once he got his air museum going, he promised her he'd get all the boxes and stuff out of the house. He assured her that when she saw how great the items would go with his future air museum, she too would be glad. He then explained that the first wave of World War II aviators was just beginning to die now and the trend would only grow bigger as that group continued to age. People at the sale who were cleaning out the attics of these aviators were bringing in all kinds of aviation things that would be lost unless he collected them. The only thing Dad admitted to was that he was late discovering these sales. He now worried he probably missed some items that might never be available again, so he was determined not to miss another sale.

For the same reasons, he vowed to search military surplus stores and salvage yards more frequently. Doing so, he got more than he bargained for late one evening. Dad was poking around at a big salvage yard when it happened. Through some rows of junk, he spotted the black streak of a German shepherd making a beeline for him. It was a good distance back to the Suburban, so Dad ran as fast as he could. He almost made it.

"I thought I was done," Dad told me and Mom. He heard the mean barking dog catching him, and when the barking changed to growling, he could feel the dog biting his coat sleeve. Dad stopped the story there and walked out as Mom and I looked at each other very puzzled. In a few moments he returned while holding up his old ragged rummage-sale coat. "Look, look, see what happened to my coat!" Dad burst out laughing. Mom and I could barely believe our eyes. One entire sleeve was missing. As Dad was running full speed with the junkyard dog sinking his teeth into the coat sleeve, the stitching in the shoulder let go, and torn insulation was all that was left around the big hole where the sleeve had ripped out.

"Did you get any dog bites?" Mom asked.

"Not a scratch!" Dad laughed. The dog didn't realize for a few moments that he only had the sleeve. "I kept running like hell, and after about ten steps the dog figured it out." Dad then had just enough time to get in the Suburban and shut the door. "Wow, was that dog pissed!" Dad continued laughing. We all had a good laugh as Dad joked about the benefits of not owning a good coat. But despite his entertaining junkyard dog story, he was oblivious to the pain his new binge for collecting was causing.

I still hadn't decided what I would do or where I would go after high school, and Dad already had his sights on warehousing giant loads of stuff in my tiny bedroom. As I looked around the house, already overflowing with his collectibles, I thought how I'd *die* if my girlfriend were here to see this. I was very glad to honor her mother's rule that all visits be at their house. As the year wore on, Dad did exactly what I feared worse. He found more big sales to go to and often came home with the Suburban fully packed.

My girlfriend's father and I got along great, and he was a much-needed breath of fresh air. To begin with, he was a father figure who sometimes reminded me of Fred MacMurray starring as the dad on TV's *My Three Sons*. He'd also been a B-24 bomber mechanic during World War II, and we soon began exchanging airplane stories. From there we talked about cars, and what each of us had done to fix things on our own. By now I was very mechanically inclined, and it felt good to see that this man whom I quickly looked up to was showing me respect for my abilities. Beyond the mechanical common ground, I found this father figure to be an intriguing man who in one major way was the flip side of my dad.

Being employed as an engineer and having his master's degree, he had a strong commitment to education. Tall and handsome with black hair showing a few streaks of gray, smoking his pipe, he had an academic appearance about him that made it easy to imagine him as a college dean in some engineering school. As a result, I quickly realized I was in a home where academics were very important. Until now, I was never real excited about doing homework, but if it made a good excuse to be with my gal, I was for it.

As we did our schoolwork together, I learned a lot from my girlfriend, but not just about the subject material. I learned that the secret to her high grades was no secret. She simply worked real hard. When we got hung up on things like physics problems, I was ready to give up and let the teacher explain it. But not her. She'd go back and forth from the problem to the reading assignment. If that didn't help, then she'd see if a similar problem we understood provided a clue to the one we didn't. By chopping away at it in those kinds of ways, she'd eventually solve almost any problem. Academically, I'd never been exposed to such tenacity and drive. I long knew I'd been a slacker at school, and simply through her work she inspired me to change my ways.

Dad's sudden increase in collecting, combined with three of my sisters living away from home, caused me to feel like our family life was slipping away fast. I wanted the slide to stop and hoped Grandma Murray could somehow push Dad to make things right. That was a long shot, as she'd had some tough times recently. There were no rules against age discrimination back then, and she lost her job, simply being told she was too old. A fight with Mom and Dad the previous summer had put her a bit distant from both of them. So it truly was a long shot. Still, I looked back to her toughness and hoped she'd somehow put the brakes on where things were heading. Another pivotal moment under Dad's rule was at hand.

Early in the summer of 1971, Grandma Murray suddenly got ill and went into the hospital. I was getting dressed to visit her when we got a phone call. My visit was off. Margaret C. Murray, age 69, was dead. I felt so close to her that my sense of loss completely overwhelmed me. If any part of my childhood was normal, it in many ways was thanks to her. Having known Grandma Murray to be so full of life, I found her passing almost impossible to accept. Along with her death, I found the implications for my family hard to accept as well. In many ways, I long felt like she was the electricity that powered our family circle. Now, the plug had just been yanked out.

25

In the Grip of Obsession

Grandma Murray warned Dad for years that if he preceded her in death, she'd have a garbage truck haul everything to the dump. Now that she was gone, it seemed Dad sought revenge by collecting everything he could. Just weeks after her passing in June of 1971, a man named Ralph Huffman stopped by to see Dad's planes. Tall, gray, and definitely blue collar, he appeared to be about fifty and was dressed in a light blue utility shirt and pants. As Dad gave him the typical tour, it quickly became obvious the man knew his airplanes.

"I feel guilty you've worked so hard to save all this," Huffman said.

"What do you mean?" Dad asked.

"For years I made my living scrapping these things—thousands of them," he said sounding regretful.

"Corsairs?" Dad asked.

"Oh yeah, a huge number of Corsairs." Huffman went on, estimating thousands of Corsairs, Hellcats, Mustangs, Thunderbolts, you name it, he melted them down. He even told of a portable furnace he took to boneyards to melt the warbirds. "I've put entire fields of airplanes into the furnace," he finished, sounding sad. We walked for a while, and Dad was speechless. He was visibly stunned. It was almost like Dad was the airplane pope, and the devil dropped in to confess his terrible sins. I could tell Dad wanted to let this guy have it. But the man seemed nice, almost repentant, and Dad didn't have it in him to give the guy a bad time.

"Did you ever think of saving a few of each type of aircraft?" Dad asked.

"Sure wish I had, they'd be worth a lot now," Huffman said. Dad then went on his familiar spiel about how hard it now was to find anything. But upon learning Huffman was still an airplane scrapper, he asked repeatedly for Huffman to keep him posted on whatever airplane scrap he was acquiring. Huffman answered, "You know, I do have something right now we're about to scrap, but I doubt you'd be interested."

"What's that?" Dad asked.

"We won a scrap bid to cut up a KC-97 tanker at Selfridge Air Force Base."

"Oh wow, I don't think so," Dad laughed. "Those tanker planes are huge—that's a lot more than we can handle." We finished giving Huffman the tour and I didn't give his visit another thought until a few days later when I found a mess Dad made digging his airplane manuals out of boxes. I looked where he was sitting and noticed he had a KC-97 manual in his lap.

"Why are you looking at a KC-97 manual?" I asked, fearing the answer.

"I'm thinking of buying the KC-97 fuselage and using it as a metal warehouse for all

25. In the Grip of Obsession

the stuff I'm buying," Dad said plainly. He'd been studying the dimensions of the KC-97 he found in his manuals, and had gleefully concluded the double-deck fuselage of the huge tanker plane would be "almost impossible to fill!"

"Since you need more storage space, why don't you put up a building?" Mom asked.

"Or just quit collecting stuff," I chimed in.

"Now wait," Dad said. "To put up a building, I'll need a building permit. With all the junk I've got laying around, there's no way they'd give me a permit." On that I had to agree. Though I did what I could to keep the yard looking neat, Dad's unbounded passion for dragging stuff home made the situation nearly hopeless. Still, I just couldn't see us hauling home a KC-97 fuselage for a storage building or any other reason. At airshows, I toured enough of these planes to know they were giants, sometimes referred to as "flying gas stations." Nothing we hauled to date came close to being half the size of a KC-97 tanker. Even by today's standards, the plane was big, as it approximates the size of a modern Boeing 767 airliner.

"There's absolutely no way we can haul a giant KC-97 down the highway!" I was outraged by the very idea of it.

"Well, of course we'll have to cut it up to get it home," Dad sounded unconcerned.

"How in the heck will you put it back together—after it's all cut to pieces?" I barked.

"You'll see," Dad said. He then described how we'd drill holes, and bolt steel bars between the sections to connect them back together. Then we'd cut strips of aluminum to cover all the places where the fuselage was cut. He proclaimed no one would be able to tell the tanker had been apart when that was all done. It was like this was going to be his greatest airplane resurrection yet. Almost like his personal *Flight of the Phoenix*. Just add Jimmy Stewart and you'd think Dad was gonna make this old tanker fly again.

Boeing KC-97L Stratofreighter (National Museum of the United States Air Force).

Dad's in a lighthearted mood after my high school graduation in 1971. Forced to work at a young age, he was denied the opportunity to finish high school, so among his happiest days were the ones when each of his five children graduated. I look unsure here. Perhaps my instincts are telling me a giant Boeing airplane is heading my way.

I looked at Mom and tried to read whether she was going to fight Dad on this. She looked back and shrugged her shoulders. I felt sick. Altogether, I could give a thousand reasons why it was a bad idea to haul this thing home. But none of that mattered. Dad had his mind made up, and if Mom wasn't even going to squabble about something of this magnitude, it gave me great fear about the future.

That evening, Dad got on the phone with Huffman and tried to work out a deal. They settled on a price easily. Then Dad wanted the fuselage cut to certain specifications. Huffman refused. He reminded Dad he was under contract with the Air Force to have the plane off base within 30 days, and the clock was ticking. If he had to mutilate the plane to meet the deadline, so be it. Another problem for Dad: a house construction surge had his company working hard as ever, including some Saturdays. He figured his boss would have a fit if he asked for too much time off. At work the next day, he got the bad news he expected. Maybe two days off, but no more.

The next evening, I got home from my shift at the Manor House when Dad greeted me at the door. He was exceptionally pleasant, all smiles and obviously anxious to say something. "Me and your mother talked it over and have an idea," he began. As he told it, they both agreed I should quit my job at the Manor House and work full-time getting the KC-97 home.

"Ugh, gee, well, I don't know." I was lost for words.

"I'll pay you whatever they're paying you," Dad said plainly. He added that since it was all in the family, I'd make more money because I would not have to pay taxes on money from my parents. He quickly made his point, and his manner of delivery suggested I was getting a fantastic deal.

"I'll have to think about it for a minute," I answered, totally caught off guard.

"What the hell's there to think about?" Dad got terse. "I *already told you* you'll make more money." He was insistent on hearing "yes" immediately. I looked at Mom, and in response she yet again shrugged her shoulders. In a way I understood, but still I felt my mother had really let me down. That really hurt. If she agreed to let Dad rule the roost on raising kids and other family matters, I expected that. If she approved of *him* hauling giant planes, that was fine too. But for both of them to expect me to haul a giant tanker plane with a Suburban and trailer was stretching the limits of parent-child obedience in a really big way. The speeches I just heard at my high school graduation about graduates beginning their new journey seemed moot. The sudden sense that I had no right of refusal living in Newbury spoke very loudly. My ordered servitude also stirred a recent memory that suddenly seemed connected.

About six months after I got the Ford Falcon, Dad took the car because he wanted it. My first clue was to find its rear seat removed and his carpenter benches and tools on the car's rear floor. I was paid back the money I spent fixing it up, but I had no right of refusal: he took the car. I replaced the Falcon with a car that needed an engine. After I got it going, I duded up the car in a way that made it very unlikely my parents would want it.

I largely considered the Ford Falcon experience an anomaly and I got over it—I thought. But now, forced to quit my job and forced to haul this enormous air refueling tanker, it all suggested that losing my car to Dad had actually signaled the beginning of an alarming trend. Dad had long been a very controlling man of me and the others in our family. As a child I expected and accepted that. But seeing these new signs that the grip of his control was demanding this kind of servitude into my early adult years was disturbing. What made this reality even more painful was to realize my mother was almost entirely under his control. That left little if any wiggle room for me as *his* son.

For this KC-97 misadventure, I fortunately saw a few outs. First, if I was 200 miles away at Selfridge, I would make all the decisions there. Thank God no one had cell phones then. Next, I was enrolled at an electronics technical school for the fall session in Cuyahoga Falls. It was far enough away that I'd have to live there. With all Dad continued to put me through, I was more than ready to move. With my September class date only about six weeks away, I figured I'd survive working for him at least that long.

For now, he got his way. As I said my goodbyes to my coworkers at the Manor House, I felt very sad. In the year and a half I worked there, I got to know many wonderful people. Almost like a family, my coworkers included elderly people, teenagers, and parental role models in between. Throughout the group, I felt an enjoyable sense of camaraderie. Though nothing sounds special about a teenager working at a restaurant and hotel, to me the people there made it very special. The rustic lake and country setting of the former mansion was also captivating and memorable.

The objective of the first trip was to set the stage for the things Dad wanted done in his absence. About the only good thing I could think of for the KC-97 trips was that we weren't driving the old rusted-out '57 Chevy Suburban anymore. A few months earlier, Dad had spotted a '66 Chevy Suburban that was in excellent condition. When he told me he'd decided to buy it, I almost couldn't believe my ears. Of great importance for hauling, this Suburban had a V-8 engine and a four-speed truck transmission, which gave it the towing power we were long overdue for. It also had a radio! We took turns driving on the road to Selfridge, and the drive was rather quiet with neither of us having much to say. The airbase people were friendly as always. They gave us directions out to the site of the plane, which was in a grass field about a mile from the end of one of the runways.

Driving across the base, we could see rows of KC-97s parked neatly on the flight line. A few other KC-97s always seemed to be flying. Others on the ground were slowly going down a taxiway with their giant props turning lazily, powered by the same 28-cylinder R-4360 engines like the one on Dad's race Corsair 74. I found the view of the big planes operating there to be very inspiring. Part of our route took us down a remote taxiway that had thirty or so RF-101 Voodoo jets painted in camouflage parked in a tight and neat long row. I felt my yearning to fly perk up every time I drove by those jets. We finally drove onto the grassy field, where our KC-97 contrasted greatly with the other tankers. It was sitting on its belly with no landing gear or engines, so at least it was easy to climb inside the giant plane.

As expected, no one was at the plane when we arrived. Huffman told Dad they'd be there the next day, which suited him fine. By getting there first, he felt he could control exactly how the plane would be cut. Walking through the tall grass, we quickly surveyed the plane. While the cockpit was stripped of instruments and radios, the near perfect condition of the fuselage delighted Dad as he envisioned the giant double-deck storage building it would become for the waves of shopping he had in mind.

The structure of the KC-97 fuselage would have to be cut in numerous places, and Dad planned for Huffman's crew to do most of the work. Since they used metal cutting

Despite resting on the ground with no landing gear, the KC-97 is still a tall and intimidating giant looking down its nose at our dinky Suburban and trailer.

power saws to cut aircraft they scrapped, this job would be rather routine for them. Dad's biggest worry about the project was that Huffman's crew wouldn't cut the plane the way he wanted it done. Since there was no way to communicate with the crew face to face, we brought some paint with us and planned to mark all the places on the fuselage where Dad wanted it cut.

Deciding how to cut the KC-97 fuselage took some planning. Besides the fuselage's being far too big to haul down the highway, the double-deck arrangement added complexity to its structure. The KC-97 was a major link in the evolution of airliners, and as in a modern wide-body jet today, the upper deck was very spacious, while the lower deck was considerably smaller. After our brief tour of the plane was finished, Dad made up his mind on how he wanted to cut the plane and haul it. As we stood on the upper deck cargo floor, he explained wanting the upper deck cut in long sections nose to tail.

"It'll be a giant mess to put all the chopped metal back together," I said, casting my doubts. Dad calmly disagreed. As I sort of expected, his behavior was completely tamed. Without hinting a word about it, I knew that he knew there was a risk I'd walk if he really ticked me off. And I had a secret he knew nothing about.

A dear sweet lady named Vi Lord stunned me by insisting I refuse my father's demands to haul this plane. Just over age 50, her ever elegant and gracious appearance made her look much younger. A sweet motherly role model, she long befriended and mentored me along with many other young teens working with her at the Manor House. Fighting a few tears, she told me her dreadful fears I'd be seriously injured or killed working on and hauling the giant chopped-up plane. A saintly good woman, she reminded me of Julie Andrews caring for the Von Trapp children in *The Sound of Music*. So concerned was she was for my safety, she offered to find a place for me to stay if I had to refuse my father and leave home. I appreciated it, but I was also quite startled and confused by what she had to say. Here was an adult woman I admired greatly, like a wonderful aunt, who was—suddenly telling me to disobey my parents? What was she seeing that I was missing, to advise me so strongly to consider the unthinkable?

Illustrating his KC-97 vision for chopping now and reconstructing later, Dad showed me his reasons for some new optimism. As we walked across the upper deck's cargo floor, he led me to a spot on the tanker's wall and pulled back some insulation. As I looked, he pointed to a long row of bolts that ran from the floor up over our heads and down the other side. Then he walked me to other locations built the same way. He was thrilled that so much of the upper fuselage could be unbolted, which of course would simplify its reconstruction. Still, between those bolted sections, we had to chop the aluminum nose to tail. He did not find similar bolted sections in the heavy structure located in the bottom deck. He figured he'd just have to trust Huffman's crew to use their metal-cutting power saws to cut the lower section the way he wanted. The main thing he hoped Huffman's crew could avoid was cutting the cargo floor. If they could preserve the cargo floor, then his giant aluminum KC-97 would be a delightful and enormous storage building for him.

So for now, the plan was to cut the top of the fuselage into strips, with the length of each strip determined by the seams where the plane bolted together. Still, Dad was unsure how wide to cut each strip. I helped him with a tape measure as we found how big each of the round fuselage sections could be without greatly exceeding an eight-foot width when loaded on the trailer. It was soon obvious the top compartment needed to be cut into three sections. Simply put, there would be one cut section for the left wall, another cut section for the ceiling, and a third cut section for the right wall.

I was ready to go get the paint and start marking the places for Huffman's men to cut when Dad stopped me. "The top fuselage up here is built a lot lighter than the bottom fuselage," Dad said as his experienced junkman's hands tapped a screwdriver on the plane's thin metal skin. "We can cut this ourselves and not have to worry about Huffman's crew messing it up," he said with a can-do spirit.

"Do what?" I asked, dismayed. I knew what Dad just volunteered us for was going to be brutally hard work. With noon fast approaching, this sunny August day was already getting hot. An ax and hacksaw were the only cutting tools we had, and my last memory of using them was really bad. It was five years earlier when we nearly froze to death cutting the crashed B-57 wings from tip to tip with these same tools at this same air base. My first assignment on the KC-97 was to begin removing the hundreds of bolts that held the top fuselage sections together. Then, to confirm his theory, Dad began working with the ax by cutting from inside the plane while standing on the cargo floor.

As he stood behind the cockpit and began chopping at the ceiling, the steel ax hitting the aluminum made two loud sounds that were painful to our ears. The first sound was the bang of the ax hitting the metal. Following the bang was an intense shrieking sound as the split aluminum rubbed the steel sides of the ax. The sounds themselves were nothing new to us, but being inside the fuselage was like being in a large drum that amplified the noise. In little time we found some cotton balls in the Suburban to stuff our ears with.

As I removed bolts, I looked at Dad periodically to see what kind of progress he was making. The good news was the ax could cut the metal. The bad news was that with such a big plane, it seemed like he had miles to go. I could tell that while the ax was getting the job done, it was going to take many hours of sweat to get all the cutting finished. Dad chopped away for about an hour, after which his white T-shirt was soaked with sweat. He looked beat. Even though we had all the hatches open on the plane, the hot sun beating down on all that metal made the inside of the plane feel like an oven.

I took my turn with the ax. Chopping above my head while trying to cut in a straight line took a bit of practice, but I soon got the hang of it. For the most part, the aluminum skin cut rather easily. However, about every 18 inches that I cut, I ran into an aluminum rib that reinforced the fuselage structure. Though the ax could handle the aluminum ribs, it took a number of hard blows to get through each one. There were also some large steel ribs that went all the way around the airplane. There was no way the ax was going to cut the steel ribs, so for those we had to use the hacksaw. Between chopping and sawing, I got tired fast. For a "break," Dad and I would go back to removing bolts. While there was a great abundance of bolts to remove, the physical labor was easy.

After a couple of hours, we had one wall section of the plane ready to remove. We left a few bolts in place to steady the section while we did the last of the cutting. Then, as Dad held the wall section from falling in on us, I removed the last bolts. Dad and I pushed the wall section out until it fell away from the plane and landed in the tall grass below. With one section removed, we got more fresh air inside, which helped. Still, it was hot, and for the rest of the afternoon, we worked like dogs.

By about 7 p.m., we had much of the upper fuselage removed from the plane, and had cut a lot on the sections that remained. Since the plane was located outside of the disposal yard, nobody cared that we worked after closing hours. Our long day finished,

25. In the Grip of Obsession

I stand bewildered next to the big and heavy Boeing KC-97 Stratofreighter at Selfridge Air Force Base, Michigan in August 1971.

we were hungry, thirsty, and really exhausted. We checked in at a motel near the base and got cleaned up. After a quick supper, we went to bed and simply crashed.

The next morning, we got an early start and had all but the cockpit cut from above the upper floor when Huffman and his crew arrived. They were astounded that the two of us had removed nearly the entire top of the plane with hand tools. Dad gave them a tour while briefing them on where he wanted the rest of the fuselage cut with their power tools. The men helped us load our trailer, and then under Dad's supervision they cut the cockpit and then the lower sections of fuselage. With their special gas-powered saws cutting the metal like butter, they had the fuselage cut the way Dad wanted in a few hours. After the intensely hard work Dad had put the two of us through, those power saws were a beautiful sight.

26

Mother Load

My next trip to Selfridge was a first. Dad didn't go. Instead, I made my hauling debut with Mom. We got up at the usual time for Dad to go to his carpenter job. After a quick breakfast, Mom and I gathered our snacks, drinks and other goodies, and headed for the door. Dad seemed a little nervous. He gave me some last-minute reminders while telling Mom to remind me some more. We hopped in the Suburban and it felt strange to be going through the motions as we prepared to leave Dad behind. Maybe I wasn't really awake yet and it was just a weird dream. But within a few moments on the bumpy gravel road, there were plenty of reminders that this was real. As the windshield wipers thumped back and forth clearing off the morning dew, each bump in the road produced the familiar squeaks and rattles from our toolboxes and equipment.

On the highway, I took advantage of my no-dad trip by tuning the AM radio to my favorite rock station across Lake Erie in Detroit. Dad didn't rock and roll at all. It was strictly Glenn Miller and brass bands for him. Mom was more tolerant. And since I was drafted for this, I figured I was at least entitled to free rein of the radio. I did relent now and then for her to enjoy her classical music.

It took us about a half hour to get to the Ohio Turnpike. When we got there, we found about a dozen hippies out thumbing rides by the turnpike entrance. It was a sight we were getting more and more used to. During this summer of 1971, Cleveland-area entrances to interstates and turnpikes could have quite a crowd of ride-thumbing hippies by midday. But this early in the morning, we were both surprised. "Can't believe they're already out here," I commented.

"Yeah, me too," Mom responded. "But I don't think any of them will be interested in going to an Air Force base." The Vietnam War still had a few years to go.

We had a nice trip to Detroit on what turned out to be a perfect day. Mom didn't seem the least bit worried about my running the show on our first airplane safari together. When we arrived at the KC-97 site, no one was there, but it was obvious Huffman's crew had been busy. Most of the wing was gone. As Mom surveyed the chunks of airplane scattered around in the tall grass, I could see her mood change. "He thinks he's going to put this thing back together?" she said, looking very doubtful.

"I don't get it either," I responded. I told her how the B-25s, Corsairs, TBM and most other planes made sense to me. "But this thing—I'll never understand," I told her bluntly. Dad decided that for my first load he wanted me to haul the bottom section of the rear fuselage that was just aft of the wing. Since this section was slightly smaller and appeared lighter than the forward fuselage, Dad figured this load would be a good test to see how the Suburban and trailer handled the heavy and big lower fuselage sections.

If we could not handle the lower sections in one piece, then Huffman's crew would have to do more cutting. Such extra cutting would damage the cargo floor Dad was determined to preserve.

Ideally, the best way to haul the bottom fuselage sections would be upside down. Looking at these fuselage sections from the front or rear, each resembled a capital D in cross-section, rotated for the cargo floor to be the flat part. By turning these sections upside down, the flat cargo floor would ride perfectly on the flat trailer bed. Unfortunately, loading it this way would make it far too wide to legally go down the highway. We never had a permit to haul an oversized load. Dad had long figured it was hopeless to get the Suburban and trailer approved for one. He realized the permit people would insist on a real truck. So, instead of hauling the sections upside down, Dad wanted them hauled on their side. As a result, they'd actually resemble a capital D once resting on the trailer. By loading the sections that way, they'd be very tall, but narrower and only oversize by about a foot.

As promised, Huffman left his big forklift on site. In a few moments I got it started. Mom stood back as I experimented with the controls to raise, lower, and tilt the big long forks. A few more experiments with the gearshift and I was in business. In a few moments, I had a cable hooked from the forklift to the rear fuselage and was able to roll it onto its side. Then, driving the forklift up against the now vertical cargo floor, I was able to lift the big D. Even though the forklift was a big one, the fuselage was quite a load and wasn't very steady resting on the forks. I shut down and told Mom that instead of driving the forklift to the trailer, I was going to back the trailer under the load. I lowered the big D fuselage onto the trailer, and then we both stepped back to take a look.

"Wow, I don't know," Mom said. "It seems way too high for that small trailer." Actually, she thought the whole thing was too big for our trailer as we continued to discuss the load. After seeing Dad haul the B-25s on this trailer, I thought I'd seen everything. But the B-25s were kid toys compared to this. I suddenly realized I was going to be playing test pilot with a load much bigger than anything Dad had ever hauled on this trailer. I didn't like the thought of that at all. I also told Mom it was tail-heavy. "How can you tell?" she asked. I then showed her how the hitch was higher now than when the trailer was empty. That meant the Suburban was holding the front of the trailer down instead of holding it up. "Does that mean the load will sway?" she asked.

"Exactly. It will sway, I just don't know how bad," I answered. We both stood there silently with Mom periodically grimacing and shaking her head. Finally, she told me it was entirely up to me to make the decision to haul it or not. If I said no, she promised to do all the talking to Dad. "Your father will just have to understand, or he can come get the damn thing himself," She let out some frustration. Then I told her what I was thinking.

I would chain the load to the trailer and drive some to see how it handled. If I didn't like the way it drove, we'd come back and unload it. Mom agreed to the test drive while saying again it was entirely my decision. Huffman loaned us his chains and chain binders to tie down the wobbly load. I was never so glad to have some good equipment. With the ragged cables and U-bolts Dad normally used for tie-downs, there was always some slack in the cables. With a load this big and high, I needed it chained down tight! Still, Dad would grumble about my use of the chains upon getting home. Since he was paying by the pound, he complained Huffman was earning extra money due to the weight of the heavy steel chains on the trailer when I drove onto the scale to get weighed. The safety that Huffman's chains added to the trip was priceless, so I paid no attention to Dad's likely grumbling.

Just off base near Selfridge, we found a truck stop and decided to get set for the long trip home in case I did find the load tolerable to drive. On the short drive to the truck stop it seemed okay. Mom ran off to get some burgers, fries, drinks, and snacks while I got gas. With little delay we hit the road and were on I-94 heading south to Detroit. Since the load was tail-heavy, I knew this thing would sway. I just didn't know at what speed or how bad. Like I'd seen Dad do, I played test pilot by raising my speed in 5-mph increments to see how it handled. Things went fine until I worked my way up to just over 50 mph. Suddenly the load started swaying and I had to tap on the brakes. Even though I knew it was coming, I was pretty startled. I tried keeping my speed down, and things seemed fine from there, with one exception.

Every time a semi truck passed me at a high speed, the windblast of the semi rocked my trailer and got the load swaying again. With the huge cargo floor of the plane being vertical on the left side of the trailer, the windblast from the trucks gave the trailer quite a push. As each truck passed, I tried timing my steering inputs to offset the blast as the semis moved forward in my rearview mirror. My success was minimal at best. With more trial and error, I found that if I braked lightly as the trucks roared by, I could keep good control. Still, I was on the edge of my seat. The thought that I had 200 miles of this through Detroit, Toledo, and Cleveland was very bewildering.

"How are you doing?" Mom asked as the traffic thickened nearing Detroit. I told her I was okay and actually glad to be in rush-hour traffic going slow. The load handled great at 30 and I didn't have to worry about getting run over, I explained. "That's a good way to look at it," Mom smiled. The Detroit Expressway had four lanes going in each direction, and we were in a sea of traffic. With traffic moving at the slow pace, motorists had time to look, gawk, and point, which some did. And if ordinary people were taking such notice, I anxiously expected the police would too. Eventually we were through Detroit and traffic was back to normal speed. I was again anxious as semi after semi sped by like meteors. Though I hated the moment each one zipped by, the more miles I got under my belt, the more confident I felt.

Soon we made our way through Toledo and were approaching the entrance to the Ohio Turnpike as the sun began to set. The usual crowd of hippie hitchhikers stood by the entrance with a gaggle of crudely drawn cardboard signs listing their destinations. Of the many times I saw all those thumbs up in the air, I never saw so many thumbs fall as fast as they did when we drove up. Gawking, pointing, and staring, but not a single thumb. No hippie wanted a ride *that* bad.

When we got near the Turnpike tollbooth, I maneuvered carefully with the big load. As I stuck my arm out to get my turnpike ticket from the attendant, I was determined to act relaxed and normal. Just out for an evening cruise on the pike with my mom. I was on alert for any adverse reaction from the attendant. The giant load caught the old man's eye. "What you haulin' there, son?" the man asked as he leaned out of the booth to look at the trailer.

"Oh, just a piece of an airplane from Selfridge Air Force Base," I replied.

"Must have been a big one!" the man smiled and handed me my ticket. We were on, and I was soon happy to see the day turn to night. Under the cover of darkness, I hoped maybe we could slip the rest of the way home without being pulled over. I'd been pulled over with Dad so many times I felt like I knew every cop in three states. Still, each time I got nervous. My hopes of slipping through unnoticed soon were shattered by red flashing lights illuminating everything in my rearview mirror. I pulled over, and as the highway patrolman approached my driver's door, I rolled down my window.

"Boy, what the hell you hauling here?" the patrolman asked harshly while peering in my window with his flashlight.

"I'm, uh, uh, hauling home an airplane," I answered.

"Doin' … what?" he asked tersely.

"He's hauling home part of an airplane for his father's airplane museum," Mom answered assertively.

"I was asking the boy. Who are you, ma'am?"

"I'm his mother," Mom answered, steely eyed as ever.

"Oh, that's nice. Well, ma'am, I'd be glad to talk to you, but since your son is driving this heap, he's the one I need to talk to, okay?" The visit didn't go well at all. After doing the driver's license and vehicle registration checks, the patrolman checked the load with his flashlight and used a tape measure while sternly directing me exactly where to hold the tape while helping him. We were oversize, of course, without a permit, among other issues. He put me in the back seat of his patrol car and gave me a summary of the things he didn't like. He finished by saying he was going to let me go because most of the trip was behind me and I had my mother supervising, as he saw things. "Now be safe and get

Dad shot this photo of me in the KC-97 escape hatch opening as we examine the big tanker plane before soon being hard at work. You can see how the Boeing KC-97 was the parent in the evolution of double-deck wide-body airliners still being built today. Boeing also made a civilian airline version of this plane known as the 377 Stratocruiser. Only 55 of them saw airline service, but as a prop airplane it did pave the way for wide-body jets that would follow.

Top: Chop, chop—all in a day's work! Except for the cockpit, Dad and I have the complete upper deck of the KC-97 removed from the plane. A smooth round edge that marks where a fuselage section was removed behind the cockpit shows where this and other vertical seams were easily unbolted using wrenches. But all the horizontal work in the walls and ceiling required us to chop and cut with axes and hacksaws. The sting in my hands from the axe handle hitting solid metal left my hands sore for many days. *Bottom:* Names unknown, visitors pose by the cockpit section of the KC-97 during reassembly.

your mother home. But if I ever catch you with an oversized load like this again, I will do everything I can to get your Ohio driver's license suspended. Got it?"

"Yes sir, I understand." With that, Mom and I were back on the road. I told her about the warning I got, and like it or not, Dad wasn't getting me to haul any more oversized loads. I felt the patrolman had been unusually harsh with me. I was well experienced with Dad getting pulled over and I never saw a cop treat him like that. Then again, I had by far the biggest and bulkiest load we ever put on the trailer. I was also a snot-nosed kid just a month over 18. Mom figured my young age was part of why I got treated like that.

It was about midnight when I pulled into our driveway. I wasn't even out of my seat when I heard Dad running down the stairs. "Oh my gosh," he said as he walked out into the darkness. "I didn't know it was going to look so big."

"Yeah, neither did we—or the police," I responded.

"What? The cops pulled you over?"

I explained to Dad about my meeting with the highway patrol and the warning about a license suspension. Since it was late at night and all I cared about was getting to bed, I summarized my outlook briefly. We would have to work something else out for those other sections of the forward fuselage. Each one was bigger than what I'd just hauled. I told Dad I wasn't going to take any chances getting pulled over by that cop again.

Reassembly of the KC-97 slowly takes place at home. As shown, we did have Huffman's crew cut the cargo floor of this section to stay within size limits for trailering down the highway.

"Oh, there's not much chance of the same guy stopping you twice," Dad said, sounding unconcerned. As we continued that discussion the next day, I stood my ground. We ended up getting Huffman's crew to cut the lower forward section down to legal highway size. That included slicing the cargo floor, but so be it. Unfortunately, there was no reasonable way to do that to the wide section under the cockpit due to the complexity of the plane there. Dad continued to try to force me to haul the oversized cockpit section. Again, I stood my ground. As he persisted pushing, I finally admonished him quite sternly that he was totally out of bounds expecting me to break the law and risk losing my driver's license. Case closed. He relented, which was fortunate. He had no idea that if he kept pushing, my next move was to seek the shelter offered by Vi Lord.

Mom and I ended up hauling all the KC-97 sections cut to legal highway size by Huffman's crew. We also had several loads of top sections Dad and I had cut. No police pulled me over, and I was greatly relieved by that. For the oversize cockpit section, Mom and I went to Selfridge and got that section loaded, tied down and weighed. Then, after his day's work at his carpenter job, Dad drove a car to the off-base truck stop where his oversize load awaited him. As it should be, he and Mom then towed the oversized load home while I followed with his car. We all had a very long day, so all I could do now was try and make it a little easier. I followed just far enough behind them that my headlights would not illuminate and draw attention to the loaded trailer. I also stayed close enough

KC-97 fuselage is half-finished in top of photograph in summer of 1972. Up close is the Douglas A-26 Invader sitting on wood pallets without its landing gear or engines. Busted A-26 nosecone is visible in center of photograph as upside-down Neptune wing section and landing gear is visible left side of photograph. A junkyard look is beginning to dominate the collection and the smashed B-36 has yet to arrive.

to make it unlikely another car, police or otherwise, would get between us and light him up. Eventually we all got home fine.

My many road trips with Mom were special. Like a lot of teens and their parents, we seldom took the time to talk to each other beyond what our daily routines allowed. On these trips, it was almost like we were shipwrecked on a remote island, having contact with almost no one but each other. Of all the topics we covered, we spent some time talking about Grandma Murray. Though the emotional pain of her recent death was still fresh, I think that having the chance to share memories about her provided a well-needed sense of healing. In remembering her, we laughed as we recounted the many times and ways she tormented Dad. If only she could see the two of us now, hauling a giant chopped-up tanker plane for him.

Finished with the KC-97, I left home to attend electronics school. I enjoyed the school and did well there, but soon got a very low draft number in the lottery system used during the last years of the Vietnam War. With my airplane background, I decided to take a delayed enlistment in the Air Force rather than risk getting drafted by the Army. Though I was reluctant to move back home while awaiting my enlistment, my return to the nest worked out well. With about $200 left to my name, I quickly found a maintenance job at the local hospital that paid well.

Wading in a sea of concrete, Dad and I cement the lower deck of the KC-97 fuselage to the Earth in August 1972. The area we are working is where the center wing was removed from the plane and cut up for scrap by Huffman's crew.

Mom and Dad seemed glad I was back, and though he teased about charging me rent, nothing came of it. He knew I had other ideas about how to spend my money. At the same airport where Dad had soloed a Piper Cub many years before, I began taking flying lessons in modern Cessna 150s with their lawnmower-sounding engines and tin can aluminum airframes that Dad scoffed at years earlier. I quickly discovered that I really enjoyed flying. Though my flight instructor was very strict, I accepted the way he challenged me to fly the Cessna exactly. Looking outside and seeing the vastness of Lake Erie to the north and the lush green Ohio countryside below, I was hooked. The view was breathtaking! In about a month I had my student pilot license and was flying solo.

As I continued my flying lessons, I did whatever I could to help out at home. Dad's vehicles needed a variety of repairs, and there was a lot of mowing to do. Though I thought I'd never see it happen, Dad and I worked as a team to piece the KC-97 back together. It took many months to stitch the chopped sections of the plane together, but we finished reconstructing the fuselage as my enlistment date drew near. The last remaining problem was that the double-deck fuselage was very tall, and the bottom of the fuselage was quite round. With no wing to stabilize the structure from rolling over, we did something unconventional yet again.

When the cement truck driver climbed down from his cab and asked my father where he wanted the cement that was churning in the truck's big yellow drum, I had to fight the giggles. The driver's worn shirt, deep summer tan, and dirty scuffed hard hat told he'd been doing this a while. We walked him through the airplane collection, which he'd heard of but never seen. Between drags on his cigarette, he smiled and nodded some approving "wow" looks as we passed one plane after another. Finally, at the site of the KC-97, Dad showed him how he wanted to pour a cement floor in the lower deck of the fuselage while also pouring a thick ring of cement around the outside of the fuselage up against the aluminum skin.

"This will be a heck of a story for the guys at the cement plant," he grinned between puffs of smoke. We quickly realized the cement truck was too big to fit between all of the planes. As the clock was ticking on the load of wet cement, Dad and I raced to install the sides on his trailer and soon had the Suburban and trailer towing loads of cement to the KC-97. Then with buckets, shovels and a wheelbarrow, we raced against the clock to move and pour multiple trailer loads of cement. It was the hardest and most backbreaking work we ever did, with every bit of it a race against time. Yet, we got it done.

In a few days I was again flying solo in a rented Cessna 150. The Cessna was extremely light, it soared with ease, and unbeknown to me, its heading in flight wasn't just measured by its compass, but instead was also pointing toward my future. In contrast, the belly of the Boeing KC-97 tanker was now filled with concrete and its flying days were over, but it would also point toward Dad's future of collecting and storing things. The very different futures these two aircraft represented for each of us told that the end of our father-and-son team had indeed arrived.

27

Chasing the Dream

It's October 1978 on a sunny morning at Columbus Air Force Base in Mississippi. Six years have passed since Dad and I cemented the KC-97 to the earth, and it's been a dozen years since I first dreamed of flying the supersonic T-38 while reading *Aerospace Pilot* on the way to Earl Reinert's place in Chicago.

Right now my knees are shaking. I don't know if it's from being nervous, or from the strain of pressing hard on the brakes during my engine run-up in the cockpit of an Air Force T-38. The rearview mirror confirms the rear cockpit is empty today. My

In great contrast to the cement laden KC-97, this lightweight Cessna 150 still roams the sky today. Longtime friend and airline Captain Rick Henry continues to let me fly this 1966 model Cessna 150 that is almost identical to the one I made my first solo flight with in 1972. Rick keeps this beautiful Cessna in immaculate condition.

Even with the KC-97 fuselage completely assembled in upper left of photograph, carpenter Walter still needs more storage space. Here he has built more wood frames to reconstruct the mid fuselage of the smashed B-36. Up front in photograph, his XP-82 Twin Mustang fuselage is almost ready to join a P-63 Kingcobra fuselage inside the new B-36 storage building.

jet jock instructor pilot has cleared me to fly my first solo. In just a few seconds I will release the brakes, light the afterburners and roar rapidly down the runway—all alone. The jet will leave a lot of noise behind, and I will leave things behind as well.

Like the Beatles song, it's been a long and winding road to get here. During my enlistment in the Air Force, I continued in electronics by working on ground-based communications equipment. The five Air Force bases I traveled to in my two enlisted years gave me a great exposure to the Air Force way of life. All kinds of Air Force planes flew in and out of the bases where I served. Being far from home and out of reach of Dad's control, I was wowed by the freedom my off-duty time gave me to pursue my own goals unhindered. Using my free time to take civilian flying lessons off base, I was fortunate to have several Air Force pilots mentor me in applying for Air Force ROTC to become a college graduate, officer and pilot just like them. With their inspiration and help, plus the tireless efforts of a civil service lady named Helen Parish at the Altus Air Force Base Education Office, I found myself on the seemingly impossible path toward becoming an Air Force officer and jet pilot.

With some VA education money for my enlisted service plus the ROTC scholarship, I was able to attend college at Oklahoma State University with no help from home. Dad always said he wasn't going to spend a dime on college for his kids, and now it didn't matter. In a way, it was best that things worked out this way. What Dad and I needed from each other was a clean break. He had no interest in my attending college, and there was no future for me following in his footsteps. He continued endlessly to haul things home, and I just couldn't participate in that anymore. As the years went by, we grew further apart. I felt bad sometimes that he was all alone and still working so hard as he reached age fifty. But those were choices he made. I had to make my own.

Yet upon reaching this moment, when I'm about to blast off in my speedy Air Force jet and chart my own course, some other thoughts nag me from the past. I well remember picking my way through the Air Force F-101 Voodoo wreckage when I was a young boy and finding the busted piece of a flying helmet. It may have been of no consequence that it was there, but it was still a good reminder. Now I'm wearing likely the same type of Air Force helmet. I'd prefer to keep mine in one piece. With that background and the awareness that two fatal T-38 crashes occurred at other bases in recent months, I'm well aware that flying this high performance jet involves some unforgiving risks. Though I'm at the threshold of reaching my dream, I'm also reminded of the risks by knowing that many of the airshow pilots who inspired me as a young boy have since lost their lives while flying.

A new way of hauling. Instead of a trailer load of airplane swaying down the highway at 50 mph, the T-38's takeoff speed of 160 knots (185 mph) has me hauling down the runway with no zigzagging allowed. After flying the T-38 solo, I agree with the other students who call it the White Rocket instead of its official name the Talon.

Of the names I mentally had on that list, the hardest one to add was Dean Ortner. Three years after I saw him fly the Corsair, he was killed during an airshow performance in a T-6. I was totally devastated when Dad phoned me in Oklahoma to tell the terrible news. The news was even harder as I immediately realized the impact it had on my father. The tough as nails guy Dad so often was, I never heard him cry his heart out the way he did during that phone call. It was the first and only time as his son that I had to look past myself and help my grief-stricken father somehow pull himself together. Of all we experienced as father and son, nothing hurt so terribly as the pain we shared that day. In just the few years I'd been gone, something sparked the friendship of Dad and Dean Ortner to grow stronger, resulting in them regularly exchanging visits and also talking on the phone. There was even talk of them joining forces to start an air museum. So as hard as it was for me, I well understood how crushed my father was by Dean Ortner's death.

A row of T-38s on the Columbus Air Force Base flight line in Mississippi await their instructor pilots (IPs) and students. I had to pinch myself now and then, almost unable to believe the Air Force was paying me to fly these hotrod jets.

Still, despite all that heartbreaking tragedy, I never had a moment of doubt about my unstoppable yearning to fly. A pilot friend once described aviation as "a cruel love affair" because it sometimes takes people from you, but as an aviator you don't let that stop you from flying. So in this T-38 moment when I'm about to blast off on my first solo in a supersonic jet, there is absolutely no place I'd rather be. Unlike Dad's KC-97, an airplane should not be cemented to the Earth. It should fly!

This is what I've fought my father over, what I've dreamed of, what I've worked for, and this is the place I've cleared hurdle after hurdle to get to. And though they are gone, if my childhood pilot heroes could see me now, I sense they'd be saying "Come on up, son—it's

"Big Wally" was a popular foam cleaner that came in a spray can in the 1970s, so I decorated the visor on my flying helmet accordingly. A label I stuck on it stated "Contents Under Pressure." The visor gave my jet jock instructor pilots some good laughs. My primary goal when flying jets with the helmet was ... to keep it in one piece.

The T-38 is a great plane for formation flying. I fly my first 4-ship solo flight as jet #3 takes this photo from the other side of the lead ship.

time to live your dream."

During the engine run-up, the powerful T-38 begins to shake and quiver, somewhat like a caged animal anticipating its release. I let go of the brakes and mash both throttles forward into full afterburner, which begins the rolling thunder that announces a new journey. The next few minutes are very busy as I'm intensely focused on flying and navigating the incredibly fast jet that climbs like a rocket and rips through big chunks of miles in very little time. Soon I'm leveled off at 24,000 feet on a speedy cruise to my assigned training area. When I reach that area to practice jet aerobatics, things will get really busy again. But for now, I can relax for a few minutes and take in the scene.

As I scan around at puffy white clouds and the countryside swiftly slipping by, my mind is filled with positive thoughts. My childhood pilot heroes were right—it's absolutely beautiful up here. Alone at the controls of the T-38, I know what's been calling me. I know I'm in a place where I belong. For years I have felt this powerful calling to come up here and fly. As my oxygen mask strains from my smile, I am happy to have pursued my own obsession and answered that call.

Epilogue
Live and Let Fly

In the years after my 1979 graduation from Air Force pilot training, my father's obsessive collecting and the lifestyle it fashioned continued down a path I found both troubling and beyond influence. That gave me enormous appreciation for the opportunity I found to focus my attention on a flying career that would far exceed my seemingly impossible childhood dream of flight. Also, shortly after I got my Air Force pilot wings, a sweet Mississippi gal named Lisa became my wife. And while the Air Force called the shots on when and where I flew, in my off-duty time I put my personal life almost entirely into her caring and loving hands. I'd already been away from Ohio for much of the 1970s when this marriage helped turn my image of my former home into a faraway land.

Had I stayed in that distant land, my efforts there would not have been spent on the preservation of warbirds like the Corsairs, B-25s, Twin Mustang or others. As a warbird magazine editor lamented in a column during that period, Dad's tireless efforts to resurrect the B-36 left his other aircraft in a state of near total neglect. Undoubtedly, the B-36 project would have been my next no-right-of-refusal task, had I stayed within his grasp. Except for a Beech AT-11 he hauled in the post-Wally years, the rest of the aircraft he acquired were the big kind you chopped apart instead of unbolting, much like the KC-97. Thus, I have never regretted that as his airplane sanctuary went in that direction, I would ironically use my newly minted pilot wings to fly away from the nest.

With no choice but to look back from the outside all these years later, I can't help but reflect and try to define the incredibly unique and strange life that my father ended up carving out. Among the things that come to mind when defining my father, the word paradox appears relentlessly. First, a political conservative, he in certain ways lived the life of an anti-establishment counterculture dropout. As for personal possessions, he led the life of a poor man, rejecting anything that hinted of being in sync with a materialistic nation, yet he in other ways collected virtually everything he could get his hands on.

In a related contradiction, he maintained a mortal fear of the alcoholism that had devastated the father figures in the generation before him, yet he succumbed to a collecting addiction that could almost be described as tsunamis of stuff arriving on his property. Likewise contradictory, despite his dedicated efforts to save World War II and other historic aircraft, he saw nothing wrong with allowing them to become increasingly derelict from half a century exposed to the elements. In these and other ways, Dad was indeed a paradox.

The ultimate truth was that it took a person who was visionary, driven, innovative, and fearless of being different to salvage and save the historic aviation treasures that he did. But in the end, it was the recklessness of his obsession that isolated him and stood in the way of his having the air museum he always dreamed of.

In summing up my father's life, it may appear that I'm disappointed and perhaps

I took the liberty of combining two photographs here. At the very same time I was learning to fly the T-38 as an Air Force student pilot, Dad was hauling this chopped Douglas DC-7 freighter. We were clearly now on very different paths.

bitter over the way things turned out. Disappointed—definitely. But bitter? No way. There's a saying that attitude is the difference between adventure and ordeal. Though the distant journey I shared with my father was a mixture of both, clearly it was much more of an adventure than anything else. Despite some hardships I endured under his roof, I got to experience and do countless things that other boys can never begin to imagine. And in today's world, where so many boys grow up without even having a father at home, I was blessed beyond measure simply to be in the shadow of this visionary man.

Speaking of a vision, I have my own about what may ultimately define part of his legacy. As I attended yet another of the breathtaking AirVenture aviation conventions at Oshkosh, I sat and watched the airshow from my lawn chair perched upon the trampled grass where other spectators had marveled at the show on this and previous days. Sitting next to me was fellow airplane enthusiast and longtime friend Rick Rice. Over many years, Rick and I have flown a Stearman and several other historic aircraft together, including his Fairchild PT-26. Rick at one time even owned and flew a Sky King Bobcat and is long familiar with Dad's collection. And so the setting and the moment were perfect.

25th Flight Training Squadron photograph of me as a T-38 Instructor Pilot (IP). I enjoyed flying the T-38 so much that I volunteered to teach in it. Training many students to fly the White Rocket truly made my long journey to the cockpit well worth the wait! A few student pilots tried their best to kill me, but my white helmet is still in one piece and is now retired in my garage in Collierville, Tennessee.

As I sat there at Oshkosh and looked beyond a parade of planes flying against the background of white puffy clouds dotting the crystal blue sky of that perfect afternoon, I shared a vision I had of a day in the future. As I explained to Rick, the day will come when a formation of planes Dad saved will fly together at AirVenture or some other big airshow. The *Wild Cargo* B-25 has been flying since 2005, and the incredibly rare XP-82 Twin Mustang was recently restored to absolute perfection by Tom Reilly and the XP-82 Team. Likewise, other warbirds Dad saved are going through the restoration process, while many rare parts he salvaged will eventually end up in dozens of yet more rare and historic aircraft now being restored.

And so the day will come when these historic aircraft, saved from annihilation by a simple carpenter, will fly together in bright and shining splendor. And when that glorious event does come to be, proof will abound that clouds can in fact have a silver lining.

Remembering My Mom and Dad: Peggy and Walter Soplata

Stronger than any bond of solid welded steel, Peggy and Walter's marriage of 62 years was every bit as profound as the airplane collection Walter built during the entire span of their marriage. From the outside, it might appear he got the better end of the deal. Yes, he had his way concerning virtually every major decision made during their decades together. But what may appear on the surface as Walter's domination of my mother was an illusion that hid what was truly a deep personal bond that was theirs, and theirs alone.

For decades, other women asked Mom how she put up with her husband. Her light-hearted reply was always the same. "I never have to wonder or worry about where my husband is," she would laugh. Measured in material terms, Dad was quite stingy. As Mom lived what people would call a minimalist lifestyle today, that begs the question of whether she did this because of her husband, or of her own choosing. To me it was clear this was a choice she made on her own and she was totally content and happy with that choice. Eventually, Dad did split most of the proceeds from his airplane sales with her 50/50 in their later years when he finally parted with his best planes. But true to her faith and to herself, she continued her minimalist lifestyle. The only objection I ever witnessed was the fury she unleashed on Dad when he surprised her by arriving home from his carpenter job with the wing of Corsair Zero Zero (see Chapter 2). Ironically, that was likely the best airplane investment he ever made.

What really mattered to her most was his true and endless devotion to her as the woman in his life. He forever had a saintly adoration for her as the most wonderful woman to ever walk the earth except perhaps for Saint Mary herself. That such a spiritual and personal bond to his wife was embedded deep in his soul is an enormous truth that I learned early as their son and never to this day have doubted for a moment.

In November 2010, Dad passed away at the age of 87 following two months of being in a coma from a stroke. I was able to visit him during that time, but it didn't go unnoticed by me that at the time of his death I was on the other side of the planet on an airline layover in Hong Kong. We had grown worlds apart over many years, and his death that day led me to reflect on how things got that way. Yet I think he'd have been happy to know I followed the advice of my crew scheduler who concluded the quickest way to the states was to pilot a Boeing 777 myself. He asked if I was okay to fly, and I assured him I was fine. It was Dad who raised me to obsess about airplanes; thus I had no problem focusing on my duties as a pilot that night. So perhaps it was our deep airplane bond that was still strong after all.

Mom lived until February 2017. She was seven years younger than Dad, so perhaps a sign of their oneness, she long endured a number of difficult medical issues to reach nearly the same age he did. During that time, she left his collection mostly untouched in the exact derelict junkyard condition he left it in. A number of airplane collectors contacted her about selling some of the valuable items that remained. Except for some small items sold to a man who long befriended her and Dad, she didn't budge. It wasn't about the money. She didn't want her husband's collection disturbed. No matter what, the deep bond that she carried her memory of him with probably made the idea of selling out seem like a betrayal.

I'd been retired from my airline job barely a month when Mom passed. Since I flew while remembering Dad, I figured I'd do the same while thinking of her. Aloft alone in my Piper J-3 Cub, I lazily roamed a crisp blue afternoon sky dotted with white scattered clouds. The abundant artistry of the sky has never disappointed me in my decades of flying, and today would be no different. As the sun set on this last day of her life, the sky painted her a beautiful and peaceful scene. Mom was always a very gifted artist, so I knew she would appreciate the view.

Appendix I

*Walter Soplata's Airplanes:
Where Are They Now?*

Below is a list of aircraft that have departed the collection. Details are incomplete in some cases for several reasons. First, my parents were not the best record keepers and the clutter of collecting made it easy to lose things. Some aircraft came with poor records to begin with, especially if purchased from scrap yards. Dad purposely resisted registering his aircraft with the FAA; thus only limited documentation is available through their records. Fortunately, a reasonable amount of records have been located. Still, documents for some aircraft remain lost.

B-25 *Wild Cargo* was sold in 1984. The initial intent of the first buyer was to use it for parts, and in particular wanted its center wing for another B-25 restoration. After a subsequent purchase by warbird collector Jerry Yagen, this B-25 was completely restored for flight in 2005 and remains flying with The Military Air Museum in Virginia Beach. It still bears its *Wild Cargo* name today. On April 18, 2012, *Wild Cargo* flew in a formation of seventeen B-25s over Wright Field in Dayton, Ohio, honoring the last surviving Doolittle Raiders on the 70th anniversary of their heroic and unimaginable mission to reach and strike Japan. Lunken Airport in Cincinnati from where we rescued *Wild Cargo* in 1964 is just over 40 miles from Wright Field. If a B-25 could smile, I think *Wild Cargo* would have done so during its flight that day.

For many years Dad told all inquirers that nothing was for sale. But the sale of B-25 *Wild Cargo* in 1984 opened the door a bit, and he soon sold the P-51 that I found in a scrap yard in the mid 1960s, described in Chapter Thirteen. The name of the P-51 buyer and its location remain unknown. Dad likewise sold the P-80 Shooting Star jet around the same time. Again, the buyer is unknown, but online postings suggest the buyer traded this early jet age Navy P-80 to the National Naval Aviation Museum in Pensacola, Florida.

The F-82E Twin Mustang was sold in the mid–1990s to a buyer in Britain, but never left the United States. It was resold several times and is currently owned by Pat Harker, who is restoring it in Minnesota. As mentioned in more detail in Appendix II, Pat now owns what remained of race Corsair *Lucky Gallon*.

Anxious for a tax write-off following the F-82 sale, Dad donated the F2G air race Corsair 74 to the Crawford Auto-Aviation Museum in Cleveland, Ohio, in 1998. The race champ Corsair was supposed to become a static display exactly as Dad wanted in a deal that was partially a donation, partially monetary, and partially a trade for museum aircraft engines. After a number of years stored in a North Dakota restoration shop, the museum sold Corsair 74 to a buyer who had it completely restored for flight. Barely a year after its first flight in 2011, a crash during an airshow practice session in 2012 resulted in fatal injuries to renowned restorer and warbird pilot Robert Odegaard. My parents became good friends with Robert over a number of years and admired him greatly. Robert's death saddened our entire family. Corsair 74 was totally destroyed in the accident. Dad's death in 2010 prevented him from realizing what for decades was among his greatest fears for Corsair 74 and other historic aircraft that might be flown and lost, as well as pilots such as Robert who would be lost flying them.

Corsair Zero Zero was sold in a private arrangement to a California warbird collector in 2007. Its current status remains unknown.

The Curtiss O-52 Owl was sold at an unknown time to an unknown buyer.

In 2008 Dad sold what remained of the XP-82 Twin Mustang to master warbird restorer Tom Reilly. In 2006 I wrote my father one of my many letters and sent him photos of a newly manufactured P-51A I saw at Oshkosh. Writing him about seeing this totally new P-51A airframe, I suggested the remaining population of four Twin Mustangs could grow to five in the same way. In 2005 Dad informed me that warbird restorers had discovered all the blueprints for the P-51 Mustang as well as the P-82/F-82 Twin Mustangs, so a resurrection of the XP-82 appeared possible to me. Other than the left fuselage of the XP-82, Dad had very little of the airframe, but I knew he had many critical components and parts including each of its steel landing gear. Tom Reilly's purchase of the XP-82 items initiated a monumental restoration that many experts said could not be done. He and his XP-82 team nevertheless spent over ten years and more than 207,000 man-hours restoring the XP. Among the many enormously talented people who helped the XP team, Pat Harker frequently shared his ex-Soplata F-82E years of Twin Mustang experience. A master restorer himself, Pat scratch-built the XP landing gear doors. On a visit to Reilly's shop in February 2019, I helped Tom install the outboard gear doors, which wasn't easy and took some time. That gave me the opportunity to appreciate Pat Harker's craftsmanship in fabricating these enormously complex doors and their highly contoured structure. They not only looked perfect, but our installation showed they fit perfectly. The XP-82 became the fourth Soplata airplane to return to the sky and was eagerly celebrated by aviation enthusiasts from around the globe when it appeared at EAA Conventions SUN 'n FUN and AirVenture in 2019.

In 2008, an F-84F Thunderstreak jet was donated to the MAPS Air Museum in North Canton, Ohio.

Mom's passing in 2017 put the remainder of the collection into an estate. That same year the Franklin B-25 was sold to warbird restorer Kevin Hooey in New York who intends to return this B-25 to flying status. Also in 2017, a partial TBM was sold to Ohio TBM restorer Charlie Cartledge.

In 2018 the estate sold a complete TBM Avenger to Brian and Mark Stoltzfus in Kidron, Ohio. Both men are grandsons of Chris Stoltzfus who originally sold the plane to Dad in 1970. We were thrilled to see this plane go back to its wonderful aviation family from fifty years ago. Tragically, Brian Stoltzfus was lost in an aviation accident in January 2019. While we mourn the loss of Brian, we look forward to the continued restoration of the TBM for flight by his brother Mark and the rest of the amazing Stoltzfus team.

Also in 2018 the ex-Dean Ortner SNJ-7 Texan told of in Chapter Twenty was sold to Nicholas Mech of Dublin, Georgia to be restored.

Numerous engines, parts, and a few cockpits including that of an F-100 Super Sabre were also sold in 2018 to a variety of collectors.

In 2019 Dave Hall, who owns MotoArt and Planetags with operations based in Mojave, California, purchased a number of predominantly big airframes from the estate. Among these are a very unusual P2V-7 Neptune, the cut-up and heavily damaged B-36, and a complete F-86L. Also in the sale was the forward fuselage of B-52B *Lucky Lady III* that led three B-52s on a non-stop round-the-world speed record flight in January, 1957. This world record display of global Air Force airpower put the B-52 on the cover of *Life* magazine on the January 28, 1957, edition. Dad acquired this B-52 fuselage after it was sold for scrap by the Air Force Museum in the 1980s. For more on B-52B *Lucky Lady III*, visit: https://www.thisdayinaviation.com/tag/53-0394/.

Also purchased by Dave Hall were a Handley Paige Victor K.2 cockpit, a Convair T-29 cockpit, and a DC-7 cockpit. Each of these aircraft Dave purchased except for the F-86L are far beyond any hope of restoration. Yet, the long and proven commitment of Dave Hall to preserve aviation history provides these aerial artifacts the best opportunity for preservation in an appropriate and meaningful way.

As of early 2020 The Cessna Bobcat and the Douglas A-26 Invader have sales and transportation pending.

As this book goes to publication, a few complete aircraft remain in the collection. These are the BT-15, F7U Cutlass, the X-prototype (XBT2D-1) Skyraider, and

Walter and Peggy Soplata in 1998 with Corsair 74 while the old racer is being prepared for shipment to the Crawford Auto-Aviation Museum in Cleveland, Ohio.

The XP-82 Twin Mustang at EAA's Airventure 2019. Tom Reilly and his XP-82 team earned four awards at AirVenture for this astonishing restoration including Grand Champion—Post WWII, Phoenix Award, and two Golden Wrench awards (courtesy Airline Captain Alexis Meaders).

the T-28A. The large fuselages of the C-82 Packet and KC-97 Stratofreighter likewise remain. The estate remains closed to visitors as the process goes on of finding a good home for what remains there. Sharp jagged metal from some of the wrecked planes Dad collected presents an injury hazard such that visitors cannot be allowed on the property for safety and liability reasons. There are possible plans for several aircraft to remain along with Dad's boom tractor and other items in order to honor his memory on the exact location where he singlehandedly accomplished so much to preserve aircraft and other artifacts of our nation's rich aviation history.

Appendix II
Aviatrix Marge Hurlburt's Hidden Treasure:
Air Race Corsair Lucky Gallon

While my memoir has been mostly focused on the father-son experiences of Dad and I hauling airplanes together, I'd be unforgivably remiss if I failed to pay tribute to the role of women aviators who have heroically pushed the frontiers of air and space. In yet one more case of Dad having the rarest of the rare, I have just the right plane for this.

I made little mention of air race Corsair *Lucky Gallon* in this book. It was actually

City of Painesville Corsair (Marge Hurlburt's *Lucky Gallon* incognito) arrives at the Soplata home in 1951. Our house in the background still has its flat roof that I don't remember, but that Dad often told me about. He got tired of constant leaks, so built the pitched roof seen in later photos. The 1942 Chevy truck seen here would later become the workhorse boom tractor Dad and I would use to attend to the needs of his ever-growing collection, including the reassembly of his B-25s and other aircraft.

the first of three Corsairs my father acquired. *Lucky Gallon* isn't featured in my memoir because much of it had been sold for scrap when I was very young, and I have no memory of the plane when it was complete. Around 1950 a severe windstorm snapped off one of then not-so-*Lucky Gallon*'s folding wings, and caused other damage while at Cook Cleland's Euclid Avenue Airport. Cleland sold the badly damaged Corsair to Dad in 1951 for $100. Sometime later after scrapping the entire wing and tail of the plane to put food on the table, Dad stored the cockpit and forward fuselage plus engine, prop, landing gear and other parts in his ever dark hangar. These sections of *Lucky Gallon* remained hidden in Dad's hangar for over sixty years until I led an effort to remove it in 2018. We always knew that Cook Cleland raced this stock Corsair #92 in the 1946 Cleveland National Air Races and placed sixth. But not until 2017 did we learn *Lucky Gallon* had some other fascinating history.

In a newspaper story on April 29, 2017, published by *The News Herald* in Willoughby, Ohio, we learned that Cook Cleland loaned Corsair *Lucky Gallon* to a woman named Margaret "Marge" Hurlburt in 1947. This story told of a "Come Fly With Marge!" event the International Woman's Air & Space Museum in Cleveland was soon having. This event was to recognize and honor Marge on the 70th anniversary of her setting an international woman's speed record with Corsair *Lucky Gallon.* Achieving a speed of 337 mph, Marge beat the previous record of 292 mph set by the ever iconic race pilot and WASP founder Jackie Cochran.

Marge Hurlburt in Corsair *Lucky Gallon* in which she set a new women's speed record in 1947. Hurlburt earlier won first place in the inaugural Halle Trophy Race, flying a T-6 Texan, in the 1946 Cleveland National Air Races. The Halle race was the first pylon air racing event that permitted women pilots (courtesy the International Women's Air & Space Museum, Cleveland, Ohio).

It was Cochran who years earlier recruited Hurlburt for the WASP program, and I imagine Cochran was proud to see her record broken by a woman she had mentored. I also doubt she was worried about that or any of her other numerous speed records as Jackie Cochran was still a long way from done. In 1953 and beyond she exploded the envelope of speed for women in the new jet age, becoming the first woman to break the sound barrier flying a Canadian F-86 Sabre. Cochran would later set new jet plane world records regardless of gender flying the T-38 Talon in 1961, and in 1964 would set three more jet world records flying the F-104 Starfighter. In one record speed dash alone, Cochran dared life and limb by blasting her way in the F-104 to an astonish-

After over sixty years of dark hibernation, the light of day finally peeks in on the *Lucky Gallon* Corsair cockpit of Marge Hurlburt on April 29, 2018. It took me most of the day to dismantle the wall of WWII engine crate boards, which were so hard it was as if they had become petrified in the decades since the war. After dulling several power saw blades, I resorted to using a chainsaw, large hammers, pry bars and, finally, an electric winch to yank the wall down. We retrieved this fuselage section of the plane the next day. The remaining engine crate boards on the left were a source of the lumber Dad used extensively for our home construction.

ing speed of 1429 mph! But back to 1947, it was Marge Hurlburt the media named "America's Queen of the Air" for beating Cochran's speed record flying Corsair *Lucky Gallon*.

What remained of *Lucky Gallon* was sold from the Soplata estate in 2018, and a rebuildable Corsair wing has already been acquired by new owner Pat Harker in Minnesota. Pat also owns the former Soplata F-82E Twin Mustang and has an amazing restoration of the F-82 underway. It will take many years and a lot of resources to restore *Lucky Gallon* to flying status. But eventually when that day comes, it's well within reason that one of today's lady warbird pilots could take *Lucky Gallon* up to roam the skies again. I will keep my hopes up that such a future flight will happen in order to pay tribute to Marge Hurlburt, Jackie Cochran, and the many other great and heroic women who have deeply enriched more than a century of *wo-manned* flight!

Appendix III
The Global Reach of Walter Soplata's Airplanes: Lockheed Neptune #40436

If airplanes could talk, some of Dad's planes would have a lot to say. And if they could speak of where they've been, you can't help wonder what they might say. Just where his Cold War B-36, later converted to an RB-36 spy plane, might have flown would be interesting to hear. But if that plane could speak, it would probably tell the joke that goes, "I can tell you, but then I have to shoot you." In Appendix I, I introduce the

Here's Dad's Navy P2V-7 Neptune 40436 in the last stages of disassembly at Clinton County Air Force Base in Wilmington, Ohio. As the photograph suggests, there are no other airplanes remaining at the base, which is all but closed. Mom stands by the boom tractor as she takes over helper duties while I'm in electronics school in Cuyahoga Falls, Ohio. This was the very last airplane I helped my father haul. The Neptune was never reassembled at home.

round-the-world record flight of B-52 *Lucky Lady III* that's obviously seen a few places. Also in Appendix I, Dad's P2V-7 Neptune gets its first mention. While we for decades suspected nothing special about Neptune #40436, it was hiding an icy story long waiting to be uncovered. Dare I say again that my father stumbled upon an extraordinary rarity.

Honestly, I was dismayed when Dad got his Neptune on an $800 military scrap bid in 1972. It wasn't a warbird in the normal sense, so I could not understand what he was thinking. While the Neptune was not as big as the KC-97, it was still a big and heavy giant compared to a B-25. Like a lot of Soplata airplanes, it survived simply because something bad happened to it. But if military airplanes could also have feelings, they wouldn't mind a bad event that prevents them from eventually being flown to an airplane boneyard to be recycled into aluminum screen doors and beer cans.

When Dad got the Neptune, it was parked at Clinton County Air Force Base in Wilmington, Ohio. The airfield later became a cargo hub for Airborne Express, which was a big operation there until 2008. But in 1972 as we hauled the plane away, the military base was in the closure process, and oddly, this Navy Neptune was the last military airplane to leave that Air Force Base. Yes, I can hear you saying and asking: "Come on Wally, we're at the end of the book. Don't you have *anything normal* to tell us?"

The story we were told at the base is that the Neptune stopped there on a gas & go trip, but made a very hard landing. The resulting maintenance inspection revealed a wing crack, so the plane was grounded and sold for scrap by the Navy. A bonus for Dad in the sale, the Neptune was fueled with about 1,000 gallons of purple 115/145 octane avgas still on board. Those high-octane aviation gasoline days are long gone now.

During the 1960s, Dad and I climbed in Navy Neptunes at many airshows, so it

Neptune 40436 in its glory days exploring Antarctica. Today it is the last survivor of its arctic-modified P2V-7 Neptune family. Old Revell model airplane kits of this exact Neptune are still advertised online with Antarctica artwork on the box cover of Neptune 40436 taking off. Talk about an old plane that just won't give up! (courtesy Larry L. Johnson).

was a plane we knew well. But we immediately noticed this one was weird and different. Really odd, we found large box structures with strange brackets and fittings around each landing gear area. The plane also had big brackets on the rear fuselage that Dad recognized as mounts for JATO "Jet-Assisted Take-off" rocket bottles. We had no idea what that was about, but no time to waste, we got busy taking the plane apart and didn't give the Neptune's oddities any significant thought thereafter.

After I wrote "The Soplata Airplane Sanctuary," published by *Air & Space/Smithsonian* mgazine in November, 2007, I was contacted by a 1950s Neptune crew member who was a radio operator in Antarctica on sister-ship Neptune 40437. He told of being a former member of the US Navy's Antarctic Development Squadron Six (VXE-6) known as the "Puckered Penguins." He further explained that Dad's Neptune was the last survivor of the snow-ski-configured Neptunes flown on historic "Deep Freeze" and other missions exploring Antarctica in the late 1950s and early 1960s. Other people including my good friend in New Zealand, aviation historian and author Simon Beck, have confirmed Dad's Neptune flew these missions. So it was the need for snow skis that finally explained the odd landing gear hardware and JATO bottle brackets we found on 40436. Numerous photos of Neptune 40436 in Antarctica, and a video of it performing a JATO takeoff in the snow can be found online. Searches for Navy VX-6 "Puckered Penguin" squadron, Antarctica Neptunes, and Deep Freeze will lead to a variety of sites. The book *Gateway to the Ice* is rich with history of these heroic missions featuring Dad's Neptune and many other planes. So I say again, if only Dad's airplanes could talk!

Sources

Chapter 1
Karl Haas, *Inside Music* (New York: Doubleday, 1984), p. 9; Simon D. Beck, *Fairchild C-82 Packet* (Jefferson, North Carolina: McFarland, 2017), p. 167; Simon D. Beck, *The Aircraft-Spotter's Film and Television Companion* (Jefferson, North Carolina: McFarland, 2016), pp. 94–97.

Chapter 2
Roger Huntington, *Thompson Trophy Races* (Osceola, Wisconsin: Motorbooks International, 1989), p. 187; Moose Peterson, "Simply Super," *Classic Wings Magazine* 18, No. 5, Issue 83, pp. 14–19.

Chapter 3
B. Sims (writer) & J. Copeland (director), *The Golden Burro* [Television series, Season 2, Episode 9, 1956]; Jack Chertok (Executive Producer), *Sky King*, Apple Valley, California; Beck, *Aircraft-Spotter's Companion*, pp. 230–231.

Chapter 4
Carl Hoffman, *Hunting Warbirds* (New York: Ballantine Books, 2001), chap. 4; William T. Larkins, *Surplus WWII U.S. Aircraft* (Upland, California: BAC Publishers, 2005).

Chapter 5
Warren Thompson, "Vought's Visionary Fighter," *Aviation History Magazine* (September 2016): Steve Ginter, *Chance Vought F7U Cutlass* (Simi Valley, California: Naval Fighters, 1982), pp. 83–84.

Chapter 9
General James H. "Jimmy" Doolittle with Carroll Glines, *I Could Never Be So Lucky Again* (New York: Bantam Books, 1991); James P. Harrison, *Mastering the Sky* (New York: Sarpedon, 1996), p. 139; Bruce Orris, "Thirty Seconds Over Tokyo," *Air Classics Magazine* 55, Number 5 (May 2019): pp. 50–54.

Chapter 10
1944 North American B-25J Mitchell [Wild Cargo], Warbirds Over the Beach Program Guide (Virginia Beach, Virginia: Military Aviation Museum, 2016), p. 6.

Chapter 11
Watty Piper, *The Little Engine That Could* (New York: Platt & Munk, 1954).

Chapter 14

R.A "Bob" Hoover with Mark Shaw, *Forever Flying* (New York: Pocket Books, 1996), p. xxi; Bill Sweet, as told to Bob Stailey, *They Call Me Mr. Airshow* (Milwaukee, Wisconsin: Ken Cook Transnational, 1972); Louis Keefer, "Around the Pylons, Cleveland's National Air Races," *Ohio Historical Society* 13, Number 5 (September–October 1996): pp. 2–21.

Chapter 15

Charles Coombs, *Aerospace Pilot* (New York: William Morrow, 1964); Joe Christy, *Racing Planes & Pilots* (Blue Ridge Summit, Pennsylvania: Tab Books, 1982), p. 154; Geoffrey Norman, "The incredible life and terrible death of the Navy's first World War II ace," *Military History Magazine* (August 2008); Doug Goss, "Adventures with Earl," *Warbirds International Magazine* 24, Number 4 (July–August 2005): pp. 44–51; William N. Hess, *P-47 Thunderbolt at War* (New York: Doubleday & Company, 1977), pp. 60–63; *North American F-86A Sabre,* National Museum of the United States Air Force. Last edited May 4, 2015, https://www.nationalmuseum.af.mil/Visit/Museum-Exhibits/Fact-Sheets/Display/Article/196118/north-american-f-86a-sabre/.

Chapter 16

Michael J.H. Taylor, *Jane's Encyclopedia of Aviation* (New York: Portland House, 1989), pp. 283, 392, 584, 593, 604–605; "See the USA in your Chevrolet," Wikipedia, last modified August 14, 2019. http://en.wikipedia.org/wiki/See_the_USA_in_Your_Chevrolet.

Chapter 19

Joseph Heller, *Catch-22* (New York: Simon & Schuster, 1961); *Catch-22,* directed by Mike Nichols (1970; Guaymas, Mexico, Paramount Home Video 2013), DVD; Beck, *Aircraft-Spotter's Companion,* pp. 55–58; Marshall Wainwright, "Cobra's Final Flight," *Warbirds International Magazine* 28, Number 6 (September–October 2009): pp. 24–26.

Chapter 20

Otha C. Spencer, *Flying the Hump* (College Station: Texas A&M University Press, 1992); Don Vaughan, "Lost in the Himalayas," *Military Officer Magazine* (September 2009): pp. 94–99.

Chapter 21

Michael O'Leary, "Before Warbirds," *Warbirds International Magazine* 23, Number 6 (November–December 2004): p. 29; Richard R. Burgess and Warren E. Thompson, *AD Skyraider Units of The Korean War* (Oxford, UK: Osprey, 2016); Byron E Hukee, *USAF and VNAF A-1 Skyraider Units of the Vietnam War* (Oxford, UK: Osprey, 2013).

Chapter 22

Beck, *Aircraft-Spotter's Companion,* pp. 201–208; "*Tora! Tora! Tora!* Postscript," *Air Classics Magazine* 8, Number 7 (May 1972): pp. 20–25, 63.

Chapter 23

"Grumman TBF Avenger," Military Factory.com, last edited June 6, 2019, https://www.militaryfactory.com/aircraft/detail.asp?aircraft_id=300.

Chapter 25

"Boeing KC-97L Stratofreighter," National Museum of the United States Air Force, last edited July 21, 2015, https://www.nationalmuseum.af.mil/Visit/Museum-Exhibits/Fact-Sheets/Display/Article/196737/-boeing-kc-97l-stratofreighter/.

Bibliography

Books

Beck, Simon D. *The Aircraft-Spotter's Film and Television Companion.* Jefferson, North Carolina: McFarland, 2016.
_____. *Fairchild C-82 Packet: The Military and Civil History.* Jefferson, North Carolina: McFarland, 2017.
Burgess, Richard R., and Warren E. Thompson. *AD Skyraider Units of The Korean War.* Oxford, UK: Osprey, 2016.
Berliner, Don. *Airplane Racing: A History, 1909-2008.* Jefferson, North Carolina: McFarland, 2010.
Christy, Joe. *Racing Planes & Pilots.* Blue Ridge Summit, Pennsylvania: Tab Books, 1982.
Coombs, Charles. *Aerospace Pilot.* New York: William Morrow and Company, 1964.
Doolittle, General James H., with Carroll V. Glines. *I Could Never Be So Lucky Again.* New York: Bantam Books, 1991.
Ginter, Steve. *Chance Vought F7U Cutlass.* Simi Valley, California: Naval Fighters, 1982.
Haas, Karl. *Inside Music.* New York: Doubleday, 1984.
Harrison, James P. *Mastering the Sky.* New York: Sarpedon, 1996.
Heller, Joseph. *Catch-22.* New York: Simon & Schuster, 1961.
Hess, William N. *P-47 Thunderbolt at War.* New York: Doubleday & Company, 1977.
Hoffman, Carl. *Hunting Warbirds.* New York: Ballantine Books, 2001.
Hoover, R.A., and Mark Shaw. *Forever Flying.* New York: Pocket Books, 1996.
Hukee, Byron E. *USAF and VNAF A-1 Skyraider Units of the Vietnam War.* Oxford, UK: Osprey, 2013.
Huntington, Roger. *Thompson Trophy Races.* Osceola, Wisconsin: Motorbooks International, 1989.
Larkins, William T. *Surplus WWII U.S. Aircraft.* Upland, California: BAC Publishers, 2005.
Ogden, Bob. *Great Aircraft Collections of the World.* New York: Gallery Books, 1986.
Phillips, Tony. *Gateway to the Ice.* Christchurch, New Zealand: Christchurch International Airport Ltd., 2001.
Spencer, Otha C. *Flying the Hump.* College Station: Texas A&M University Press, 1992.
Sweet, Bill, as told to Bob Stailey. *They Call Me Mr. Airshow.* Milwaukee, Wisconsin: Ken Cook Transnational, 1972.
Taylor, Michael J.H. *Jane's Encyclopedia of Aviation.* New York: Portland House, 1989.
Veronico, Nicholas A. *Hidden Warbirds.* Minneapolis, Minnesota: Zenith Press, 2013.
Yeager, General Chuck, and Leo Janos. *Yeager: An Autobiography.* New York: Bantam Books. 1985.

Newspapers and Periodicals

Busha, Jim. "Fate, Circumstance, and Necessity—The Resurrection of the XP-82 Twin Mustang." *Sport Aviation* (August 2018): pp. 60–68.
Editors, Air Classics. "*Tora! Tora! Tora!* Postscript." *Air Classics Magazine* 8, Number 7 (May 1972): pp. 20–25, 63.
Felton, Chad. "Forgotten Aviatrix, Record Setter Celebrated." *The News Herald* (Willoughby, Ohio), Apr 29, 2017.
Goss, Doug. "Adventures With Earl." *Warbirds International Magazine* 24, Number 4 (July–August 2005): pp. 44–51.
Keefer, Louis. "Around the Pylons: Cleveland's National Air Races." *Ohio Historical Society* 13, Number 5 (September–October 1996): pp. 2–21.

Norman, Geoffrey. "The incredible life and terrible death of the Navy's first World War II ace." *Military History Magazine* (August 2008).
O'Leary, Michael. "Before Warbirds." *Warbirds International Magazine* 23, Number 6 (November–December 2004): p. 29.
_____. "Restoration of the Century—How Tom Reilly and the XP-82 Restoration Team Made Aviation History." *Air Classics Magazine* 55, Number 4 (April 2019): pp. 30–44.
Orris, Bruce. "Thirty Seconds Over Tokyo." *Air Classics Magazine* 55, Number 5 (May 2019): pp. 50–54.
Peterson, Moose. "Simply Super." *Classic Wings Magazine* 18, Number 5, Issue 83 (2012): pp. 14–19.
Scholler, Ray. "Museum in the Making." *Sport Aviation* (January 1971): pp. 22–23.
Soplata, Wally. "The Soplata Airplane Sanctuary." *Air & Space/Smithsonian* (November 2007): pp. 30–35.
Tanner, Kevin S. "Backyard Bomber—After 42-years, another B-25 Mitchell is up and flying." *Air Classics Magazine* 42, Number 2 (February 2006): pp. 6–8.
Thompson, Warren. "Vought's Visionary Fighter." *Aviation History Magazine* (September 2016).
Vaughan, Don. "Lost in the Himalayas." *Military Officer Magazine* (September 2009): pp. 94–99.
Volpe, Randall F. "Backyard Air Force." *Air Progress Magazine* (January 1972): pp. 78–79.
Wainwright, Marshall. "Cobra's Final Flight." *Warbirds International Magazine* 28, Number 6 (September–October 2009): pp. 24–26.
_____. "Super Corsair!" *Air Classics Magazine* 50, Number 12 (December 2014): pp. 14–19.
Wilson, Kenneth D. "The Soplata Collection." *Model Aviation Magazine* (October 1986): pp. 87–92, 168–172.

Websites

National Museum of the United States Air Force. 2015. Boeing KC-97L Stratofreighter, //www.nationalmuseum.af.mil/Visit/Museum-Exhibits/Fact-Sheets/Display/Article/196737/boeing-kc-97l-stratofreighter/.
National Museum of the United States Air Force. 2015. North American F-86A Sabre, https://www.nationalmuseum.af.mil/Visit/Museum-Exhibits/Fact-Sheets/Display/Article/196118/north-american-f-86a-sabre/.

Aircraft Make and Model Index

Beech Aircraft
AT-11 Kansan 204
Beech Model-18, "Twin Beech" 12, 143, 150

Bell Aircraft
P-39 Airacobra, "Cobra II" 134
P-59 Airacomet 117
P-63 Kingcobra 88, 200

Boeing Aircraft
B-47 Stratojet 72
B-52B Stratofortress 72, 211, 218
Boeing 777 207
KC-97L Stratofreighter 182-190, 193-200, 202, 204, 212, 218, 222, 224
PT-17 Stearman 51, 94, 96, 206

Cessna Aircraft
Cessna 150 198-199
Cessna 172 112
Cessna 310 18-19
Cessna T-50 Bobcat, and UC-78 Army Bobcat, "Bamboo Bomber" 18-24, 29, 34, 47-48, 50, 54, 65, 98, 105, 109, 117, 124, 126-127, 135, 206, 211

Chance Vought Aircraft
F4U-7 Corsair 139, 146, 159, 161-162, 165
F7U-3 Cutlass 22, 32-42, 44-45, 47-50, 52, 60, 72-73, 88, 123, 135, 137, 157

Consolidated Aircraft
PBY Catalina 108-109

Convair Aircraft
B-36, YB-36, RB-36 Peacemaker 136-138, 196, 200, 204, 211, 217

B-58 Hustler 72
T-29 Flying Classroom 211

Curtiss Aircraft
C-46 Commando 7-8, 16, 50, 81, 143-145
O-52 Owl 151-153, 210
SB2C Helldiver 128

Douglas Aircraft
A-26 Invader 151, 166, 176, 196, 211
AD-5 Skyraider 60, 86-87, 155, 157, 222-223
DC-3 143-144
DC-7 205, 211
RB-26C Invader 109
XBT2D-1, X-prototype—Dauntless II (renamed Skyraider) 86-87, 153, 155, 157-158, 166, 177, 211, 222-223

Fairchild Aircraft
C-82 Packet 9, 11-13, 15, 81, 114, 116, 126
C-119 Flying Boxcar 106, 129, 132, 168
PT-26 206

Fleetwings Aircraft
BT-12 Sophomore 151-153, 167

General Motors Aircraft
TBM Avenger 28, 172-174, 176, 190, 210

Goodyear Aircraft
FG-1A Corsair, "Lucky Gallon" 50, 209, 213, 214-216
FG-1D Corsair, "Zero Zero" 15-16, 28, 37, 83, 85, 102, 122, 129, 139-141, 143, 146, 149, 159, 207, 210
F2G Corsair, Race #57 17
F2G Corsair, Race #74 16, 57,

95, 99, 122, 130, 163, 169-170, 176, 186, 209-211

Grumman Aircraft
F4F Wildcat 101, 105-106
F6F Hellcat 87, 101, 109
F8F Bearcat 85, 86, 94-97, 101, 109, 134
S-2 Tracker 168
TBF Avenger 173, 222

Lockheed Aircraft
F-104 Starfighter 215
P2V-7 Neptune 168, 196, 211, 217-219
P-80 Shooting Star 116-124, 126, 175, 209
T-33 Shooting Star, "T-Bird" 60, 117

McDonnell Aircraft
F-101, RF-101 Voodoo 89-90, 186, 201

North American Aviation (NAA) Aircraft
AT-6 Texan 61, 109, 143-145, 159, 201, 214, see also SNJ Texan
B-25 Mitchell, Doolittle Raiders 59
B-25 Mitchell: Earl Reinert 100
B-25J Mitchell, "Franklin B-25" 88, 124-125, 139, 166, 170, 176, 210
B-25J Mitchell, "Wild Cargo B-25" 59, 61, 63, 67, 69, 72, 74, 77, 79-80, 82, 84, 87, 89, 100, 114, 122, 124, 173, 206, 209, 221
F-82E Twin Mustang 5-7, 11, 13, 17, 26, 37, 47, 57, 86, 94, 98, 126, 131, 163, 175, 209-210, 215
F-86 Sabre 110-111, 114, 124,

Aircraft Make and Model Index

163, 174-175, 211, 215, 222, 224
P-51 Mustang 5, 57, 88, 92-94, 99-100, 109, 126, 142-143, 178, 209-210
SNJ Texan 143-144, 146-149, 160, 163, 171, 211
T-28A Trojan 27, 116-117
XP-82, X-prototype Twin Mustang 7-8, 17, 50, 64, 126, 200, 206, 210, 212, 223-224

Northrop Aircraft
T-38 Talon, "White Rocket" 105, 117, 199, 201-203, 205-206

Piper Aircraft
J-3C Piper Cub 95, 105, 142, 198, 208

Republic Aircraft
F-84 Thunderstreak 60, 87, 210
P-47 and Odom/Reinert YP-47M Thunderbolt 80, 99-105, 107-111, 113, 115-117, 124, 126, 133, 222-223

Sikorsky Aircraft
H-34 Seabat, helicopter

Vultee Aircraft
BT-13 Valiant 7, 87, 126, 151, 159
BT-15 Valiant 11, 83, 126-127, 151, 164, 211

General Index

Adams, Bill 51, 94, 96
Adventures in Good Music (AM radio show) 8
Aerospace Pilot (book) 104, 199
Air Classics 60, 221-224
Air&Space/Smithsonian 219, 224
AirVenture 206, 210, 212
Akron Naval Air Station 28
Allison 128-129
American Pickers (television series) 103
astronaut 19, 40, 96, 104, 107, 153, 158

Becker, Dick 95, 130-131
Bell 117
Boeing 183-184, 189, 193, 198, 207, 222, 224
boom tractor 5, 7, 10, 26, 47, 81-82, 103, 109, 128, 151, 168, 170, 212-213, 217
A Boy Named Sue (song) 168
Burke Lakefront Airport 94, 168
Burton Library 9

Cash, Johnny (singer) 168
Catch-22 (movie and book) 135-136
Cessna 18-20, 23, 61, 73, 105, 112-113, 127, 198, 199, 211
Chance Vought 40, 221-223
Chardon Maple Festival 12
Cleland, Cook 56, 95, 99, 130, 143
Cleveland Browns 94
Cleveland Hopkins International Airport 93-94, 147
Cleveland Indians 94
Cleveland National Air Races 2, 16-17, 37, 56, 92-93, 95, 99-100
Cleveland Plain Dealer 96
Cochran, Jacqueline "Jackie" 95, 105, 214-216

Columbus Air Force Base, MS 199, 202
Commemorative Air Force, CAF 60
Concord Airport 112
Confederate Air Force, CAF 60, 167
Convair 138, 211
Cuban Missile Crisis 72
Curtiss 128, 144, 151-152, 210

Deliverance (movie) 163
Doolittle, Gen. James H. 59, 92, 95, 105, 137, 209, 221-223
Doolittle Raiders 59, 137, 209
Douglas 109, 151, 196, 205, 211

EAA (Experimental Aircraft Association) 210, 212
Euclid Avenue Airport 214
Euclid Beach, amusement park 12

Fairchild 11, 129, 206, 221, 223
Flight of the Phoenix (movie) 12, 183
Fornoff, Bill 94
Franklin Airport 88, 124-125, 139, 166, 170, 176, 210
Flintstone, Fred (cartoon character) 54

Gann, Ernest K. (author) 166
Geauga County Fair 12
Geauga Lake (amusement park) 12
General Motors 114, 138, 173
Go Go Construction Company 71, 84
The Golden Burro (*Sky King* episode) 18, 221
Goldwater, Berry (US senator) 100
Goodyear 5-16, 27, 98
Grant, Kirby (actor) 119

Great Depression 29, 51, 56, 71, 107
Grosse Ile, Naval Air Station 60
Grumman 101, 173, 176, 222

Haas, Karl (classical music radio show host) 8, 221, 223
Hackett, Buddy (actor) 12
Hank's junkyard 76
Henschel Hs129 108
Hickory Lake 6
Higbee's Department Store 54-55
Hippies 107, 153-154, 190, 192
Hoover, R.A. "Bob" 92-94, 222-223
Hornet, USS 59, 105
Horn's Flying School 95
Huffman, Ralph 182, 184, 186-192, 195-197
Hurlburt, Margaret "Marge" 213-216

International Women's Air & Space Museum 214
It's a Mad, Mad, Mad, Mad World (movie) 12

Johnson, Alvin M. "Tex" 134

Kamikaze 17
Kennedy, John F. (US president) 27
Kent State University 154
Kirtland Invitational 174
Korean War 111, 117, 141, 153, 222-223
Kucera, Bob 85-86, 95, 97, 134

Lake Erie 12, 53, 94, 113, 162, 190, 198
Lockbourne Air Force Base 90, 93
Lockheed 109, 117, 119, 217
Lost Nation Airport 96-97

General Index

Lunken Airport 61, 63, 68, 72, 77, 209

MacMurray, Fred (actor) 180
Maloney, Ed 60
McKinney, J. Curtis 124
Meig's Field 151
Merlin, engine 92
The Military Air Museum 209
Mission Impossible (television series) 116
MIT 26, 59
Moran, Father James J. 114, 150-151, 167
My Three Sons (television series) 180

NACA 7
NASA 7, 14, 40, 59
Naymick, John 133
New York State Thruway 44-45
Newbury 6, 34, 53, 76, 142, 185
North American Aviation (NAA) 149, 221-222, 224

Odom, Bill 99-100
O'Hare, Lt. Cdr. Edward "Butch" 106
Oklahoma State University 128, 200
Ortner, Andy 143
Ortner, Dean 94, 142-149, 159-162, 165, 171, 201, 211
Ortner Air Service 143-144

Palwaukee Airport 105
Pearl Harbor 5, 59, 159, 162
Piper 61, 73, 95, 105, 112, 142, 198, 208
Popular Mechanics (magazine) 130
Pratt & Whitney R-2800 (engine) 85, 145
Pratt & Whitney R-4360 (engine) 95, 163, 186
Punderson Manor House 178, 184-185, 187

Reinert, Earl 80, 98-103, 105-111, 113-117, 132-133, 151, 199
Republic 87, 103
Restful Lake 55
Rooney, Mickey (actor) 12

St. Helen Catholic Church and School 8, 114
Schirra, Wally (astronaut) 40-41
Selfridge Air Force Base 90, 112, 182, 185, 186, 189-190, 192, 196
Shell Oil 59
Sky King (television series) 18-20, 22, 24, 105, 206, 211
South Weymouth Naval Air Station 34, 36
Star Trek (television series) 148
Stewart, Jimmy (actor) 12, 183
Strategic Air Command (SAC) 72
Strube, Bill 115-120
Sweet, Bill 51, 94, 222

Thirty Seconds Over Tokyo (movie) 59, 65
Those Magnificent Men and Their Flying Machines (movie) 12
Tora! Tora! Tora! (movie) 159-160, 162, 164-165, 222-223
Tracy, Charles 96
Trade-A-Plane 30
Turner, Roscoe 95
Twentieth Century Fox-Film Corporation 159, 164-165

US Air Force Museum 129-131, 211
US Marine Corps Museum (Quantico) 129, 141, 146, 159-160, 165
US Naval Air Museum 102, 129

Vietnam War 93, 95, 153-154, 190, 197, 222-223

Wakeman, Ohio 143
Wayne, John (actor) 162
White Motor Company 36
The Wizard of Oz (movie) 147, 150
Wright Field 127, 209
Wright-Patterson Air Force Base 90, 93
Wright R-2600, engine 74, 77, 128

Yagen, Jerry 209

www.ingramcontent.com/pod-product-compliance
Lightning Source LLC
Chambersburg PA
CBHW060341010526
44117CB00017B/2923